Patterns

A Short Prose Reader

Patterns

A Short Prose Reader

Fourth Edition

Mary Lou Conlin
Cuyahoga Community College

Houghton Mifflin Company   **Boston**   **Toronto**
Dallas   Geneva, Illinois   Palo Alto   Princeton, New Jersey

Sponsoring Editor: Mary Jo Southern
Managing Development Editor: Melody Davies
Project Editor: Susan Lee-Belhocine
Electronic Production Specialist: John Robbins
Senior Manufacturing Coordinator: Priscilla Bailey
Marketing Manager: George Kane

Acknowledgments for reprinted materials begin on page 369.

Cover art and photograph: Fabric art on cover is the property of, and is used with permission of, BellSouth Corporation. Fabric art designed and produced by B. J. Adams of Washington, D.C. © BellSouth Corporation, 1991.

Cover design by Harold Burch, Harold Burch Design, New York City.

Printed in the U.S.A.

Library of Congress Catalog Card Number: 93-78632

Instructor's Edition ISBN: 0-395-68425-0

Student Text ISBN: 0-395-59343-3

123456789-AM-96 95 94 93

Contents

3   Description   59

4   Examples   109

5   Classification and Division   145

6 Comparison and Contrast

Contents

Contents

Glossary   361

Acknowledgments   369

Index   375

Thematic Table
of Contents

6 Expectations and Reality

7 Education and Learning

13   Communication

Preface

Patterns: A Short Prose Reader provides students with an understanding of the process, organizational principles, and rhetorical strategies involved in producing clear and effective writing. In this Fourth Edition, students are introduced to the uses of freewriting and brainstorming in getting started on and defining ideas for their writing. The study apparatus provides complete and clear explanations of the various rhetorical modes, and the paragraph and essay-length readings provide students with examples of how the modes can be used in organizing and developing their ideas.

New to the Fourth Edition

Patterns, Fourth Edition, strives to give students a variety of models for their own writing and the stimulus for lively classroom discussion. Features of the new edition include:

- 40 percent new selections. Selections by traditional favorites such as John Updike, Joan Didion, and E. B. White are joined by many new works by women and minority authors Amy Tan, Brent Staples, Gary Soto, and Paula Gunn Allen.
- Introductory chapter and chapter introductions have been revised to include more student work and expanded to provide fuller treatment of the writing process.
- The Glossary has been expanded to include creative writing and writing process terms presented in the chapter introductions and in the end-of-selection apparatus.
- Beginning-of-selection apparatus has been expanded to include a "Getting Started" question that assists students in recalling information that will aid in reading the selection and, later, writing about it.

An Overview of Patterns

Chapter 1, an introductory chapter, describes the prewriting process and the basics of paragraphs and essays. In Chapters 2 through 9, the various techniques in developing the main idea—*narration, description, examples, classification and division, comparison and contrast, process, cause and effect,* and *definition*—are taken up in individual chapters. These techniques are the traditional *rhetorical modes*—the strategies for development that have proven effective in providing starting points for many student writers. Chapter 10, "Extra Readings," contains essays that illustrate the ways writers combine various modes of development within a single essay.

Professional and student selections in *Patterns* were specifically chosen to build students' confidence by showing them that writing a short, effective composition is within their reach. Selections range from simple, accessible paragraphs to longer, more challenging essays. The student writing included throughout the text will make students aware of the level of skill they can realistically expect to acquire.

The breadth of reading selections also allows the instructor a wide choice of topics—from serious and timely discussions about hidden racism and the constitutionality of gun control to lighthearted pieces that reveal human foibles. As a stimulus to discussion, two sides of a controversial subject are sometimes provided; students will probably respond quite differently to the definitions of success offered by Ellen Goodman and Michael Korda.

Apparatus

Patterns offers a full range of study apparatus:

- *Headnotes* provide context for each reading selection, helping students to understand and enjoy the selection more easily.
- *Words to Know* define unfamiliar words and clarify allusions that might be unfamiliar or regional.
- *Getting Started* question prepares students to draw on prior knowledge and think critically about the topic presented in the selection that follows.
- *Exercises* elicit various levels of thinking from the student:

  Questions About the Reading are designed to stimulate thinking about the selection's meaning—expressed and implied—and help students gain fuller understanding of the writer's message.

  Questions About the Writer's Strategies ask students to discuss the writer's *thesis statement, mode of development, point of view, figurative language*—or whatever strategy is particularly appropriate to a given selection—and thereby promote analytical thinking.

Writing Assignments are related to the topic or mode of the reading selection and are designed to encourage the student to generate ideas and develop these ideas into paragraphs and essays.

- The *thematic table of contents* groups the readings in the text by themes such as "The Individual and Society," "Values," and "The Working World."
- The *Glossary* provides definitions of all writing process, creative writing, rhetorical, and literary terms boldfaced throughout the chapter introductions and end-of-selection questions.

Support for Instructors

The Instructor's Resource Manual for *Patterns* offers instructors a wide variety of supplemental materials:

- Part I supplies teaching suggestions that will allow flexibility in determining course content and structure.
- Part II provides suggested answers to the reading comprehension and Writer's Strategies questions appearing at the end of each reading selection in Chapters 2 through 9.
- Part III offers suggested questions and answers for the Extra Readings that are included in Chapter 10.
- Part IV includes a list of the reading levels according to the Fry and Dale-Chall readability formulas. Reading levels are arranged by chapter and by grade.

Acknowledgments

I want to thank my good friends Ruth Silon, Cuyahoga Community College, for sharing her students' essays, "The Pediatrician" and "Students," and Kim Flachmann, California State University, Bakersfield, for providing "Intruder in the House." I am also indebted to the following persons for their help on the fourth edition of the text:

Diane S. Fitton, Monroe Community College: Rochester, NY
Sylvia H. Gamboa, College of Charleston
Douglas R. Garrison, Southwestern College: Chula Vista, CA
Laurance J. Riley, Milwaukee Area Technical College
Denis Sivack, Kingsborough Community College, CUNY
Donald K. Skiles, Chabot College: Hayward, CA

Joy Stone, Montclair State College: Upper Montclair, NJ
Barbara P. Thompson, Columbus State Community College: OH
Linda S. Weeks, Dyersburg State Community College: TN

Mary Lou Conlin

Patterns

A Short Prose Reader

1

The Basics
of Paragraphs
and Essays

WRITING IS A way of communicating, and of course you communicate all the time, mainly by talking to other people. Whenever you talk to anyone—a friend, a teacher, an employer—you want your listener to understand your ideas as clearly as possible. Usually you make your main point and then go on to provide some clear examples or to tell a lively story that clarifies your idea. In any case, you continue to explain or develop your main idea until you feel your listener grasps the point you are making.

In your writing, your purpose is similar. You want your reader to understand your idea—the main point you are making. Suppose you have an idea that people should participate in some volunteer activity. In your opinion, people benefit from helping others. You will want to think of clear-cut examples to back up your statement, or you may choose to tell a story drawing from your experience as a volunteer. Perhaps you will want to write a comparison of how you felt before and after you started participating in volunteer activities. In whatever way you choose to clarify your idea—by an example, a story, or a comparison—you want to present your main idea in a clear and effective manner.

This book tells you about the strategies, techniques, and process that you can use to produce effective writing. It includes many paragraphs and essays by other writers—both students and professionals—that you can study as models for your own writing. By studying the techniques and strategies these writers use to communicate their ideas, by understanding the process involved in writing, and by practicing in paragraphs and essays of your own, you can develop the skill and confidence needed to write effectively on many different subjects.

It is important that you learn a variety of writing strategies because you will find yourself, in school and afterward, writing for different **purposes**, to different types of **audiences**, and for varied **occasions**. Your purpose might be to instruct (in a description of how you successfully handled a lab assignment), or to inform (in a letter to the editor explaining errors in a newspaper article). Your audience, or reader, and the occasion for your writing will vary too. In one situation, your audience might be fellow students or friends and the occasion an informal activity. Or your audience could be your economics or history professor and the occasion an assigned essay or term paper. In each case, you will need to make choices about the organization, content, and words you use in your paragraph or essay.

As a student, you will have assignments that require you to write either a **paragraph** or an **essay**. Although such compositions may differ in their length and content, a paragraph and an essay are alike in two important ways. First, each one should have a **main idea**. Second, the main idea should be fully explained or developed. In this book, you will learn how many writers go about finding a main idea and the methods they use in explaining or developing it.

Finding a Main Idea

If you are like many writers, you may find it difficult to come up with a main idea of your own. You may stare out the window, get something to eat, or in some way put off starting to write. Many writers find it helps to do some prewriting exercises to warm up and to generate ideas. One method for doing this is to sit down and write without stopping for five or ten minutes. This is called **freewriting**, and its purpose is to get you started writing.

As its name implies, freewriting may be disorganized and may lack clear focus. For example, suppose your instructor has asked you to write a paragraph describing the room you are in. Instead of staring at the blank page and agonizing over the best way to start, you could just begin to write down your thoughts as they occur. Your freewriting might read like this:

> Looks like rain. Wonder if I closed my bedroom windows. What can I say about this classroom except that it's pretty much like all college classrooms. Seats with writing arms, blackboard, teacher's desk, tan walls with lots of dents in them. Have to pick Chad up from the day care center at 4. Hope he won't be crabby like he was yesterday. What should I say about this classroom?

Chapter 1 / The Basics of Paragraphs and Essays

After you have completed your freewriting, read it over and underline anything that strikes you as being interesting or important. Besides getting you started writing, freewriting may also trigger an idea for you to write about. When you looked around your classroom, you noticed that it was like all classrooms, except for having lots of dents in its walls. Choosing this as a main idea, you might then write a paragraph something like this:

Main Idea	⌈ The classroom is like all college classrooms except for the ⌊ many dents in its walls. Like all classrooms, it has thirty chairs with writing arms, lined up in five rows with six chairs in each row; a blackboard that still has the assignment on it from the previous class and needs a good washing; the professor's desk, with a podium on it to hold his oft-used lecture notes; and tan, finger-marked walls. But for some unknown reason, chairs have been shoved hard and often against the walls, which have more and deeper dents than
Main Idea restated	⌈ those in other classrooms. Only its dented walls make this ⌊ classroom different from all college classrooms.

Suppose, however, that your assignment is to write an essay, and you have been given the environment as the subject to write about. Again, you may want to do some freewriting in order to get started. But you may now find it helpful to do some **brainstorming**, either on your own or with some classmates.

Brainstorming involves listing whatever you know or perhaps feel about a subject—in this case, the environment. Now you must focus your thinking and list, note, or write down only what you think of that relates to the environment. A list might look like this:

trees	water
pollution	diapers
landfills	food
harmful	resources
paper	waste disposal
flowers	cars, airplanes—noise
smog	cars—exhaust
plastics	wasting resources—oil, coal, water
land	

After you finish your brainstorming list, read it over and look for relationships between the words and ideas. For instance, the previous list could be divided into two groups or categories: (1) things that the environment provides and (2) things that can harm or damage the environment.

Environment provides:	Environment damaged by:
trees	waste disposal—diapers, plastics
flowers	cars—exhaust fumes, noise
food	airplanes—noise
resources—water, oil, coal	wasting resources—water, oil, coal, trees

Based on these categories, the main idea for the essay could be: "We depend on our environment for food, water, and other resources, but we are damaging our environment in several ways." If we then further group or classify the *ways* we are damaging the environment, we could say we are "*polluting* the land and our water supply with waste disposal," "*poisoning* the air with the exhaust from cars and airplanes," and "*wasting* our resources by the overuse of paper and oil."

Brainstorming, like freewriting, can help you decide on the main idea for a paragraph or essay. Such prewriting techniques can also provide you with some of the specific ideas you need to support or develop your main idea.

The main idea of a paragraph is called the **topic**. This topic is usually stated in a sentence, called a **topic sentence**. The topic sentence, usually a general rather than a specific idea, may be placed anywhere within the paragraph. However, you will find it generally helps to keep your writing clear and focused if you state your main idea at the *beginning* of the paragraph. In the sample paragraph that follows, the main idea (or topic) of the paragraph is stated in the first sentence.

Topic sentence

Americans are probably the most pain-conscious people on the face of the earth. For years we have had it drummed into us—in print, on radio, over television, in everyday conversation—that any hint of pain is to be banished as though it were the ultimate evil. As a result, we are becoming a nation of pill-grabbers and hypochondriacs, escalating the slightest ache into a searing ordeal.

Norman Cousins,
Anatomy of an Illness

In the paragraph that follows, the writer has stated the topic in the first and second sentences.

Topic sentences

Example 1 of main idea

For as far back as I can remember, people have been saying the youth of the nation [are] getting soft and losing [their] moral fiber. I just doubt it. They certainly aren't wearing as much underwear, but I doubt if there's any less moral fiber. I'll bet the very day Andy Robustelli put on his first jockstrap, some old athlete was saying athletes weren't what

Chapter 1 / The Basics of Paragraphs and Essays

Example 2 of
main idea

they used to be. I'll bet the day little Ike Eisenhower was
planting that sweet corn, someone was saying kids wouldn't
work anymore.

Andy Rooney,
"Youth"

As you become more experienced, you may sometimes find it effective
to place the topic sentence at the *end* of the paragraph. In the following
paragraph the writer has stated the topic in the last sentence.

When a motorist, driving at 65 miles per hour, sights a
sudden hazard, his foot moves sharply to the brake pedal.
But, incredibly, the car has traversed another 70 feet between
the sighting and contact with the brake. Another 250 feet will
be covered before the car is brought to a halt. The total procedure [takes] a distance longer than a football field. So brakes
are important and they deserve a checkup at least twice a
year.

Topic sentence

Saturday Evening Post,
January/February, 1975

As you study the student and professional writings that follow, you
will find that writers do not always state outright the main idea of their
paragraphs and essays. Instead, they may prefer to suggest or to **imply**
the idea. Notice that the writer must provide enough clues to allow the
careful reader to determine the main idea. In the following paragraph,
for example, the writer implies rather than states the idea that the man
saw the berries reflected rather than actually floating in the water. The
writer provides the clues the reader needs by saying that the man struck
the bottom of the river when he dived in and that he then looked up and
saw the berries hanging over him.

While walking along the river, he saw some berries in the water. He
dived down for them, but was stunned when he unexpectedly struck the
bottom. There he lay for quite a while, and when he recovered consciousness and looked up, he saw the berries hanging on a tree just above him.

Paul Radin,
"Manbozho and the Berries"

If you experiment with implying your main idea, be sure to give the
reader enough clues to determine your meaning.

In a longer piece of writing, such as an essay, the main idea is called the
thesis (rather than the topic). The thesis is usually stated in one or more
sentences called the **thesis statement**. Like the topic sentence of a paragraph, the thesis statement is often placed near the beginning of an essay.
In the sample essay that follows, the thesis is stated in the opening paragraph.

Thesis statement	Scientists all agree that packages are very necessary. They also agree that packages are a problem. But they do not agree on what to do about it.
Topic sentence of paragraph 2	There is the make-it-attractive group. These designers concentrate on making the package so interesting that the buyer cannot bring himself to part with it—thus keeping it out of the trash. . . .
Topic sentence of paragraph 3	Next there are the no-package-package groups. They have ideas like spraying a protein coating, derived from corn, on foods to protect them against loss of vitamins and spoilage. . . .
Topic sentence of paragraph 4	In the no-package-package group is a new type of glass that may be the answer to the 26 billion bottles thrown away every year. The glass is coated on the inside as well as on the outside by a water-resistant film. When the bottle is smashed, the glass will dissolve in plain water. . . .
Topic sentence of paragraph 5	Another no-package is the plastic bag used to hold laundry bleach or bluing. Tossed into the laundry, it dissolves before the washing is finished. But the prize will go to the scientist who can come up with a container that is as successful as the ice cream cone.

Suzanne Hilton,
How Do They Get Rid of It?

In addition to the thesis statement, notice how each paragraph has its own individual topic sentence.

Experienced writers may place the thesis statement in later paragraphs or at the end of the essay. They may, indeed, only imply the thesis. For your own writing, the important point to remember is that an effective essay has a clear thesis statement, just as a well-made paragraph has a topic sentence. When you are reading, your task is to discover the writer's thesis. When you are writing, your task is to make your own thesis as clear as possible to your reader. And your best strategy, initially, is to *state your thesis at or near the beginning of your essay.*

Developing the Main Idea

The second important way in which paragraphs and essays are alike is that their main ideas must be explained or **developed** by the writer. Among the methods of development most frequently used by writers are:

narration	cause and effect
description	definition
examples	
classification and division	
comparison and contrast	
process	

Chapter 1 / The Basics of Paragraphs and Essays

These methods of developing the main idea are called **modes of development**. Although they have different characteristics, the modes of development have a common purpose in written compositions. That purpose is to provide the reader with the specific information needed to **support** or clarify the main idea. As stated earlier, the main idea is a general statement; the development provides the details to support or explain the main idea.

In developing a paragraph, the writer usually (1) begins with a topic sentence, (2) develops the main idea (topic) by a series of related sentences that explain the idea fully, and (3) concludes with a sentence that restates or summarizes the main idea. Look at the following paragraph diagram and compare it with the example paragraph about the classroom on page 3. Notice that the example paragraph begins with a topic sentence; develops the main idea (topic) with the sentences about the chairs, blackboard, desk, and walls; and then concludes by restating the topic sentence.

Paragraph

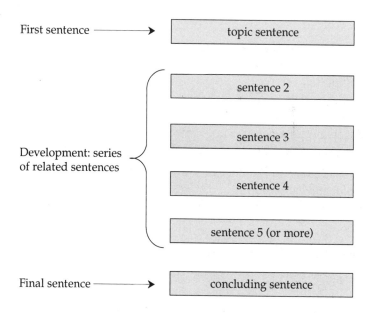

Next, compare the paragraph diagram with the essay diagram that follows. Notice that in developing the essay, the writer starts with a thesis statement, which is generally part of the introduction and may make up the whole first paragraph. Then the writer develops the thesis in a series of related paragraphs, usually called the **body** of the essay. Often, each paragraph has its own individual topic sentence. The conclusion, which may restate the thesis or summarize the essay's important points, is usually found in the final paragraph.

Essay

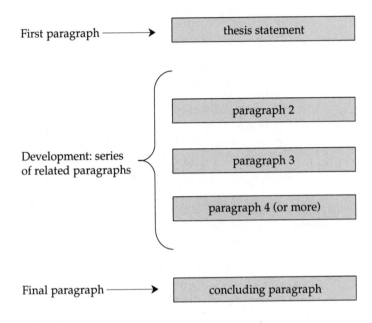

First paragraph ⟶ thesis statement

Development: series of related paragraphs

paragraph 2

paragraph 3

paragraph 4 (or more)

Final paragraph ⟶ concluding paragraph

Now compare the following first draft of a student's essay about the environment with the previous essay diagram. Notice that the thesis is stated in the first paragraph, which is called the **introduction** of the essay. The thesis is developed, or supported, by the next three paragraphs that make up the body of the essay. The final paragraph, called the **conclusion** or concluding paragraph, restates the thesis and sums up the main points of the essay.

Thesis statement (introduction)

Modern conveniences have made our lives easier, but often at the expense of our environment. Science and society, which have been so quick to create and adopt new consumer goods, have been slow in creating and adopting practices to protect the environment from the same consumer goods. As a result, just through everyday living, we are damaging the environment we depend on and wasting our resources.

Development (body paragraphs)

For one thing, we pollute the land and our water supply with the by-products of modern life. We fill our garbage dumps and landfills with throw-away plastic products and "disposable" diapers that will not disintegrate for hundreds of years, if ever. Industries accidentally or willfully spill oil and chemicals into the ground or streams and pollute our water supply.

Chapter 1 / The Basics of Paragraphs and Essays

For another thing, we poison the air with exhaust from the cars and airplanes that have become such an important part of our lives. In some areas, the exhaust from cars creates smog that poisons our lungs and causes respiratory ailments. Air pollution also causes acid rain that, in turn, destroys rivers, lakes, woods, and farm crops.

Finally, we are wasting our resources shamefully. For example, we use far more water than we need to in brushing our teeth and taking showers. Even something as "harmless" as letting dripping faucets go unrepaired wastes a lot of valuable water. We water our lawns through automatic sprinkler systems that run even in rainstorms. We also waste oil by driving millions of cars hundreds of millions of needless miles each year and by keeping our houses warmer than we need to. We are even dangerously close to depleting our "renewable" resources. We cut down our forests with abandonment in order to eat from paper plates, drink from paper cups, and carry products home from the store.

Thesis and important points restated (concluding paragraph)

Yes, we have come to depend on technology to fulfill our needs, but we still need our natural environment. Unless we start developing technology to protect our natural world, it may soon pollute and poison us.

Although the essay can and should be developed more fully in a second draft and in subsequent revisions, notice that the writer's essay is structured like the diagram. The thesis is stated in the introductory paragraph. Each classification of the *ways* the environment is being damaged has been used as the topic for a body paragraph, and items from the brainstorming list have been used as examples to develop the topics. The concluding paragraph restates the thesis and sums up the important points.

The essay has also been developed by using three modes of development: **classification, examples,** and **cause and effect.** The *classifications* are the *ways* we are damaging the environment: polluting, poisoning, wasting. *Examples* are plastics, diapers, and oil and chemical spills; exhaust fumes from cars and airplanes; and brushing our teeth, watering our lawns, driving needlessly, overheating our houses, and using paper products. In turn, the examples are *causes* of three *effects:* pollution, poisoning, and wasting. The smog created by car exhaust is also a *cause* of lung and respiratory ailments *(effects).*

Although the modes of development are often combined in this and other ways, a single mode of development will often be dominant in a composition. For instance, if you are writing a **descriptive** essay, that does not mean you cannot use **examples** to illustrate your description, but it means that the essay's purpose and most of the paragraphs will be descriptive. Or you might write a **cause-and-effect** essay in which you **narrate** a series of events that constitute a cause and another event that is the effect. In general, though, you will learn to be comfortable with the modes of development if you first study them individually, and this text is organized so you can do that. You will see that each chapter that follows deals with a single mode of development and brings together paragraphs and essays in which that mode dominates.

Before each paragraph or essay you will find a note that tells you something about the reading, definitions of words that might be unfamiliar to you, and a question that will help you begin to think about the reading, as well as a writing idea. Following each reading selection you will find questions about the reading and about the writer's strategies and suggestions for your own writing assignments.

The Glossary at the back of the book defines and explains the technical terms you will learn to use. These terms are boldfaced throughout the text. If you encounter a boldfaced term and cannot recall what it means, turn to the Glossary to refresh your memory.

The ability to state an idea and to develop it so that it is clear to your reader is essential to all forms of writing. Mastery of the writing principles covered in this text will help give you that ability. You can then apply it to the many kinds of writing projects you will encounter both now at school and later in your career or business.

2

Narration

AT ONE TIME or another, you may have rushed a friend to the hospital for emergency treatment or warned your sleeping neighbors that their apartment was full of fire and smoke—and they had to get out. If you later mention one of these **events** to friends, they will probably want to know more about it. What individual **incidents** made up the event? How did it happen? At what time? Where did it take place? On the spot, you become a narrator or storyteller and try to give a clear and lively account of the event. Thus you are already familiar with **narration**, one of the modes of development that writers frequently use to illustrate and explain their ideas. Using narration, the writer hopes to interest the reader in a good story while illustrating a particular idea clearly.

Narration is frequently used to tell about personal experiences. You have a variety of personal experiences every day. Your car won't start, you miss the bus, and then you are late for your seminar. Such experiences, although important to you, will not necessarily make an effective narrative. For a narrative to be effective, the writer needs to have some goal in mind that will attract the reader's interest. The goal might be to portray a unique or exciting event that the reader has never experienced, or it might be to stir the reader's emotions—a sad story or a humorous story.

Most often, the goal of narration is to describe an experience that has some unusual meaning or significance both for the writer and for the reader. Usually an experience is significant because it taught you—and may teach your reader—something new, something you never realized before about life. For example, in the following paragraph, the writer tells about a personal experience that taught her about being responsible not only for making decisions but also for accepting the consequences of those decisions.

Topic sentence

Incident 1

Incident 2

Incident 3

Topic restated: significance of narrative

As I was growing up, my father and I sometimes disagreed about how I should spend my time. He began telling me, "If you get yourself into it, you'll have to get yourself out." But I learned what it meant to be responsible for the consequences of my decisions only after I went to a weekend party when I should have studied for a chemistry exam. I needed a good grade on the exam to stay in the nursing program, and the consequences of my decision to go to the party were clear when I got my exam back with a notice that I was on academic probation. I spent two semesters of almost steady studying before I was back in good standing. Now, whenever I have a difficult decision to make, I remind myself, "If you get yourself into it, you'll have to get yourself out." I've learned that making a decision means taking the responsibility for its consequences.

Effective narrative writing, like all good writing, is carefully organized. Since a narrative describes events, its organization must be governed by some form of time **order**. The writer often tells about events in the order in which they took place. This method, called **chronological order**, ensures that the time and sequence of the incidents will be logical.

Sometimes, though, a writer may reorder events to achieve an effect that will increase the reader's interest. Experienced writers, using what is called *flashback style,* may start near the end of the narrative or even in the middle and then work their way back to the beginning. Or a writer may withhold a key event that preceded the incidents in the narrative. Doing so can add emphasis to the narrative's main idea. Consider, for instance, what the effect would have been if the writer of the example paragraph above had introduced her father's advice at the end of the paragraph instead of at the beginning.

You may want to avoid complicated time schemes like these, at least at first. But no matter at what point you choose to start a narrative, the reader must be able to understand the order of the incidents and not feel confused or unclear about what happened. You may want to jot down the incidents in a rough list and then order them so that the time and sequence of the incidents will be logical and clear to your reader.

In the following sample paragraph, the writer uses narration to give a factual account of an event—the discovery of Wheaties. Notice that this writer has chosen to explain the different incidents in a simple chronological order.

Topic sentence

Like gravity and penicillin, Wheaties was discovered by accident. In 1921, a health clinician named Minnenrode, in

	Minneapolis, was mixing up a batch of bran gruel for his pa-
Incident 1	tients when he spilled some on a hot stove. He heard it
Incident 2	crackle and sizzle, and had a taste. Delicious, he thought. He took his cooled gruel to the Washburn Crosby Company,
Incident 3	which in 1928 would merge with three mills to become Gen-
Incident 4	eral Mills. Favorably impressed, Washburn Crosby gave Minnenrode use of a laboratory. Alas, his flakes crumbled
Incident 5	too easily and turned to dust in a box. Exit Minnenrode, en- ter George Cormack, Washburn Crosby's head miller. Cor-
	mack tested 36 varieties of wheat. He cracked them, he
Conclusion	steamed them, he mixed them with syrup, he cooked them, he dried them, he rolled them. Finally he found the perfect flakes.

Steve Wulf,
"The Breakfast of Champions"

Notice the **details** in this paragraph. In addition to re-creating the incidents that are significant to his topic, the writer colors those incidents with details that help describe what happened. Minnenrode's spilled gruel *crackled* and *sizzled,* but his flakes "turned to dust in a box." By using words that provide descriptive detail, the writer adds variety and clarity to his narrative. (**Description**, a mode of development in its own right, is the subject of the next chapter.)

Notice, too, that this paragraph contains only the incidents or details that contribute directly to the story. Avoiding irrelevant incidents and details is essential to effective narrative writing. Perhaps you have had some long-winded person tell you a story and have found yourself wishing that person would skip some of the trivial details. You should keep this in mind when you are writing and limit yourself to the details that are *essential* to the main idea of your narrative. In the following essay, for example, the writer does not include any incidents that happened before or after the robbery. He concentrates on those incidents and details that explain his actions and reactions only during key moments. As you read the essay, think about the details the writer provides and try to form an image of the scene in your mind.

Thesis statement	Recently I was unfortunate enough to be in a store when a robbery took place. I learned from that experience that a pointed gun makes people obey.	1
Incidents ar-ranged as they occurred in time	I had stopped at the store on my way home from work to get a loaf of bread. I was at the check-out counter when a man standing nearby pulled out a gun and yelled, "Everyone on the floor and away from the cash register!"	2
Frozen in place	My first reaction was fear. Around me, people dropped to the floor. But I felt frozen where I stood.	3
Gun pointed	As I hesitated, the robber pointed his gun at me and yelled again, "On the floor!" Then I felt angry. I was bigger	4

and stronger than he was. I was sure I could put *him* on the floor in a fair fight.

But the gun, small enough to be cradled in the palm of my 5 hand, was bigger and stronger than I was. I sank obediently to the floor.

All of us watched silently as the robber scooped money 6 out of the cash register into a paper bag. Then he ran out the door, jumped into a car that was waiting, and the car raced away.

Everyone stood up and started talking. A clerk called the 7 police, who asked if anyone could describe the robber or the car. No one could.

Then one man, blustering defensively, told the clerk just 8 what I was thinking. "Listen. Tell them when a gun is pointed at me, it's all I'm looking at. One look and I'm going to do whatever I'm told."

(Marginal notes: Sank to floor — Robbery took place — After robbery — Dialogue / Significance of narrative restated)

Look at each paragraph in this essay. The first paragraph is an introduction in which the main idea or thesis of the essay is stated. Each successive paragraph deals with an incident or set of incidents in the narrative. Each incident contributes key information to the essay, and each incident moves the story forward in time. The final paragraph concludes the narrative by restating the main significance of the essay.

As you can see from the example essay, the narrative mode is used for more than just retelling what happened. In addition to reporting the action, narrative writing often explains the *reactions*—emotions and feelings—of the narrator and others involved. At other times, the writer may leave it to the reader to determine the narrator's feelings and reactions.

In this and other ways, the writer establishes a particular **point of view** for the essay. Point of view involves three elements: **Person, time**, and **tone**. The essay may be written in the **first person** (*I/we*), **second person** (*you*), or **third person** (*he/she/it/they*). The time in which the essay is set may be past, present, or future, and the tone is the attitude (serious, humorous, angry, sad) the writer adopts. The writer's point of view thus establishes the setting for an essay and greatly influences the essay's meaning and how the reader will interpret it. In a narrative essay, the point of view creates the context for the incidents described.

In narration and the other modes of development, an important factor in point of view is whether the writer is being objective or subjective. An **objective** essay presents the **facts**—the basics of what occurred or what is being described—without including the writer's own interpretations or personal opinions of those facts. The writer tries to portray the subject of the essay as truly as possible and does not try to influence how the reader will react. A **subjective** essay, by contrast, expresses how the writer feels and may try to get the reader to feel a certain way. It may give an opinion or reveal the writer's emotions, or it may present facts in such a way that the reader will draw a conclusion favored by the writer. The Wheaties story is an example of objective writing; it presents the facts without interpreting them. The other two preceding examples are written more subjectively, expressing the writers' own feelings about and interpretations of the events described.

Often, writers give clues that indicate that they are being subjective. Phrases like "in my opinion" or "I felt" or "I learned" signal a subjective interpretation. (Just because an essay is written in the first person does not mean it is entirely subjective, however.) As you will see in some of the selections in this text, writers may not always tell you when they are being subjective. Some writers may even take an objective tone when they are being quite subjective—perhaps, for instance, by presenting certain facts about a subject but not others. No matter what mode of development is used in an essay, you should try to make sure just how subjective or objective the writer is being.

Narrative writing is called **nonfiction** if the story or event is true and actually happened. All of the preceding examples are nonfiction accounts. This kind of factual narrative is found in biography, history, and newspaper writing. Narrative is also the mode used in short stories and novels. If a story is not true or did not actually occur, it is called **fiction**.

In fiction and nonfiction narrative writing, writers use **dialogue** to recreate what people or characters in the narrative said. In the essay on the store robbery, notice that the writer often tells you exactly what was said and encloses the statement using quotation marks to let you know he is quoting word-for-word conversation. Quoted dialogue can help the writer accurately express the incidents in a narrative and can add variety and color. To practice working with dialogue, listen to your friends talking with one another and see if you can reproduce dialogue something like their conversation in your own narratives.

Writers use narration to tell about personal experiences, about other people's lives and experiences, and about factual or historical events, such as the discovery of Wheaties. Narration adds interest, suspense, and clarity to writing, as you will find in the reading selections that follow. Consequently, it is a writing skill well worth mastering.

The questions and assignments at the ends of the readings in this chapter will help you recognize and apply the principles of narration. They will give you practice with the concepts of chronological order, narrative detail, subjective and objective writing, and dialogue.

The Movie House

John Updike

Our fondest childhood memories are often laced with terror. This paragraph from John Updike's memoir of life in a small town is filled with details that provide a vivid description of just how exciting it is to be terrified.

Words to Know

glowered   scowled, stared angrily

indulgent   not strict, tolerant

supersensory   beyond or above awareness of senses, supernatural

Getting Started

Can you recall a frightening incident from your childhood that haunts you to this day?

It was two blocks from my home; I began to go alone from the age of six. My mother, so strict about my kissing girls, was strangely indulgent about this. The theater ran three shows a week, for two days each, and was closed on Sundays. Many weeks I went three times. I remember a summer evening in our yard. Supper is over, the walnut tree throws a heavy shadow. The fireflies are not out yet. My father is off, my mother and her parents are turning the earth in our garden. Some burning sticks and paper on our ash heap fill the damp air with low smoke; I express a wish to go to the movies, expecting to be told no. Instead, my mother tells me to go into the house and clean up; I come into the yard again in clean shorts, the shadows slightly heavier, the dew a little wetter; I am given eleven cents and run down Philadelphia Avenue in my ironed shorts and fresh shirt, down past the running ice-plant water, the dime and the penny in my hand. I always ran to the movies. If it was not a movie with Adolphe Menjou, it was a horror picture. People turning into cats—fingers going stubby into paws and hair being blurred in with double exposure—and Egyptian tombs and English houses where doors creak and wind disturbs the curtains and dogs refuse to go into certain rooms because they sense something supersensory. I used to crouch down into the seat and hold my coat in front of my face when I sensed a frightening scene coming, peeking through the buttonhole to find out when it was over. Through the buttonhole Frankenstein's monster glowered; lightning flashed; sweat poured over the bolts that held his face together. On the way home, I ran again, in terror now. Darkness had come, the first show was from seven to nine, by nine even the longest summer day was ending. Each porch along the street seemed to be a tomb crammed with shadows, each shrub seemed to shelter a grasping arm. I ran with a frantic high step, trying to keep my ankles away from the reaching hands. The last and worst terror was our own porch; low brick walls on either side concealed possible cat people. Leaping high, I launched myself at the door and, if no one was in the front of the house, fled through suffocating halls past gaping doorways to the kitchen, where there was always someone working, and a light bulb burning. The icebox. The rickety worn table, oilcloth-covered, where we ate. The windows solid black and fortified by the interior brightness. But even then I kept my legs away from the dark space beneath the table.

Questions About the Reading

1. Did the writer enjoy horror movies as a young boy? How can you tell?
2. What gives this paragraph a breathless, frightened quality? Try to identify specific **details** that contribute to this quality.
3. As a young boy, the writer spent many hours at the movies. Does he ever mention being there with friends? What does the writer **imply** about his social experiences in this paragraph?

Questions About the Writer's Strategies

1. Is the **main idea** of the paragraph directly stated? If so, in which sentence(s)? If not, state the main idea in a sentence of your own.
2. What is the **point of view** in the narrative? Could another point of view be used? Using the first two sentences of the paragraph as an example, explain how you could change the point of view.
3. If you had never seen a horror movie, what **details** in the paragraph would give you an idea of what one would be like?
4. In what ways is this paragraph **subjective**? In what ways is it **objective**?

Writing Assignments

1. Recall the most frightening episode from your childhood. Write a narrative paragraph describing the feelings you experienced.
2. Write a narrative paragraph that describes the neighborhood in which you grew up. Try to include details that will help the reader infer the size and type of town.
3. Think of an activity that you loved as a child. Write a narrative paragraph in the **third person** that describes a child participating in that activity.

Grandma's Last Day

Ivan Doig

After his grandmother died, Ivan Doig set out to trace the events of her last day. He found that her day had been filled with activity, work, and— most of all—life. The following paragraph is from the last chapter of This House of Sky, *Doig's beautifully written memoir of growing up on the sheep and cattle ranches of Montana. In the paragraph, Doig tells us the details of his grandmother's last day.*

Words to Know

thorned   irritated, pained, aggravated

Getting Started

How significant do you think the daily activities of an ordinary person could be?

Wonder built in me as I traced out her last day. The morning, Grandma had spent working on a quilt, another of her rainbow-paneled splendors, for a helpful neighbor who looked in on her often. Sometime she had telephoned to a friend at a ranch out of Ringling, asking to be brought a fresh supply of eggs when the woman came to town. At noon she was phoned by her son, and as usual in those checking calls, they talked for several minutes. In the afternoon a funeral was held for a member of one of the last families of the Sixteen country: Grandma did not go to the rites, but at the coffee hour held afterward at the Senior Citizens Club she helped with the serving and chatted with friends for an hour or more. Someone had driven her home, where she had her supper alone. In the evening, there was to be the weekly card party back at the Senior Citizens Club, and she phoned to ask for a ride with her best friend in the group—a woman who had run one of the White Sulphur saloons that had so often thorned Grandma's earlier life. They had nearly arrived at the card party when, in the midst of something joked by one or the other of them, Grandma cut off in the middle of a chuckle and slumped, chin onto chest. The friend whirled the car to the hospital a block away. A doctor instantly was trying to thump a heartbeat-rhythm into Grandma, but could work no flicker of response from her. She had gone from life precisely as she had lived it, with abruptness and at full pace.

Questions About the Reading

1. If the writer had not called the woman "Grandma," you would still have some idea of her age. Which **details** indicate her age?
2. On the surface, this paragraph appears to tell about a series of **incidents**, but in the end it tells you a great deal about Grandma's character. Which sentences tell you that Grandma was helpful to and considerate of other people?
3. Did Grandma live in a town or in the country? Which details help you decide where she lived? Did she live alone? Which details tell you?
4. What are some conclusions you might draw about Grandma's character from the statements that "saloons . . . had so often thorned Grandma's earlier life" and that a woman who had run one of the saloons was Grandma's best friend in the Senior Citizens Club?

Questions About the Writer's Strategies

1. What is the **main idea** of the paragraph?
2. What are the specific incidents or events that the writer uses to support the main idea of the paragraph? What words and phrases does he use to let you know the **order** in which the incidents occurred?
3. The writer left out some details about incidents and time. Which details are missing? Why do you think Doig did not include them?
4. The writer says the friend "whirled" her car to the hospital. Would *turned* be as effective a word? Why or why not?
5. The **point of view** used by the writer indicates that he was not with his grandmother on her last day. Using the first three sentences as an example, explain how you could change their wording to indicate that he was with her that day.

Writing Assignments

1. Write a narrative paragraph in which you tell about the daily activities of a person you admire or, if you prefer, of a person you dislike. Be sure the actions provide your reader with an understanding of the character of that person.

2. Think of someone who has influenced your life in some way. In a narrative paragraph, tell about several things that person did that influenced you. Narrate the incidents in **chronological order**.
3. Write a narrative paragraph in which you tell about one single event that was significant to a friend of yours.

The Discovery of Coca-Cola

E. J. Kahn, Jr.

Kahn has written about the American scene for The New Yorker *for over forty years. He has written about America at war, about Frank Sinatra, about Harvard, and about burlesque. He has also discussed that most American of drinks, Coca-Cola, in a book titled* The Big Drink. *In a paragraph from that book, he tells us of the invention of Coca-Cola as a medicine and the discovery that led to its becoming a soft drink.*

Words to Know

audit   analyze, figure out, verify
composition   contents, ingredients
concoction   mixture of ingredients
dollop   a large portion or serving
factotum   employee
testimonially   in honor of

Getting Started

How do you suppose some of the world's most common inventions were discovered?

The man who invented Coca-Cola was not a native Atlantan, but on the day of his funeral every drugstore in town testimonially shut up shop. He was John Styth Pemberton, born in 1833 in Knoxville, Georgia, eighty miles away. Sometimes known as Doctor, Pemberton was a pharmacist who, during the Civil War, led a cavalry troop under General Joe Wheeler. He settled in Atlanta in 1869, and soon began brewing such patent medicines as Triplex Liver Pills and Globe of Flower Cough Syrup. In 1885, he registered a trademark for something called French Wine Coca—Ideal Nerve and Tonic Stimulant; a few months later he formed the Pemberton Chemical Company, and recruited the services of a bookkeeper named Frank M. Robinson, who not only had a good head for figures but, attached to it, so exceptional a nose that he could audit the composition of a batch of syrup merely by sniffing it. In 1886—a year in which, as contemporary Coca-Cola officials like to point out, Conan Doyle unveiled Sherlock Holmes and France unveiled the Statue of Liberty—Pemberton unveiled a syrup that he called Coca-Cola. It was a modification of his French Wine Coca. He had taken out the wine and added a pinch of caffeine, and, when the end product tasted awful, had thrown in some extract of cola (or kola) nut and a few other oils, blending the mixture in a three-legged iron pot in his back yard and swishing it around with an oar. He distributed it to soda fountains in used beer bottles, and Robinson, with his flowing bookkeeper's script, presently devised a label, on which "Coca-Cola" was written in the fashion that is still employed. Pemberton looked upon his concoction less as a refreshment than as a headache cure, especially for people whose throbbing temples could be traced to overindulgence. On a morning late in 1886, one such victim of the night before dragged himself into an Atlanta drugstore and asked for a dollop of Coca-Cola. Druggists customarily stirred a teaspoonful of syrup into a glass of water, but in this instance the factotum on duty was too lazy to walk to the fresh-water tap, a couple of feet off. Instead, he mixed the syrup with some charged water, which was closer at hand. The suffering customer perked up almost at once, and word quickly spread that the best Coca-Cola was a fizzy one.

Questions About the Reading

1. Why did the drugstores in Atlanta honor Pemberton by closing on the day of his funeral?
2. How is Frank M. Robinson significant to the story of Coca-Cola's origins?
3. Sherlock Holmes, the fictional detective in a series of books written by Arthur Conan Doyle, and the Statue of Liberty appeared in the same year as Coca-Cola. Why would Coca-Cola officials like to point out these facts?
4. The writer describes the way Pemberton mixed Coca-Cola and distributed it. What does the writer's explanation tell you about the standards that existed in 1886 for the production and sale of patent medicines? Which words and phrases help describe the standards?

Questions About the Writer's Strategies

1. Is the **main idea** of the paragraph directly stated? If so, in which sentence(s)? If not, state the idea in a sentence of your own.
2. What is the **point of view** in "The Discovery of Coca-Cola"? Could the writer have used another point of view, such as **first person**? Why or why not?

3. Does the writer include any **details** that are not essential to the idea of the narrative? If so, why did he include them?
4. What **tone** does the writer achieve by his description of how Frank M. Robinson checked a batch of syrup? What is the effect of using the word *nose?* Why is the word *audit* appropriate?
5. The writer uses the words *dollop* and *factotum* in telling about the customer being served Coca-Cola in the drugstore in 1886. Why are these words more effective than *large serving* and *employee* would be?

Writing Assignments

1. Write a narrative paragraph in which you tell about an experience or event that had an unexpected ending.
2. Write a narrative paragraph in which you describe the incidents that you imagine led to the discovery of fire or of the wheel.
3. Write a narrative paragraph in the **first person** telling about something you did to help a friend, relative, or organization. Try to show how your action was significant to *you.*

Pearl Harbor Echoes in Seattle

Monica Sone

The bombing of Pearl Harbor by the Japanese drew America into World War II. It also inspired a time of discrimination against and intimidation of Japanese Americans. The FBI began "calling" on Japanese families, often taking the men away for questioning. This policy eventually led to an internment order, which forced Japanese Americans to live in camps until the end of the war. In this paragraph, Monica Sone recalls what it was like to be a Japanese American child living in Seattle, Washington, during this tense and frightening time.

Words to Know

pandemonium   chaos, confusion, uproar
routed   driven out, ejected
stoicism   without emotion, expression, or interest

Getting Started

Can you recall an incident from your childhood when you believed that you and your family were in danger?

Once when our doorbell rang after curfew hour, I completely lost my Oriental stoicism which I had believed would serve me well under the most trying circumstances. No friend of ours paid visits at night anymore, and I was sure that Father's hour had come. As if hypnotized, I walked woodenly to the door. A mass of black figures stood before me, filling the doorway. I let out a magnificent shriek. Then pandemonium broke loose. The solid rank fell apart into a dozen separate figures which stumbled and leaped pell-mell away from the porch. Watching the mad scramble, I thought I had routed the FBI agents with my cry of distress. Father, Mother, Henry and Sumi rushed out to support my wilting body. When Henry snapped on the porch light, one lone figure crept out from behind the front hedge. It was a newsboy who, standing at a safe distance, called in a quavering voice, "I . . . I came to collect for . . . for the *Times*."

Questions About the Reading

1. Why did the sound of the doorbell terrify the writer?
2. What did the writer do that signified she had lost her "Oriental stoicism"?
3. Why do you think the newsboy first came to the door accompanied by so many other people?

Questions About the Writer's Strategies

1. What is the **point of view** in the narrative? Could another point of view be used? Using the first two sentences of the paragraph as an example, explain how you could change the point of view.
2. In which sentence is the **main idea** of the paragraph stated?
3. What specific **incidents** or events does the writer use to support the main idea?
4. What are some of the descriptive words the writer uses to re-create the scene on the porch? Is her choice of words effective? Why or why not?

Writing Assignments

1. Recall an incident in which you were frightened or in which you frightened someone else. Write a narrative paragraph describing the feelings you experienced.
2. Write a narrative paragraph that describes an episode in which a child acts courageously. Try to include **details** that will help the reader infer the child's anxiety.
3. Imagine being mistaken for someone else. Write a narrative paragraph in which you are mistaken for a famous entertainer, a wanted criminal, or a family member. Include details that will help the reader understand your feelings.

Vital Signs

Natalie Kusz

When Natalie Kusz was seven, she was nearly killed in an accident that cost her the loss of one eye. The following paragraph, taken from her later account of her experience, tells us how a hospital worker helped her understand that, like Kusz's kindergarten teacher who had also suffered the loss of an eye, she could still have a full life when she grew up.

Getting Started

When a person is seriously ill, what heals first, the body or the mind?

Within Janine's playroom, we were some of us handicapped, but none disabled, and in time we were each taught to prove this for ourselves. While I poured the flour for new playdough, Janine asked me about my kindergarten teacher: what she had looked like with an eyepatch, and if she was missing my same eye. What were the hard parts, Janine said, for a teacher like that? Did I think it was sad for her to miss school sometimes, and did she talk about the hospital? What color was her hair, what sort was her eyepatch, and did I remember if she was pretty? What would I be, Janine asked, when I was that age and these surgeries were past? Over the wet salt smell of green dough, I wished to be a doctor with one blue eye, who could talk like this to the sick, who could tell them they were still real. And with her feel for when to stop talking, Janine turned and left me, searching out volunteers to stir up new clay.

Questions About the Reading

1. What does the writer mean when she says, "[W]e were some of us handicapped, but none disabled"?
2. Why did Janine ask so many questions about Natalie's teacher?
3. How was Natalie reassured that she was still "real"?

Questions About the Writer's Strategies

1. Is the **main idea** of the paragraph directly stated? If so, in which sentence(s)? If not, state the main idea in a sentence of your own.
2. What **incidents** does the writer use to support the main idea?
3. How is **dialogue** handled in this paragraph? Do you think the writer recalls the exact words that were said?
4. Is this paragraph **subjective** or **objective**? Support your answer.

Writing Assignments

1. Recall an incident from your childhood in which you were seriously sick or injured. Write a **first-person** paragraph that describes your state of mind at the time.
2. Rewrite Natalie Kusz's paragraph using quoted dialogue. Make sure the pronouns reflect the point of view you have chosen.
3. In a paragraph, describe an incident when an adult, other than a parent, had a positive impact on your life.

Freedom

Iu-choi Chan (student)

Sometimes a single event can tell us a great deal about a person, culture, or way of life. In the following paragraph a young Chinese man tells about his daring attempt to escape from a country where he felt oppressed to a place where he could be free. Although this attempt failed, Iu-choi Chan has since managed to come to the United States. He wrote this paragraph while he was a student at California State University in Bakersfield.

Words to Know

Hong Kong   a British colony on the coast of China
sentries   persons or soldiers posted to guard an area or position

Getting Started

When have you had to overcome obstacles to fulfill an important dream?

Two years ago, I attempted to escape from mainland China to Hong Kong. I planned and prepared well. I dressed up like a farmer and walked for two days from my village to the border between China and Hong Kong. That night, I was very excited and nervous, but I tried to keep calm. At the border there were a lot of sentries who tried to catch people like me, so I put some mud on myself to avoid being noticed. It was not easy for me to pass through the sentries, but I bit my tongue and climbed across the swampy area. Finally, I reached the river that runs across the border. I plunged into it. It was icy cold, and I used all my strength to swim as fast as I could. In about twenty minutes, I touched land. I had made it! My happiness was beyond description. But when I stood up, a Hong Kong policeman was immediately beside me. My dream was shattered. I was taken to a police station to wait for a truck that takes unsuccessful refugees back to China. The police put me in the truck with a great many other people, and we were driven like a herd of buffalo back to China. I had lost my freedom again.

Questions About the Reading

1. Which statement indicates the distance the young man lived from the Hong Kong border?
2. Describe the border area between China and Hong Kong.
3. Do many people try to leave mainland China and go to Hong Kong? Which **details** support your answer?
4. Why do you think the young man dressed like a farmer when he tried to escape?
5. The writer says, "I had lost my freedom again." What does the word *again* tell you about what has happened to him before? Do you think the sentence indicates his opinion of life in mainland China?

Questions About the Writer's Strategies

1. Is the **main idea** of the paragraph directly stated? If so, in which sentence(s)? If not, state the main idea in a sentence of your own.
2. In what **order** are the major incidents of the story arranged? Could the order be changed? If so, in what way?
3. The writer compares the return of the refugees to China to being "driven like a herd of buffalo." Does this comparison help you see his situation?
4. What is the **point of view** in the narrative? Could another point of view be used? Using the first three sentences of the paragraph as an example, explain how you could change the point of view.

Writing Assignments

1. Think of a goal you have set for yourself but that you have not yet reached. Write a narrative paragraph in which you (a) state the goal, (b) explain what has happened to prevent you from reaching the goal, and (c) tell what you will do in the future to achieve the goal.
2. Write a narrative paragraph in which you tell what you or another person did to succeed in reaching a particular goal.
3. What career have you chosen for yourself? Write a narrative paragraph in which you tell what you have done or what experiences you have had that made you choose the career.

Learning to Write

Russell Baker

Russell Baker is a Pulitzer Prize winner noted for his humorous writing. However, although this passage from his autobiographical book Growing Up *is lighthearted, we learn in the end that Baker is earnestly describing an event of serious, almost touching, personal importance.*

Words to Know

antecedent   the word to which a pronoun refers
listless   without energy, boring
prim   formal and neat, lacking humor
reminiscence   memory of a past experience

Getting Started

Can you describe an experience that changed the way you thought about yourself?

W hen our class was assigned to Mr. Fleagle for third-year English I 1
anticipated another grim year in that dreariest of subjects. Mr. Fleagle
was notorious among City students for dullness and inability to inspire.
He was said to be stuffy, dull, and hopelessly out of date. To me he looked
to be sixty or seventy and prim to a fault. He wore primly severe eye-
glasses, his wavy hair was primly cut and primly combed. He wore prim
vested suits with neckties blocked primly against the collar buttons of his
primly starched white shirts. He had a primly pointed jaw, a primly
straight nose, and a prim manner of speaking that was so correct, so
gentlemanly, that he seemed a comic antique.

I anticipated a listless, unfruitful year with Mr. Fleagle and for a long 2
time was not disappointed. We read *Macbeth.* Mr. Fleagle loved *Macbeth*
and wanted us to love it too, but he lacked the gift of infecting others
with his own passion. He tried to convey the murderous ferocity of Lady
Macbeth one day by reading aloud the passage that concludes

> . . . I have given suck, and know
> How tender 'tis to love the babe that milks me.

I would, while it was smiling in my face,
Have plucked my nipple from his boneless gums. . . .

The idea of prim Mr. Fleagle plucking his nipple from boneless gums was too much for the class. We burst into gasps of irrepressible snickering. Mr. Fleagle stopped.

"There is nothing funny, boys, about giving suck to a babe. It is the— 3 the very essence of motherhood, don't you see."

He constantly sprinkled his sentences with "don't you see." It wasn't 4 a question but an exclamation of mild surprise at our ignorance. "Your pronoun needs an antecedent, don't you see," he would say, very primly. "The purpose of the Porter's scene, boys, is to provide comic relief from the horror, don't you see."

Late in the year we tackled the informal essay. "The essay, don't you 5 see, is the . . ." My mind went numb. Of all forms of writing, none seemed so boring as the essay. Naturally we would have to write informal essays. Mr. Fleagle distributed a homework sheet offering us a choice of topics. None was quite so simpleminded as "What I Did on My Summer Vacation," but most seemed to be almost as dull. I took the list home and dawdled until the night before the essay was due. Sprawled on the sofa, I finally faced up to the grim task, took the list out of my notebook, and scanned it. The topic on which my eye stopped was "The Art of Eating Spaghetti."

This title produced an extraordinary sequence of mental images. Surg- 6 ing up out of the depths of memory came a vivid recollection of a night in Belleville when all of us were seated around the supper table—Uncle Allen, my mother, Uncle Charlie, Doris, Uncle Hal—and Aunt Pat served spaghetti for supper. Spaghetti was an exotic treat in those days. Neither Doris nor I had ever eaten spaghetti, and none of the adults had enough experience to be good at it. All the good humor of Uncle Allen's house reawoke in my mind as I recalled the laughing arguments we had that night about the socially respectable method for moving spaghetti from plate to mouth.

Suddenly I wanted to write about that, about the warmth and good 7 feeling of it, but I wanted to put it down simply for my own joy, not for Mr. Fleagle. It was a moment I wanted to recapture and hold for myself. I wanted to relive the pleasure of an evening at New Street. To write it as I wanted, however, would violate all the rules of formal composition I'd learned in school, and Mr. Fleagle would surely give it a failing grade. Never mind. I would write something else for Mr. Fleagle after I had written this thing for myself.

When I finished it the night was half gone and there was no time left 8 to compose a proper, respectable essay for Mr. Fleagle. There was no choice next morning but to turn in my private reminiscence of Belleville. Two days passed before Mr. Fleagle returned the graded papers, and he returned everyone's but mine. I was bracing myself for a command to report to Mr. Fleagle immediately after school for discipline when I saw him lift my paper from his desk and rap for the class's attention.

"Now, boys," he said, "I want to read you an essay. This is titled 'The 9 Art of Eating Spaghetti.'"

And he started to read. My words! He was reading *my words* out loud 10 to the entire class. What's more, the entire class was listening. Listening attentively. Then somebody laughed, then the entire class was laughing, and not in contempt and ridicule, but with openhearted enjoyment. Even Mr. Fleagle stopped two or three times to repress a small prim smile.

I did my best to avoid showing pleasure, but what I was feeling was 11 pure ecstasy at this startling demonstration that my words had the power to make people laugh. In the eleventh grade, at the eleventh hour as it were, I had discovered a calling. It was the happiest moment of my entire school career. When Mr. Fleagle finished he put the final seal on my happiness by saying, "Now that, boys, is an essay, don't you see. It's—don't you see—it's of the very essence of the essay, don't you see. Congratulations, Mr. Baker."

Questions About the Reading

1. Why did the writer not want to write an essay? What discovery changed his mind?
2. Why did eating spaghetti so delight the people at the supper table?
3. What comment does the writer make on the role of formal rules in writing?
4. What is your opinion of Mr. Fleagle? How did it change during the course of reading the essay?
5. What was the significance of the essay's main event for the writer?

Questions About the Writer's Strategies

1. What is the **main idea** in this essay?
2. At what point in the essay did you begin to figure out what the main idea would be?
3. What **order** does the writer use in describing the **incidents** in his narrative?
4. Is this essay written **objectively** or **subjectively**? Cite examples from the essay to help explain your answer.

Writing Assignments

1. Write a narrative essay about the most important event you experienced in school. Use **chronological order** to describe the event and the incidents leading up to it.
2. Write a narrative essay on one of the following events in your own life: leaving high school, learning to read a novel, using a computer for the first time, learning to have confidence, learning not to jump to conclusions, or controlling your temper. Try to indicate the significance that the event has had for you since it took place.

The Pie

Gary Soto

Childhood pranks and misdemeanors often become bigger than life in the retelling. In this selection, Gary Soto recalls the day he gave in to temptation and committed a sin.

Words to Know

proximity   closeness
retrieve   to get back

Getting Started

Can you describe an incident from your childhood that involved a petty crime?

I knew enough about hell to stop me from stealing. I was holy in almost 1
every bone. Some days I recognized the shadows of angels flopping on
the backyard grass, and other days I heard faraway messages in the
plumbing that howled underneath the house when I crawled there looking for something to do.

But boredom made me sin. Once, at the German Market, I stood before 2
a rack of pies, my sweet tooth gleaming and the juice of guilt wetting my
underarms. I gazed at the nine kinds of pie, pecan and apple being my
favorites, although cherry looked good, and my dear, fat-faced chocolate
was always a good bet. I nearly wept trying to decide which to steal and,
forgetting the flowery dust priests give off, the shadow of angels and the
proximity of God howling in the plumbing underneath the house,
sneaked a pie behind my coffee-lid frisbee and walked to the door, grin-
ning to the bald grocer whose forehead shone with a window of light.

"No one saw," I muttered to myself, the pie like a discus in my hand, 3
and hurried across the street, where I sat on someone's lawn. The sun
wavered between the branches of a yellowish sycamore. A squirrel
nailed itself high on the trunk, where it forked into two large bark-
scabbed limbs. Just as I was going to work my cleanest finger into the pie,
a neighbor came out to the porch for his mail. He looked at me, and I got
up and headed for home. I raced on skinny legs to my block, but slowed

to a quick walk when I couldn't wait any longer. I held the pie to my nose and breathed in its sweetness. I licked some of the crust and closed my eyes as I took a small bite.

In my front yard, I leaned against a car fender and panicked about 4 stealing the apple pie. I knew an apple got Eve in deep trouble with snakes because Sister Marie had shown us a film about Adam and Eve being cast into the desert, and what scared me more than falling from grace was being thirsty for the rest of my life. But even that didn't stop me from clawing a chunk from the pie tin and pushing it into the cavern of my mouth. The slop was sweet and gold-colored in the afternoon sun. I laid more pieces on my tongue, wet finger-dripping pieces, until I was finished and felt like crying because it was about the best thing I had ever tasted. I realized right there and then, in my sixth year, in my tiny body of two hundred bones and three or four sins, that the best things in life came stolen. I wiped my sticky fingers on the grass and rolled my tongue over the corners of my mouth. A burp perfumed the air.

I felt bad not sharing with Cross-Eyed Johnny, a neighbor kid. He 5 stood over my shoulder and asked, "Can I have some?" Crust fell from my mouth, and my teeth were bathed with the jam-like filling. Tears blurred my eyes as I remembered the grocer's forehead. I remembered the other pies on the rack, the warm air of the fan above the door and the car that honked as I crossed the street without looking.

"Get away," I had answered Cross-Eyed Johnny. He watched my fin- 6 gers greedily push big chunks of pie down my throat. He swallowed and said in a whisper, "Your hands are dirty," then returned home to climb his roof and sit watching me eat the pie by myself. After a while, he jumped off and hobbled away because the fall had hurt him.

I sat on the curb. The pie tin glared at me and rolled away when the 7 wind picked up. My face was sticky with guilt. A car honked, and the driver knew. Mrs. Hancock stood on her lawn, hands on hip, and she knew. My mom, peeling a mountain of potatoes at the Redi-Spud factory, knew. I got to my feet, stomach taut, mouth tired of chewing, and flung my frisbee across the street, its shadow like the shadow of an angel flee-ing bad deeds. I retrieved it, jogging slowly. I flung it again until I was bored and thirsty.

I returned home to drink water and help my sister glue bottle caps 8 onto cardboard, a project for summer school. But the bottle caps bored me, and the water soon filled me up more than the pie. With the kitchen stifling with heat and lunatic flies, I decided to crawl underneath our house and lie in the cool shadows listening to the howling sound of plumbing. Was it God? Was it Father, speaking from death, or Uncle with his last shiny dime? I listened, ear pressed to a cold pipe, and heard a howl like the sea. I lay until I was cold and then crawled back to the light,

Chapter 2 / Narration

rising from one knee, then another, to dust off my pants and squint in the harsh light. I looked and saw the glare of a pie tin on a hot day. I knew sin was what you take and didn't give back.

Questions About the Reading

1. Is the boy anxious about being caught stealing the pie? What **details** support your answer?
2. Does the fact that the pie was stolen prevent the boy from enjoying eating it? How do you know?
3. What conclusions can you draw about the boy's feelings about God and religion?
4. Do you think the boy ever stole another pie from the market? Explain your answer.

Questions About the Writer's Strategies

1. In what **order** does the writer arrange the main incidents in the story? Could he have rearranged the order? If so, in what way?
2. In what ways is this paragraph **subjective**? In what ways is it **objective**?
3. What is the **point of view** in **person, time,** and **tone** in the essay?
4. What are some of the descriptive words the writer uses to describe the act of eating the pie? Is his choice of words effective? Why or why not?

Writing Assignments

1. Write a narrative essay that describes what would have happened to the writer if he had been caught in the act of stealing.
2. Recall an episode from your childhood in which you "sinned." Write a narrative essay describing the feelings you experienced.
3. Describe eating your favorite childhood food from the point of view of yourself as a six-year-old.

The Jeaning of America— and the World

Carin C. Quinn

In "The Jeaning of America—and the World," Carin Quinn tells about Levi Strauss's development of blue jeans, the sturdy and reliable American pants that are now famous worldwide. Quinn also explains some of the reasons for the popularity and success of blue jeans.

Words to Know

Alexis de Tocqueville (1805–1859)   French aristocrat, traveler, and author; noted for his four-volume work, *Democracy in America* (1835–1840), which was based on his travels in the United States in 1831 to study the American penitentiary system and democracy.

appropriated   took over

bureaucrats   government officials, particularly those who follow rules and regulations rigidly

ensuing   following, subsequent

idiosyncratic   individual, unique

mother lode   rich, original vein of ore

proletarian   working class

rigors   hardships

ubiquitous   seeming to be everywhere at the same time

Getting Started

Do you believe that success in life comes from hard work or good luck or a combination of the two?

This is the story of a sturdy American symbol which has now spread 1 throughout most of the world. The symbol is not the dollar. It is not even Coca-Cola. It is a simple pair of pants called blue jeans, and what the pants symbolize is what Alexis de Tocqueville called "a manly and legitimate passion for equality. . . ." Blue jeans are favored equally by bureaucrats and cowboys; bankers and deadbeats; fashion designers and beer drinkers. They draw no distinctions and recognize no classes; they are merely American. Yet they are sought after almost everywhere in the world—including Russia, where authorities recently broke up a teen-aged gang that was selling them on the black market for two hundred dollars a pair. They have been around for a long time, and it seems likely that they will outlive even the necktie.

This ubiquitous American symbol was the invention of a Bavarian-born Jew. His name was Levi Strauss. 2

He was born in Bad Ocheim, Germany, in 1829, and during the Euro-pean political turmoil of 1848 decided to take his chances in New York, to which his two brothers already had emigrated. Upon arrival, Levi soon found that his two brothers had exaggerated their tales of an easy life in the land of the main chance. They were landowners, they had told him; instead, he found them pushing needles, thread, pots, pans, ribbons, yarn, scissors, and buttons to housewives. For two years he was a lowly peddler, hauling some 180 pounds of sundries door-to-door to eke out a marginal living. When a married sister in San Francisco offered to pay his way West in 1850, he jumped at the opportunity, taking with him bolts of canvas he hoped to sell for tenting. 3

It was the wrong kind of canvas for that purpose, but while talking with a miner down from the mother lode, he learned that pants—sturdy pants that would stand up to the rigors of the diggings—were almost im-possible to find. Opportunity beckoned. On the spot, Strauss measured the man's girth and inseam with a piece of string and, for six dollars in gold dust, had [the canvas] tailored into a pair of stiff but rugged pants. The miner was delighted with the result, word got around about "those pants of Levi's," and Strauss was in business. The company has been in business ever since. 4

When Strauss ran out of canvas, he wrote his two brothers to send more. He received instead a tough, brown cotton cloth made in Nîmes, France—called *serge de Nîmes* and swiftly shortened to "denim" (the word "jeans" derives from *Gênes*, the French word for Genoa, where a similar cloth was produced). Almost from the first, Strauss had his cloth dyed the distinctive indigo that gave blue jeans their name, but it was not until the 1870s that he added the copper rivets which have long since become a company trademark. The rivets were the idea of a Virginia City, Nevada, tailor, Jacob W. Davis, who added them to pacify a mean-tempered miner called Alkali Ike. Alkali, the story goes, complained that the pockets of his jeans always tore when he stuffed them with ore samples and demanded that Davis do something about it. As a kind of joke, Davis took the pants to a blacksmith and had the pockets riveted; once again, the idea worked so well that word got around; in 1873 Strauss appropriated and patented the gimmick—and hired Davis as a regional manager. 5

By this time, Strauss had taken both his brothers and two brothers-in-law into the company and was ready for his third San Francisco store. 6

The Jeaning of America—and the World / Carin C. Quinn

Over the ensuing years the company prospered locally and by the time of his death in 1902, Strauss had become a man of prominence in California. For three decades thereafter the business remained profitable though small, with sales largely confined to the working people of the West—cowboys, lumberjacks, railroad workers, and the like. Levi's jeans were first introduced to the East, apparently, during the dude-ranch craze of the 1930s, when vacationing Easterners returned and spread the word about the wonderful pants with rivets. Another boost came in World War II, when blue jeans were declared an essential commodity and were sold only to people engaged in defense work. From a company with fifteen salespeople, two plants, and almost no business east of the Mississippi in 1946, the organization grew in thirty years to include a sales force of more than twenty-two thousand, with fifty plants and offices in thirty-five countries. Each year, more than 250,000,000 items of Levi's clothing are sold—including more than 83,000,000 pairs of riveted blue jeans. They have become, through marketing, word of mouth, and demonstrable reliability, the common pants of America. They can be purchased pre-washed, pre-faded, and pre-shrunk for the suitably proletarian look. They adapt themselves to any sort of idiosyncratic use; women slit them at the inseams and convert them into long skirts, men chop them off above the knees and turn them into something to be worn while challenging the surf. Decorations and ornamentations abound.

The pants have become a tradition, and along the way have acquired 7 a history of their own—so much so that the company has opened a museum in San Francisco. There was, for example, the turn-of-the-century trainman who replaced a faulty coupling with a pair of jeans; the Wyoming man who used his jeans as a towrope to haul his car out of a ditch; the Californian who found several pairs in an abandoned mine, wore them, then discovered they were sixty-three years old and still as good as new and turned them over to the Smithsonian as a tribute to their toughness. And then there is the particularly terrifying story of the careless construction worker who dangled fifty-two stories above the street until rescued, his sole support the Levi's belt loop through which his rope was hooked.

Questions About the Reading

1. What reasons does Quinn give for the success of blue jeans? Identify the sentences that support your answer.
2. What are the main **incidents** in the development of blue jeans?

3. Speculate about why Levi's brothers lied to him about their position in America. Why do you think the writer included this **detail**?
4. What conclusions can you draw about Strauss's character?
5. How do you think Quinn feels about Levi's jeans and their popularity?

Questions About the Writer's Strategies

1. What **order** does the writer use for paragraphs 3–6? What is the purpose of the first paragraph of the essay? What is the purpose of the last paragraph?
2. Is the **thesis** of the essay stated? If so, in which sentence(s)? If not, state the thesis in a sentence of your own.
3. What are the **main ideas** in paragraphs 3, 4, 5, and 6? Are the main ideas directly stated?
4. What is the **point of view** in **person**, **time**, and **tone** in the essay?
5. Could the first sentence in paragraph 5 be made into more than one sentence? Why or why not? Could the third sentence in paragraph 5 be made into more than one sentence? If so, how? If not, why not?

Writing Assignments

1. Write a narrative essay in which you explain an achievement—either your own or that of another person—resulting from one of the following: working hard, being lucky, taking a risk, or being innovative. Describe the series of events that led to success.
2. Write a narrative essay about an important opportunity that you once had. Explain how the opportunity arose, how you did or did not take advantage of it, and what the results of your action were.

Healthy Bodies, Healthy Minds?

Paul Theroux

Paul Theroux is a novelist, essayist, and world traveler. In The Old Patagonian Express, *he wrote about his journey from the suburbs of Boston
to the southern tip of South America—a journey that he took entirely by
train. The following essay tells of an encounter he had during that journey with a young woman whose absorption with the health of her body
has closed her mind to thinking about other viewpoints.*

Words to Know

betrothal   promise to marry
Buddhism   a form of religion practiced principally in eastern
and central Asian countries
commissar   official of the Communist party
devoid   absent, lacking
effulgent   splendid, glorious
Leopold Bloom   character in James Joyce's *Ulysses*
magnum   about two-fifths of a gallon
Mahatma Gandhi   Hindu spiritual leader
Marx   Karl Marx, German-born founder of communism
pedantic   boring and overlearned
savored   enjoyed
wraithlike   like a ghost, not like a living person
Zen   form of Buddhism

Getting Started

How could it be possible to have a dialogue with a fanatic?

T here would be no food until Albany, when the New York section, with   1
its diner, was hooked to this train. So I went into the lounge car and had
a beer. I packed my pipe and set it on fire and savored the effulgent blur
of lazy reflection that pipe smoke induces in me. I blew myself a cocoon
of it, and it hung in clouds around me, so comforting and thick that the
girl who entered the car and sat down opposite seemed wraithlike, a

child lost in fog. She put three bulging plastic bags on her table, then tucked her legs under her. She folded her hands in her lap and stared stonily down the car. Her intensity made me alert. At the next table a man was engrossed in a Matt Helm story, and near him, two linesmen—they wore their tools—were playing poker. There was a boy with a short-wave radio, but his racket was drowned by the greater racket of the train. A man in a uniform—a train man—was stirring coffee; there was an old greasy lantern at his feet. At the train man's table, but not speaking, a fat woman sneaked bites at a candy bar. She did it guiltily, as if she feared that at any moment someone would shout, *Put that thing away!*

"You mind not smoking?" 2

It was the girl with the bags and the stony gaze. 3

I looked for a NO SMOKING sign. There was none. I said, "Is it bothering 4 you?"

She said, "It kills my eyes." 5

I put my pipe down and took a swig of beer. 6

She said, "That stuff is poison." 7

Instead of looking at her I looked at her bags. I said, "They say peanuts 8 cause cancer."

She grinned vengefully at me and said, "Pumpkin seeds." 9

I turned away. 10

"And these are almonds." 11

I considered relighting my pipe. 12

"And this is cashews." 13

Her name was Wendy. Her face was an oval of innocence, devoid of 14 any expression of inquiry. Her prettiness was as remote from my idea of beauty as homeliness and consequently was not at all interesting. But I could not blame her for that: it is hard for anyone to be interesting at twenty. She was a student, she said, and on her way to Ohio. She wore an Indian skirt, and lumberjack boots, and the weight of her leather jacket made her appear round shouldered.

"What do you study, Wendy?" 15

"Eastern philosophy. I'm into Zen." 16

Oh, Christ, I thought. But she was still talking. She had been learning 17 about the Hole, or perhaps the Whole—it still made no sense to me. She hadn't read all that much, she said, and her teachers were lousy. But she thought that once she got to Japan or Burma she would find out a lot more. She would be in Ohio for a few more years. The thing about Buddhism, she said, was that it involved your whole life. Like everything you did—it was Buddhism. And everything that happened in the world— that was Buddhism, too.

"Not politics," I said. "That's not Buddhism. It's just crooked." 18

"That's what everyone says, but they're wrong. I've been reading 19 Marx. Marx is a kind of Buddhist."

Was she pulling my leg? I said, "Marx was about as Buddhist as this 20 beer can. But anyway, I thought we were talking about politics. It's the opposite of thought—it's selfish, it's narrow, it's dishonest. It's all half truths and short cuts. Maybe a few Buddhist politicians would change things, but in Burma, where . . ."

"Take this," she said, and motioned to her bags of nuts. "I'm a raw- 21 foodist-nondairy vegetarian. You're probably right about politics being all wrong. I think people are doing things all wrong—I mean, completely. They eat junk. They *consume junk*. Look at them!" The fat lady was still eating her candy bar, or possibly another candy bar. "They're just destroying themselves and they don't even know it. They're smoking themselves to death. Look at the smoke in this car."

I said, "Some of that is my smoke."   22

"It kills my eyes."   23

" 'Nondairy,' " I said. "That means you don't drink milk."   24

"Right."   25

"What about cheese? Cheese is nice. And you've got to have calcium." 26

"I get my calcium in cashews," she said. Was this true? "Anyway, milk 27 gives me mucus. Milk is the biggest mucus-producer there is."

"I didn't know that."   28

"I used to go through a box of Kleenex a day."   29

"A box. That's quite a lot."   30

"It was the milk. It made mucus," she said. "My nose used to run like 31 you wouldn't believe."

"Is that why people's noses run? Because of the milk?" 32

"Yes!" she cried.   33

I wondered if she had a point. Milk drinkers' noses run. Children are 34 milk drinkers. Therefore, children's noses run. And children's noses do run. But it still struck me as arguable. Everyone's nose runs—except hers, apparently.

"Dairy products give you headaches, too."   35

"You mean, they give *you* headaches."   36

"Right. Like the other night. My sister knows I'm a vegetarian. So she 37 gives me some eggplant parmyjan. She doesn't know I'm a nondairy raw foodist. I looked at it. As soon as I saw it was cooked and had cheese on it, I knew that I was going to feel awful. But she spent all day making it, so what else could I do? The funny thing is that I liked the taste of it. God, was I sick afterwards! And my nose started to run."

I told her that, in his autobiography, Mahatma Gandhi stated that eat- 38 ing meat made people lustful. And yet at thirteen, an age at which most

American children were frolicking with the Little League team or concentrating on making spit balls, Gandhi had got married—and he was a vegetarian.

"But it wasn't a real marriage," said Wendy. "It was a kind of Hindu 39 ceremony."

"The betrothal took place when he was seven years old. The marriage 40 sealed the bargain. They were both thirteen. . . ."

Wendy pondered this. I decided to try again. Had she, I asked, noticed 41 a falling off of her sexual appetite since her conversion to raw vegetables?

"I used to get insomnia," she began. "And sick—I mean, really sick. 42 And I admit I lost my temper. I think meat *does* cause people to be hostile."

"But what about sexual desire? Lechery, cravings—I don't know quite 43 how to put it."

"You mean sex? It's not supposed to be violent. It should be gentle and 44 beautiful. Kind of a quiet thing."

Maybe if you're a vegetarian, I thought. She was still droning on in her 45 pedantic college student way.

"I understand my body better now . . . I've gotten to know my body a 46 whole lot better . . . Hey, I can tell when there's just a little difference in my blood sugar level. I can sense it going up and down, my blood sugar level. When I eat certain things."

I asked her whether she ever got violently ill. She said absolutely not. 47 Did she ever feel a little bit sick?

Her reply was extraordinary: "I don't believe in germs."   48

Amazing. I said, "You mean, you don't believe that germs exist? 49 They're just an optical illusion under the microscope? Dust, little specks—that sort of thing."

"I don't think germs cause sickness. Germs are living things—small, 50 living things that don't do any harm."

"Like cockroaches and fleas," I said. "Friendly little critters, right?"   51

"Germs don't make you sick," she insisted. "Food does. If you eat bad 52 food it weakens your organs and you get sick. It's your organs that make you sick. Your heart, your bowels."

"But what makes your organs sick?"   53

"Bad food. It makes them weak. If you eat good food, like I do," she 54 said, gesturing at her pumpkin seeds, "you don't get sick. Like I never get sick. If I get a runny nose and a sore throat, I don't call it a cold."

"You don't?"   55

"No, it's because I ate something bad. So I eat something good."   56

I decided to shelve my inquiry about sickness being merely a question 57 of a runny nose, and not cancer or the bubonic plague. Let's get down to particulars, I thought. What had she had to eat that day?

"This. Pumpkin seeds, cashews, almonds. A banana. An apple. Some 58 raisins. A slice of wholemeal bread—toasted. If you don't toast it you get mucus."

"You're sort of declaring war on the gourmets, eh?" 59

"I know I have fairly radical views," she said. 60

"I wouldn't call them radical," I said, "They're smug views, self- 61 important ones. Egocentric, you might say. The funny thing about being smug and egocentric and thinking about health and purity all the time is that it can turn you into a fascist. *My* diet, *my* bowels, *my* self—it's the way right-wing people talk. The next thing you know you'll be raving about the purity of the race."

"Okay," she conceded in a somersault, "I admit some of my views are 62 conservative. But so what?"

"Well, for one thing, apart from your bowels there's a big world out 63 there. The Middle East. The Panama Canal. Political prisoners having their toenails pulled out in Iran. Families starving in India."

This rant of mine had little effect, though it did get her onto the subject 64 of families—perhaps it was my mention of starving Indians. She hated families, she said. She couldn't help it; she just hated them.

I said, "What does a family make you think of?" 65

"A station wagon, a mother, a father. Four or five kids eating ham- 66 burgers. They're really awful, and they're everywhere—they're all over the place, driving around."

"So you think families are a blot on the landscape?" 67

She said, "Well, yes." 68

She had been at this college in Ohio for three years. She had never in 69 that time taken a literature course. Even more interesting, this was the first time in her life that she had ever been on a train. She liked the train, she said, but didn't elaborate.

I wondered what her ambitions were. 70

"I think I'd like to get involved in food. Teach people about food. What 71 they should eat. Tell them why they get sick." It was the voice of a com- missar, and yet a moment later she said dreamily, "Sometimes I look at a piece of cheese. I know it tastes good. I know I'll like it. But I also know that I'm going to feel awful the next day if I eat it."

I said, "That's what I think when I see a magnum of champagne, a rab- 72 bit pie, and a bowl of cream puffs with hot chocolate sauce."

At the time, I did not think Wendy was crazy in any important sense. 73 But afterward, when I remembered our conversation, she seemed to me profoundly loony. And profoundly incurious. I had casually mentioned to her that I had been to Upper Burma and Africa. I had described Leo- pold Bloom's love of "the faint tang of urine" in the kidneys he had for breakfast. I had shown a knowledge of Buddhism and the eating habits of Bushmen in the Kalahari and Gandhi's early married life. I was a fairly interesting person, was I not? But not once in the entire conversation had she asked me a single question. She never asked what I did, where I had come from, or where I was going. When it was not interrogation on my part, it was monologue on hers. Uttering rosy generalities in her sweetly tremulous voice, and tugging her legs back into the lotus position when they slipped free, she was an example of total self-absorption and desperate self-advertisement. She had mistaken egotism for Buddhism. I still have a great affection for the candor of American college students, but she reminded me of how many I have known who were unteachable.

Questions About the Reading

1. What is the writer's opinion of the girl? Does he state his opinion? If so, in which sentences particularly?
2. When the girl talks about wanting to teach other people about foods, the writer says, "It was the voice of a commissar." Explain what he means. Would you want to be taught by the girl? Why or why not?
3. Is there anything in the first paragraph to suggest that the writer had already formed an opinion of the girl before she began to speak? Do you think his opinion of her changed during their conversation?
4. Does the writer reveal himself as being almost as convinced of his own opinions as the girl is of hers? Support your answer by citing sentences and passages from the essay.

Questions About the Writer's Strategies

1. The writer's principal strategy for creating an impression of the girl is **dialogue**. Identify **examples** of her conversation that help you determine her character and personality.
2. What is the purpose of the first paragraph of the essay?
3. Does the writer state the **thesis** of the essay? If so, in which sentence(s)? If not, state the thesis in a sentence of your own. What is the significant point the writer is making in this narrative?
4. The paragraphs of the essay are short and often contain only one sentence. Why is the paragraphing appropriate to the principal writing strategy that the writer uses in the narrative?
5. This essay touches on a great many subjects, but the main topic of conversation is food. In this discussion, how is food used to represent a larger idea?

Writing Assignments

1. Write a narrative essay about an interesting conversation you had during a bus ride or a plane ride, while waiting in a long line, or in some similar situation. Use **dialogue** to recount what was said.
2. Write a narrative essay describing an argument between two people on some important issue, such as the death penalty, the nuclear freeze movement, acid rain, or teenage pregnancy. If you like, make this an imaginary argument.
3. At some time a person has probably talked you into doing something against your better judgment. Write a narrative essay about that event.

Just Walk on By: A Black Man Ponders His Power to Alter Public Space

Brent Staples

Journalist Brent Staples offers his readers a rare opportunity to change lives with another human being. Staples's forceful words and images allow each of us to walk in the shoes of a young black male in today's urban environment, where fear and racism are intricately linked.

Words to Know

ad hoc with a specific purpose or cause

bandolier a belt soldiers wear over the shoulder to carry cartridges

constitutional a walk taken regularly

dicey dangerous, risky

labyrinthine like a maze

quarry object of a hunt; prey

SoHo an area of New York City with many art galleries, restaurants, and specialty shops

unwieldy difficult to carry or manage

warrenlike overcrowded

Getting Started

If you have ever been judged solely on the basis of your sex, skin color, ethnic origin, or external appearance, how did it feel?

$\mathbf{M}$y first victim was a woman—white, well dressed, probably in her 1
early twenties. I came upon her late one evening on a deserted street in Hyde Park, a relatively affluent neighborhood in an otherwise mean, impoverished section of Chicago. As I swung onto the avenue behind her, there seemed to be a discreet, uninflammatory distance between us. Not so. She cast back a worried glance. To her, the youngish black man—a broad six feet two inches with a beard and billowing hair, both hands shoved into the pockets of a bulky military jacket—seemed menacingly close. After a

few more quick glimpses, she picked up her pace and was soon running in earnest. Within seconds she disappeared into a cross street.

That was more than a decade ago. I was twenty-two years old, a graduate student newly arrived at the University of Chicago. It was in the echo of that terrified woman's footfalls that I first began to know the unwieldy inheritance I'd come into—the ability to alter public space in ugly ways. It was clear that she thought herself the quarry of a mugger, a rapist, or worse. Suffering a bout of insomnia, however, I was stalking sleep, not defenseless wayfarers. As a softy who is scarcely able to take a knife to a raw chicken—let alone hold it to a person's throat—I was surprised, embarrassed, and dismayed all at once. Her flight made me feel like an accomplice in tyranny. It also made it clear that I was indistinguishable from the muggers who occasionally seeped into the area from the surrounding ghetto. That first encounter, and those that followed, signified that a vast, unnerving gulf lay between nighttime pedestrians—particularly women—and me. And I soon gathered that being perceived as dangerous is a hazard in itself. I only needed to turn a corner into a dicey situation, or crowd some frightened, armed person in a foyer somewhere, or make an errant move after being pulled over by a policeman. Where fear and weapons meet—and they often do in urban America— there is always the possibility of death.

In that first year, my first away from my hometown, I was to become thoroughly familiar with the language of fear. At dark, shadowy intersections in Chicago, I could cross in front of a car stopped at a traffic light and elicit the *thunk, thunk, thunk, thunk* of the driver—black, white, male, or female—hammering down the door locks. On less traveled streets after dark, I grew accustomed to but never comfortable with people who crossed to the other side of the street rather than pass me. Then there were the standard unpleasantries with police, doormen, bouncers, cabdrivers, and others whose business is to screen out troublesome individuals *before* there is any nastiness.

I moved to New York nearly two years ago and I have remained an avid night walker. In central Manhattan, the near-constant crowd cover minimizes tense one-on-one street encounters. Elsewhere—visiting friends in SoHo, where sidewalks are narrow and tightly spaced buildings shut out the sky—things can get very taut indeed.

Black men have a firm place in New York mugging literature. Norman Podhoretz in his famed (or infamous) 1963 essay, "My Negro Problem— And Ours," recalls growing up in terror of black males; they "were tougher than we were, more ruthless," he writes—and as an adult on the Upper West Side of Manhattan, he continues, he cannot constrain his nervousness when he meets black men on certain streets. Similarly, a decade later, the essayist and novelist Edward Hoagland extols a New York where once "Negro bitterness bore down mainly on other Negroes." Where some see mere panhandlers, Hoagland sees "a mugger who is clearly screwing up his nerve to do more than just *ask* for money." But Hoagland has "the New Yorker's quick-hunch posture for broken-field maneuvering," and the bad guy swerves away.

I often witness that "hunch posture," from women after dark on the 6 warrenlike streets of Brooklyn where I live. They seem to set their faces on neutral and, with their purse straps strung across their chests bandolier style, they forge ahead as though bracing themselves against being tackled. I understand, of course, that the danger they perceive is not a hallucination. Women are particularly vulnerable to street violence, and young black males are drastically overrepresented among the perpetrators of that violence. Yet these truths are no solace against the kind of alienation that comes of being ever the suspect, against being set apart, a fearsome entity with whom pedestrians avoid making eye contact.

It is not altogether clear to me how I reached the ripe old age of 7 twenty-two without being conscious of the lethality nighttime pedestrians attributed to me. Perhaps it was because in Chester, Pennsylvania, the small, angry industrial town where I came of age in the 1960s, I was scarcely noticeable against a backdrop of gang warfare, street knifings, and murders. I grew up one of the good boys, had perhaps a half-dozen fistfights. In retrospect, my shyness of combat has clear sources.

Many things go into the making of a young thug. One of those things 8 is the consummation of the male romance with the power to intimidate. An infant discovers that random flailings send the baby bottle flying out of the crib and crashing to the floor. Delighted, the joyful babe repeats those motions again and again, seeking to duplicate the feat. Just so, I recall the points at which some of my boyhood friends were finally seduced by the perception of themselves as tough guys. When a mark cowered and surrendered his money without resistance, myth and reality merged—and paid off. It is, after all, only manly to embrace the power to frighten and intimidate. We, as men, are not supposed to give an inch of our lane on the highway; we are to seize the fighter's edge in work and in play and even in love; we are to be valiant in the face of hostile forces.

Unfortunately, poor and powerless young men seem to take all this 9 nonsense literally. As a boy, I saw countless tough guys locked away; I have since buried several, too. They were babies, really—a teenage cousin, a brother of twenty-two, a childhood friend in his mid-twenties— all gone down in episodes of bravado played out in the streets. I came to doubt the virtues of intimidation early on. I chose, perhaps even unconsciously, to remain a shadow—timid, but a survivor.

The fearsomeness mistakenly attributed to me in public places often 10
has a perilous flavor. The most frightening of these confusions occurred
in the late 1970s and early 1980s when I worked as a journalist in Chicago. One day, rushing into the office of a magazine I was writing for
with a deadline story in hand, I was mistaken for a burglar. The office
manager called security and, with an ad hoc posse, pursued me through
the labyrinthine halls, nearly to my editor's door. I had no way of proving
who I was. I could only move briskly toward the company of someone
who knew me.

Another time I was on assignment for a local paper and killing time 11
before an interview. I entered a jewelry store on the city's affluent Near
North Side. The proprietor excused herself and returned with an enormous red Doberman pinscher straining at the end of a leash. She stood,
the dog extended toward me, silent to my questions, her eyes bulging
nearly out of her head. I took a cursory look around, nodded, and bade
her good night. Relatively speaking, however, I never fared as badly as
another black male journalist. He went to nearby Waukegan, Illinois, a
couple of summers ago to work on a story about a murderer who was
born there. Mistaking the reporter for the killer, police hauled him from
his car at gunpoint and but for his press credentials would probably have
tried to book him. Such episodes are not uncommon. Black men trade
tales like this all the time.

In "My Negro Problem—And Ours," Podhoretz writes that the hatred 12
he feels for blacks makes itself known to him through a variety of avenues—one being his discomfort with that "special brand of paranoid
touchiness" to which he says blacks are prone. No doubt he is speaking
here of black men. In time, I learned to smother the rage I felt at so often
being taken for a criminal. Not to do so would surely have led to mad-
ness—via that special "paranoid touchiness" that so annoyed Podhoretz
at the time he wrote the essay.

I began to take precautions to make myself less threatening. I move 13
about with care, particularly late in the evening. I give a wide berth to
nervous people on subway platforms during the wee hours, particularly
when I have exchanged business clothes for jeans. If I happen to be entering a building behind some people who appear skittish, I may walk by,
letting them clear the lobby before I return, so as not to seem to be following them. I have been calm and extremely congenial on those rare occasions when I've been pulled over by the police.

And on late-evening constitutionals along streets less traveled by, I 14
employ what has proved to be an excellent tension-reducing measure: I
whistle melodies from Beethoven and Vivaldi and the more popular classical composers. Even steely New Yorkers hunching toward nighttime

destinations seem to relax, and occasionally they even join in the tune. Virtually everybody seems to sense that a mugger wouldn't be warbling bright, sunny selections from Vivaldi's *Four Seasons*. It is my equivalent of the cowbell that hikers wear when they know they are in bear country.

Questions About the Reading

1. What does the title of this essay mean?
2. Why does Staples describe the woman in paragraph 1 as his "first victim"?
3. Give some **examples** of what Staples refers to, in paragraph 3, as the "language of fear." At what age did he become familiar with this new language?
4. List the things that Staples believes go into the making of a "young thug."
5. What are some of the precautions Staples takes to make himself appear less threatening in public places?
6. What conclusions can you draw about the writer's attitude about his predicament? Does he like or dislike his "power to alter public space"? Give specific **details** from the essay to support your opinion.

Questions About the Writer's Strategies

1. What type of **order** does Staples use to organize his essay? List the biographical details the writer includes that support this kind of order.
2. Does the writer state the **thesis** of this essay? If so, in which sentence(s)? If not, state the thesis in a sentence of your own.
3. What is the **point of view** of this essay? Could the writer have used another point of view? Do you think the essay would have been more or less effective from another point of view? Why?
4. Staples uses words and details that appeal to the imagination to make the incidents in his essay come alive to his readers. For example, in paragraph 2, the insomniac writer "was stalking sleep, not defenseless wayfarers." Would "I was taking a walk because I couldn't sleep" be as effective a choice of words? Why or why not? Find other examples of effective word choice in paragraph 3.
5. At the end of his essay, Staples compares his humming classical music to a hiker's wearing a cowbell in bear country. What does this comparison mean?

Writing Assignments

1. Have you ever been judged unfairly by someone else's preexisting stereotypes? Write a narrative essay about that incident. Include both **objective** details about the incident and **subjective** details about your feelings.
2. Have you ever had an experience in which you felt a sense of overwhelming fear? Write a narrative essay about that incident. Use strong details so that your fear comes alive through your words, and use **chronological order** to organize your essay.

The Deli

Carmen Machin (student)

Carmen Machin was a student at East Los Angeles College when she wrote this account of running a small food store in New York. She is especially effective at letting us see what happened exactly as she saw it at the time. Her account gives us a good idea of her own refreshing character—a bit wide-eyed and innocent, but ready to discover things, to learn, and to take the world as it comes.

Words to Know

naiveté innocence
purloined stolen
sorties entries, invasions

Getting Started

In what ways are people and situations not always as they first appear?

My husband and I were about a year into wedded bliss, when we were 1 made an offer we couldn't refuse. There was a delicatessen whose owner was anxious to sell. He was moving to another state. We could have the store at payments we could afford. We accepted. There was an apartment behind and connected to it which was included in the deal. We had no idea what the neighborhood was like, but with youthful energy and optimism, we moved in.

The first week was tragic. As the days passed and the end of the month 2 approached, we realized that if things continued as they were, we would not only be unable to make the payments, but would probably have to close the doors. In the midst of this anxiety was the surly attitude of the customers. One lady in particular seemed to relish my discomfort and attempts at self-control while she, on each of her sorties into the establishment, accused us, now of underweighing the cold cuts and salads, or then, of miscounting her change. For weeks I remained courteous and patient before her onslaught. I did not want to alienate the very few customers that we had.

Then suddenly, we began to see new faces. Our business started a defi- 3
nite upward swing. Even our first customers seemed more pleasant. All,
that is, except HER. The day came when I felt I could no longer tolerate
her attacks, and still smiling, I suggested that since we did not seem to be
able to satisfy her, that it might be a good idea if she went elsewhere. She
burst out laughing and in her thick Irish brogue, proclaimed to the other
customers who were there at the time, that at last she had made me show
some "backbone." Then she turned to me and said: "I wondered how
long you'd be taking it." She went on to marvel at the intestinal fortitude
or innocence of two "spics" moving into an Irish neighborhood. I stood
there in complete awe, as the other customers assured me that they had,
at first, abandoned the store when they heard that "spics was buying,"
but that, thanks to Madeline Hannon, for that was our tormentor's name,
they had, one by one, come back.

New York is a great big city; most folks call it unfriendly, and yet, I 4
never found it so. This area, from 96th Street to 100 Street, between Am-
sterdam and Columbus avenues, was absolutely small townish. Everyone
knew everybody else and most were related in some way. Outsiders who
moved in had to prove themselves worthy of acceptance or remain forever strangers. We were fortunate. Even the local gang, called "The Dukes,"
on whose turf our place was located, accepted us wholeheartedly.

The "Dukes," unknown to us, had terrorized all the shopkeepers in the 5
area. In order to be able to stay in business without being harassed by
vandalism, shoplifting, out and out robberies, and, in certain cases, beat-
ings, the Dukes were paid whatever they felt the traffic could bear. In
their opinion, we were to be no exception.

One day three of the young men swaggered into the store. At the time, 6
my husband was in the cellar arranging a shipment of merchandise that
had just arrived, and I, expecting him momentarily, was preparing a
sandwich which was to be my lunch. As I glanced up, I saw one of them
quickly grab some Hostess Cupcakes and put them in his pocket; another
leaned against the fruit bin which was immediately minus an apple. Such
was my naiveté that I firmly believed the only reason anyone stole food
was hunger. My heart broke and at the same time opened and embraced
them in the mother syndrome. They asked to speak to my husband. "He's
not here at the moment, but if you don't mind waiting, he should be back
in a jiffy." They nodded.

As they started to turn to walk around the customer area, I proceeded 7
to introduce myself and, at the same time, commenced making three
more sandwiches. While I made small talk (actually, it was a monologue),
they stood silent, looking fiercely, albeit hungrily at the masterpieces I
was concocting: Italian rolls, piled high with juicy roast pork and, on top,
my husband's wonderful homemade cole slaw. I placed them on paper

plates along with pickles and plenty of potato chips, then I said, "Come on, you'll have to eat in the kitchen, because we're not licensed to serve in the store. Do you want milk or soda?" "Don't you know who we are?" "I've seen you around, but I don't know your names," I replied. They looked at me in disbelief, then shrugging their shoulders, marched as one into the kitchen which was the first room behind the store. They ate to their hearts' content and, before they left, emptied their pockets, depositing each purloined article in its appointed place. No apologies were given, none were expected. But from that day on, we were protected, and the only payment we ever made was that which we also received: friendship, trust, and acceptance.

Questions About the Reading

1. Explain how the writer proved she was "worthy of acceptance." Did she use the same method in each of the two **incidents** she tells about in the narrative?
2. What final conclusion can you draw about Madeline Hannon's character? Was she prejudiced? Were her friends prejudiced?
3. Why do you think Madeline and her neighbors behaved as they did?

Questions About the Writer's Strategies

1. In paragraph 4, the writer says, "Outsiders who moved in had to prove themselves worthy of acceptance." What purpose does this statement serve in the essay?
2. What **order** does the writer use in explaining the incidents that took place? Are there any paragraphs in which the writer seems to change that order?
3. What is the **point of view** of the narrative? If the writer had known at the time of the incidents what she knew when she was writing, do you think the **events** would have proceeded in the same way with the same outcomes?
4. The writer does not use very much **dialogue** in her narrative. Rewrite paragraphs 6 and 7, changing some of the descriptive statements into quoted dialogue.

Writing Assignments

1. Write a narrative essay about an experience in which you did not fully understand what was happening until after the event—perhaps, for

instance, when you were the target of a practical joke, or when you misinterpreted a friendly gesture as a romantic overture.

2. Write a narrative essay in which you tell about a person who achieves a goal only after standing up to another person.

3. Write a narrative essay about a situation in which you were at a serious disadvantage. Tell how you were able to work around that disadvantage.

3

Description

BY USING *DESCRIPTION*, the writer can provide the reader with a "word picture" of a specific person, the flavor of a special place, or the look of a particular object. To help the reader visualize the object, the writer chooses key details to develop the description: a certain liveliness in a person's eyes, the movement of ocean waves, the design of a favorite chair.

We saw in Chapter 2 that writers use descriptive words to add color and vividness to the details they describe. The specific descriptive words the writer chooses depend on the particular **impression**, or image, the writer wants to create. For example, the writer can create the impression of a person who is likable by describing the person's face as "friendly" and "good-natured." The writer can create the opposite impression by using such descriptive words as "shifty" or "scowling." In the following paragraph, the writer develops an effective impression of a chair by the buildup of details and descriptive words that re-create the object for the reader.

Detail: location

Detail: appearance

Detail: appearance

The chair was the one piece of furniture I wanted to take with me when I closed up my parents' house for the final time. To look at it, sitting in the same kitchen corner where it had been for fifty years, you'd wonder how it could be my favorite chair. It was nothing but a straight-backed wooden chair, its seat scratched here and there from the soles of a small boy's shoes. The only thing unusual about it was the intricate design carved into its back. But the carving was what made the chair meaningful to me. I had sat in that chair many times as punishment for errors in my ways. I suppose my mother thought it was defiance that led me to sit cross-legged on the seat with my back to her in the kitchen.

But it was not defiance. Rather, in that position my eyes and then my fingers could trace the intertwining leaves and flowers of the design carved in the back of the chair. Each time I sat there I seemed to see lines and shapes I hadn't seen before: a heart-shaped leaf, a budding rose, a blade of grass. Perhaps that chair had something to do with my lasting interest in well-made antique furniture. Who knows? I do know that when I drove away on that last day, the chair, carefully wrapped in several old quilts, lay tenderly cradled on the back seat of my car.

Details: decoration of chair

Notice that the chair is described only as being a straight-backed wooden chair with a scratched seat and a design carved into its back. However, the writer creates the dominant impression that the chair—in spite of being associated with childhood punishment—remained beautiful to him and probably influenced his lifelong interest in fine woods and antiques. The words *intricate, trace, intertwining, heart-shaped,* and *budding* describe and help the reader picture the design in the back of the chair. And in the last sentence, the phrases *carefully wrapped* and *tenderly cradled* convey indirectly the writer's feelings about the chair. The reader must be given enough detail not only to picture an object but also to understand what touched or moved the writer to single it out.

In descriptive writing you will often find stylistic devices that help convey both the essential qualities of the subject and its significance to the writer. Consider the following paragraph.

Details: simile

Erethizon dorsatus, an antisocial character of the northern U.S. and Canadian forest, commonly called a porcupine, looks like an uncombed head, has a grumpy personality, fights with his tail, hides his head when he's in trouble, floats like a cork, attacks backing up, retreats going ahead, and eats toilet seats as if they were Post Toasties. It's a sad commentary on his personality that people are always trying to do him in.

R. T. Allen,
"The Porcupine"

In this paragraph, the writer uses a **figure of speech** called a **simile** to help enhance the description of the porcupine. A simile takes items that are considered unlike and then compares them in a way that shows an unexpected similarity. Usually, a simile uses *like* or *as* to establish the connection between the items. Two similes in this paragraph, for example, are that a porcupine "looks like an uncombed head" and "floats like a cork." (Can you find another?) A figure of speech related to the simile is the **metaphor**, which also compares unlike items, but does so without directly stating the connection with *like* or *as*. Metaphors may be used to express an idea that is rather abstract, as in "the *scales* of justice." But they can be used for other effects too, and they may only be **implied** by the use of a certain verb—"The swimmer waddled across the sand."

The organization of a description also contributes to its effectiveness. The writer may arrange the details in **order of importance**, usually moving from the less important to the more important details. The details in the paragraph above are arranged so they build to the most significant point—the deeper meaning of the chair to the writer. The writer may choose to arrange the details according to space, called **spatial order**. When a description is organized according to space, the writer takes a physical position in a room or at a scene and then describes what can be seen from that position, using some consistent order such as moving from left to right, from foreground to background, or from top to bottom.

In creating a description, the writer must identify the important characteristics of the object or scene being described and then find the words—nouns and verbs, as well as adjectives and adverbs—that best express these characteristics. In the essay that follows, the student describes the house in which she is living. Notice that she describes the house in **spatial order**—first from the outside and then as she walks through its rooms. Notice, too, that the descriptive details provide the reader with an image of both the house and its owner.

	It's really not a striking house, nor is it an old charming house. It is, in fact, very plain—just like the houses on each
View of the outside of the house	side of it. As I climb up the hilly driveway, its <u>whiteness</u> stares blankly back at me, reminding me that I am not the
Details: preciseness of the landscaping	owner but just a temporary, unwanted trespasser. There are flowers lining the driveway, which push their faces toward the sun as they lie in their bed <u>perfectly spaced</u>, not too close and not too far apart, <u>perfectly coordinated</u> to reflect all the colors of the spectrum. Through the windows of the house
Thesis statement	nothing but my reflection can be seen. They are like the house, clean and tinted, allowing no one a look in, keeping life in the house shut off from the rest of the world, uninviting of intrusion, only interested in cleanliness, only leading the people inside to a feeling of loneliness.
Entering the house	Upon <u>entering the house</u> the smell of Pinesol and disinfectant engulfs my nostrils and shoots directly to my brain,
Details: cleanliness and coldness of kitchen	anesthetizing any emotions that might surface. Like the windows, the kitchen floor reflects the <u>cleanliness</u> of the house with its <u>spotless white surface</u>, <u>scrubbed and shined</u>, casting off reflections from the <u>bright lights</u> overhead. There is wallpaper on the walls of the <u>kitchen</u>, but it is <u>void of any pattern</u> and lends <u>very little color</u> to the <u>whiteness</u> of the room. Only

items of importance for the duties of the kitchen are displayed, all in their properly appointed places, with the appropriate covers placed over them to hide them from prying eyes. The only personality the kitchen portrays is a cold,

calculating, suspicious one, wary of intruders who may
cause unnecessary filth to enter.

Around the corner from the kitchen lies the dining room.
An elegant, dark, formal table sits in the center of the room,
the surface of which is smooth as glass under my fingertips.
A white centerpiece is carefully placed at the table's center,
with two white candles that have never been lit standing
erect at the centerpiece's ends. The chairs around the table
are hard, providing support for the back but lending the
body no comfort. Above hangs a crystal chandelier—expensive, elegant, giving the room an artificial brightness. It is
made up of many dangling, teardrop-shaped crystals, all
cleaned and polished, and is the only object in the dining
room that speaks clearly of conspicuous consumption. The
drapes covering the tinted windows are a dark color and
keep out the sun of the day. This room is often cleaned, often
walked through, but never used.

Having walked through the dining room, I enter the living
room. Although this is the only room in the house where the
family can all converge to spend time together, it is not a
cheerful place. The walls are white, like the rest of the house,
with the same drapery as the dining room, and the couch and
loveseat are velvet, stiff, uncomfortable, and well maintained. A television set is placed in the corner but lies blank
with disuse. The air of coldness here seems to hold tension
though at the same time gives the impression of ossification.

I have heard it said that a person's home is a reflection of
that person, a sentiment that, with few exceptions, is true of
this home. Cleanliness is a priority of the owner, and socializ-
ing with people in this house is considered a nuisance that
only causes more work because of the dirt that people carry
in with them. The walls are kept white because it looks clean
and repainting is made easy. And the smell of disinfectant
pleases the owner, as it proves to the few who do enter that
the house is clean. This house, the place I am calling home for
this period of my life, offers me no comfort but does provide
shelter and quiet. And with the dark stillness in its rooms, I
can think, read, and plan my escape.

Carol Adams (student),
"An Intruder in the House"

In the introduction to Chapter 2 you learned about the difference between writing **objectively** and **subjectively**. Notice, in the previous
essay that although the writer's style is objective, her choice of specific
descriptive details and words supports her subjective, negative opinion
of the house and its owner.

When brainstorming for a description, it may help to begin by listing
all the features of the subject that come to mind and all the details that
seem related to those features.

Descriptive details are often combined with other modes of development. The following paragraphs, for example, are from a narrative essay about a young man's visit to the Mexican town that he had left soon after he was born. Notice his descriptions of the people and the Spanish architecture of the town.

Description: Spanish architecture

On my arrival at Morelia airport, I was greeted by the most attractive architecture I had ever seen. All the buildings had a very strong Spanish influence. Was it possible I had taken the wrong plane and landed somewhere in Spain?   1

People and their clothing

No, indeed; it was Morelia, and what a town! Its people were very plain and small-townlike. I was amused by some very oddly dressed people who wore white cotton clothing. On their heads the men wore straw hats, and the women wore large Spanish scarves called mantillas. I asked a ticket agent about the oddly dressed people. He explained that they were the native people, known as Tarascos. They were the founders of the land, and even today they are very traditional in their beliefs and ways.   2

Architectural features

I took a taxi to El Hotel Virrey de Mendoza, located in the middle of the town square. The hotel was made of hewn stone that was cut and shaped into the most captivating three-story building I had ever seen. It was built in the traditional Spanish style, with a central open patio completely surrounded by the building. My room had a spacious view of the town square and its cathedral. The cathedral was built in the seventeenth century in a baroque style that was popular in Europe. Beside the cathedral was the municipal palace and other government buildings, all in Colonial Spanish style. The feeling I had from the view was that I was back in the days when Spanish viceroys ruled the land, and the Catholic priests taught religion to the native inhabitants.   3

Arturo E. Ramirez (student),
"Back to Where the Seed Was Planted"

Descriptive words and phrases are essential to effective writing. They can make an object concrete for the reader by describing how it looks, sounds, tastes, smells, or feels. They can create a distinct impression of that which is described and thus help the reader visualize the writer's ideas. You will find specific descriptive words and details in all the paragraphs and essays that follow. As you read, notice how experienced writers select revealing details because, as with the incidents in narrative writing, the details in descriptive writing should be limited to those that contribute the most to the effectiveness of the description. In your own writing, select—as the writers of the reading selections do—the most essential qualities of whatever you describe.

The Way to Rainy Mountain

N. Scott Momaday

*Memory allows each of us to tuck meaningful images into the deepest re-
cesses of our minds. In this paragraph from* The Way to Rainy Mountain, *N. Scott Momaday has used vivid details to re-create one of his most
personal family memories: a lasting image of his beloved grandmother.*

Words to Know

exclusive   not shared among others, private
inherently   essentially, part of a basic element or nature
Kiowa   language of the Kiowa tribe of Plains Indians

Getting Started

How could you use language to paint a picture from your memory
of someone you loved very much?

Now that I can have her only in memory, I see my grandmother in the
several postures that were peculiar to her: standing at the wood stove on
a winter morning and turning meat in a great iron skillet; sitting at the
south window, bent above her beadwork, and afterwards, when her vision failed, looking down for a long time into the fold of her hands; going
out upon a cane, very slowly as she did when the weight of age came
upon her; praying. I remember her most often at prayer. She made long,
rambling prayers out of suffering and hope, having seen many things. I
was never sure that I had the right to hear, so exclusive were they of all
mere custom and company. The last time I saw her she prayed standing
by the side of her bed at night, naked to the waist, the light of a kerosene
lamp moving upon her dark skin. Her long, black hair, always drawn and
braided in the day, lay upon her shoulders and against her breasts like a
shawl. I do not speak Kiowa, and I never understood her prayers, but
there was something inherently sad in the sound, some merest hesitation
upon the syllables of sorrow. She began in a high and descending pitch,
exhausting her breath to silence; then again and again—and always the
same intensity of effort, of something that is, and is not, like urgency in
the human voice. Transported so in the dancing light among the shadows

of her room, she seemed beyond the reach of time. But that was illusion; I think I knew then that I should not see her again.

Questions About the Reading

1. What do you learn about Momaday's grandmother's physical appearance from this paragraph? Pick out some details that help you visualize her.
2. What posture does Momaday most associate with his grandmother?
3. Why can't Momaday understand his grandmother's prayers?
4. From Momaday's point of view, how do his grandmother's prayers sound? Why does Momaday think they sound like that?
5. What is the "illusion" Momaday refers to in the last sentence of the paragraph? Why is that image an illusion?

Questions About the Writer's Strategies

1. Is there a **topic sentence** in this paragraph? If so, identify it.
2. What is the **order** in which Momaday remembers his grandmother's postures?
3. Identify the **sensory details** that Momaday uses to create images that bring his grandmother to life.
4. What is the **simile** Momaday uses to describe his grandmother's hair? Does this **figure of speech** help you visualize his grandmother more clearly?

Writing Assignments

1. Use your memory to write a descriptive paragraph about someone you love or once loved. Write a **topic sentence** that describes what you remember about your loved one's physical appearance. Then include specific **details** that support your topic sentence and help your readers visualize that person.
2. Write a paragraph describing one of your special memories. Use **chronological order**, **spatial order**, or **order of importance** to organize your paragraph.

The Way to Rainy Mountain / N. Scott Momaday

Judy Schoyer

Annie Dillard

Annie Dillard is a careful observer of the everyday world. In this paragraph from An American Childhood, *Dillard uses specific details that let us "see" her childhood friend as clearly as a picture.*

Word to Know

camouflage   disguise, mask

Getting Started

Close your eyes and try to imagine one of your closest childhood friends; can you visualize every detail of that person you once knew so well?

———————

My friend Judy Schoyer was a thin, messy, shy girl whose thick blond curls lapped over her glasses. Her cheeks, chin, nose, and blue eyes were round; the lenses and frames of her glasses were round, and so were her heavy curls. Her long spine was supple; her legs were long and thin so her knee socks fell down. She did not care if her knee socks fell down. When I first knew her, as my classmate at the Ellis School, she sometimes forgot to comb her hair. She was so shy she tended not to move her head, but only let her eyes rove about. If my mother addressed her, or a teacher, she held her long-legged posture lightly, alert, like a fawn ready to bolt but hoping its camouflage will work a little longer.

———————

Questions About the Reading

1. What do you learn about Judy Schoyer's physical appearance from this paragraph? Pick out some **details** that help you visualize her.
2. What are the two personality traits that Dillard mentions about Schoyer?
3. What **examples** does Dillard use to illustrate her friend's messiness?
4. According to Dillard, what accounts for Judy's tendency to move only her eyes and not her head?

Questions About the Writer's Strategies

1. Identify the **topic sentence** in this paragraph. Does Dillard mention any other details about her friend that are not related to the topic sentence?
2. What type of **order** does Dillard use to describe her friend's physical appearance?
3. Dillard uses the repetition of certain words to create an image of her friend Judy. List the "round" details of Judy's face. Identify another example of word repetition that helps you see Judy more clearly.
4. What is the **simile** Dillard uses to describe her friend's shyness? Is it effective? Why or why not?

Writing Assignments

1. Write a paragraph describing a childhood friend. Write a **topic sentence** that describes your friend's physical appearance and personality traits. Then include specific **details** that support your topic sentence and help your readers visualize your friend.
2. Imagine you are writing to someone you have never met. Write a paragraph describing yourself. What **impression** would you want to create? Think about the specific **details** that would help a stranger visualize your physical appearance and understand your personality traits.

The Marion

Richard Ford

Sometimes an author uses a long list of objective details to help the reader visualize a specific place. Richard Ford's paragraph about the Marion Hotel, his grandfather's place of business, is full of factual details. However, when you read carefully about the fanciest hotel in Little Rock, Arkansas, you will also find some subtle judgments being made.

Words to Know

assignation   assignment or distribution of tasks

blowsy   unkempt, rundown

escritoires   a writing table or desk

mezzanine   a middle or partial story between two main stories of a building

porte-cochère   a porch roof extending over the driveway at the entrance to a building

Getting Started

What do you suppose happens behind the closed doors of a grand, ornate movie theater, restaurant, or hotel?

 The hotel was named the Marion, and it was not a small place. Little Rock was a mealy, low-rise town on a slow river, and the hotel was the toniest, plushest place in it. And still it was blowsy, a hotel for conventioneers and pols, salesmen and late-night party givers. There was a curving marble fish pond in the lobby; a tranquil, banistered mezzanine with escritoires and soft lights; a jet marble front desk; long, green leather couches, green carpets, bellboys with green twill uniforms and short memories. It was a columned brownstone with a porte-cochère, built in the twenties, with seven stories, three hundred rooms. Ladies from the Delta stayed in on shopping trips. The Optimists and the Rotarians met. Assignations between state officials went on upstairs. Senator McClellan kept a room. Visiting famous people stayed, and my grandfather kept their pictures on his office wall—Rex Allen the cowboy, Jack Dempsey the boxing champion, June Allyson and Dick Powell, Harry Truman (whose photograph I have, still), Ricky Nelson, Chill Wills. Salesmen rented sample rooms, suicides took singles. There were hospitality suites, honeymoon suites, a Presidential, a Miss America, Murphy beds, silver service, Irish napkins. There was a bakery, a print shop, an upholsterer, ten rooms (the Rendezvous, the Continental) for intimate parties, six more for large, and a ballroom with a Hammond organ for banquets. There was a beer bar in the lower lobby, a two-chair barbershop, a cigar stand, a florist, a travel agent, a news agent, a garage where you parked for nothing while you stayed. There was a drummer's rate, a service-man's rate, a monthly rate, a day rate, even an hourly rate if you knew my grandfather. Everything happened there, at all hours. Privacy had a high value. To live in a hotel as a boy knowing nothing was to see what adults did to each other and themselves when only adults were present.

Questions About the Reading

1. Why is Richard Ford so knowledgeable about the Marion Hotel?
2. What does the author think of Little Rock?
3. Why had the Marion become such a popular gathering place?
4. Why do you think it was important for the bellboys to have short memories?

Questions About the Writer's Strategies

1. In his description of the hotel, the author gives you the insider's point of view. Which **details** would not be obvious to a first-time visitor to the Marion?
2. Many of the sentences in this paragraph consist of a list of places or things. What overall **impression** is the author trying to achieve with these lists?
3. In what ways is this paragraph **subjective**? In what ways is it **objective**?

Writing Assignments

1. Write a descriptive paragraph about a public building you know well. To create a picture of the place for the reader, include as many specific details as you can.
2. Think of the grandest place in your own town and imagine what it would be like to work there. Write a paragraph describing what happens behind the scenes.
3. Do you know someone who isn't as wonderful as he or she appears to be? Write a paragraph that describes the person both as he or she appears and as the person really is.

The Subway Station

Gilbert Highet

For many years a professor at Columbia University in New York, Gilbert Highet was born in Scotland and became a U.S. citizen in 1951. The following paragraph, taken from his book Talents and Geniuses, *demonstrates the writer's appreciation of a place that many of us simply ignore.*

Words to Know

abominable   disgusting
congealed   thickened, made solid
defilement   something dirty
dubious   doubtful, suspect
encrusted   covered with a thick crust
meager   scanty, not enough
perfunctory   carelessly indifferent
vaulting   an arched structure
zest   keen enjoyment

Getting Started

If you have ever closely observed a familiar place, what made you suddenly appreciate it in a new way?

Standing in a subway station, I began to appreciate the place—almost to enjoy it. First of all, I looked at the lighting: a row of meager electric bulbs, unscreened, yellow, and coated with filth, stretched toward the black mouth of the tunnel, as though it were a bolt hole in an abandoned coal mine. Then I lingered, with zest, on the walls and ceiling: lavatory tiles which had been white about fifty years ago, and were now encrusted with soot, coated with the remains of a dirty liquid which might be either atmospheric humidity mingled with smog or the result of a perfunctory attempt to clean them with cold water; and, above them, gloomy vaulting from which dingy paint was peeling off like scabs from an old wound, sick black paint leaving a leprous white undersurface. Beneath my feet, the floor was a nauseating dark brown with black stains upon it which might be stale oil or dry chewing gum or some worse defilement; it looked like the hallway of a condemned slum building. Then my eye traveled to the tracks, where two lines of glittering steel—the only positively clean objects in the whole place—ran out of darkness into darkness above an unspeakable mass of congealed oil, puddles of dubious liquid, and a mishmash of old cigarette packets, mutilated and filthy newspapers, and the débris that filtered down from the street above through a barred grating in the roof. As I looked up toward the sunlight, I could see more débris sifting slowly downward, and making an abominable pattern in the slanting beam of dirt-laden sunlight. I was going on to relish more features of this unique scene: such as the advertisement posters on the walls—here a text from the Bible, there a half-naked girl, here a woman wearing a hat consisting of a hen sitting on a nest full of eggs, and there a pair of girl's legs walking up the keys of a cash register—all scribbled over with unknown names and well-known obscenities in black crayon and red lipstick; but then my train came in at last, I boarded it, and began to read. The experience was over for the time.

Questions About the Reading

1. What words does Highet use to demonstrate his growing appreciation of the subway?
2. Highet seems to be appreciating the subway station for the first time. Is this his first wait in a subway station, or does he ride the subway often? How can you tell?
3. At several points in the description, the writer creates the **impression** of squalor and disease. What are some of the words and phrases that he uses to create this impression?

Questions About the Writer's Strategies

1. In the second sentence, the writer uses a **simile**—"as though it were a bolt hole in an abandoned coal mine"—to describe the tunnel. Find two other similes in the paragraph. Are they effective?
2. In what **order** does the writer present the description?
3. What is the **topic sentence** of this paragraph? Where is it located?
4. The paragraph is written in the past tense. Might it be more effective in the present? Rewrite the first three sentences in the present to see how they sound.
5. Why does the writer compare the floor of the subway station to the hallway of a condemned slum building?

Writing Assignments

1. Imagine that you are riding on the subway car the writer boarded at the end of the paragraph. Describe the people you might meet.
2. Write a paragraph describing a public place, such as a shopping mall, a parking lot, or a gas station. Use **spatial order** to organize your description.
3. Describe an object, place, or event that frightened you but that you were still drawn to (for instance, a horror movie, a ride in an amusement park, or a deserted road). What frightened you? What kept you interested? Use specific details.

The Sperm Whale

Barry Holstun Lopez

Sometimes a writer can be most effective by describing what cannot be seen, as well as what can. In this paragraph from Crossing Open Ground, *Barry Lopez helps us understand his subject by creating a picture that includes more than meets the eye.*

Words to Know

ambergris a waxy goo formed in the sperm whale's intestine and collected from the ocean surface or shore for use in making perfumes

aorta the main artery of the heart

cacophony a loud, harsh sound; a racket

carnivore a meat-eating animal

corrugated shaped into folds or ridges

knots nautical miles per hour (one knot = 1.15 statute miles per hour)

rivulets small streams

subterranean underground

writhing twisting or struggling as in pain

Getting Started

What do you imagine it would be like to see inside a creature as awesome as a whale?

The sperm whale, for many, is the most awesome creature of the open seas. Imagine a forty-five-year-old male fifty feet long, a slim, shiny black animal with a white jaw and marbled belly cutting the surface of green ocean water at twenty knots. Its flat forehead protects a sealed chamber of exceedingly fine oil; sunlight sparkles in rivulets running off folds in its corrugated back. At fifty tons it is the largest carnivore on earth. Its massive head, a third of its body length, is scarred with the beak, sucker, and claw marks of giant squid, snatched out of subterranean canyons a mile below, in a region without light, and brought writhing to the surface. Imagine a four-hundred-pound heart the size of a chest of drawers driving five gallons of blood at a stroke through its aorta: a meal of forty salmon moving slowly down twelve-hundred feet of intestine; the blinding, acrid fragrance of a two-hundred-pound wad of gray ambergris lodged somewhere along the way; producing sounds more shrill than we can hear—like children shouting on a distant playground—and able to sort a cacophony of noise: electric crackling of shrimp, groaning of undersea quakes, roar of upwellings, whining of porpoise, hum of oceanic cables. With skin as sensitive as the inside of your wrist.

―――――――――

Questions About the Reading

1. Where do giant squid live?
2. Describe the type of audience you think Lopez is writing for.
3. How do you feel about the sperm whale after reading the paragraph? Commercial whaling has put sperm whales on the list of endangered species. Based on this paragraph, do you think we should continue to protect them? Why or why not?

Questions About the Writer's Strategies

1. What is the **topic sentence** of the paragraph?
2. What **metaphor** does the writer use for the whale's heart? What is the **simile** in the final sentence?
3. It is more than just its size and power that makes the sperm whale "awesome." How does the writer convince you that there is another side to the whale's awesomeness?

Writing Assignments

1. In a paragraph, describe something from the inside out, say, a roast turkey, a good book, an orange or a tomato, or some part of the human anatomy.
2. Imagine that you are in your room or some other place with which you are familiar, and that it is pitch dark. Write a paragraph describing what you would experience as you felt your way around the room in the dark. You will have to use **details** other than those gained through sight, such as touch, smell, or sound.

The Quiet Odyssey

Mary Paik Lee

History is filled with stories of the sacrifices that people have endured for their children and their children's children. In this paragraph from The Quiet Odyssey, *Mary Paik Lee takes us into the sewing factories of Los Angeles around 1950 and shows us where many Asian American families took their first difficult steps toward a better life.*

Getting Started

How would you feel about having to work for fifty cents an hour in a hot, dusty room, eight hours a day, year after year, so that your children might have a better life?

In Los Angeles in 1950 we found many minority women working in sewing factories making garments of every sort for fifty cents an hour, eight hours a day. After several years, the wage went up to one dollar an hour. The sewing rooms were dirty and very dusty, with lint and dust filling the air like fog. The rooms had no air conditioning and no windows. The dust settling on the heads of the women made their hair look gray by the end of the day. The loud power-driven sewing machines working at full speed all at once made a thundering noise that deafened the ear. It was a frightful thing to listen to for eight hours every weekday. I tried it once for several months; the experience made me admire all those women who endured it for years in order to send their children to colleges and universities. I have seen those children return home as doctors, lawyers, and engineers, thus rewarding their parents for their sacrifices.

Questions About the Reading

1. Why did the workers' hair look gray by the end of each day?
2. Why were the rooms in the sewing factories so dusty?
3. What accounted for the "thundering noise" that filled the sewing rooms?
4. What is Lee's attitude toward the workers? How do you know?
5. How are these women rewarded for their sacrifices?

Questions About the Writer's Strategies

1. What **impression** of the sewing factories does the writer offer her readers? List some descriptive words from the paragraph that create this impression.
2. Identify the **topic sentence** in this paragraph.
3. Write the **simile** Lee uses to describe the lint and dust filling the sewing rooms.
4. In what ways is this paragraph **subjective**? In what ways is it **objective**? Support your answer with details and examples from the paragraph.

Writing Assignments

1. Write a descriptive paragraph about a place where you have worked. Use specific **details** so that your readers can imagine themselves working in that place. Use one kind of **order** to organize your paragraph.
2. Write a paragraph describing the life you hope your children will have, the world you hope they will live in, and how you might sacrifice for that future world. Be as imaginative and as descriptive as you can in describing your hopes for the future.

Peace and Quiet

Nancy Pritts Merrell (student)

In the paragraph that follows, a young mother describes her discovery that she did not really want something she thought she longed for—peace and quiet. The writer is a mother of three young children, a student, and a full-time employee at a midwestern community college.

Words to Know

curtail   to limit

phenomenon   an unusual or unaccountable fact or occurrence

Getting Started

If you have ever regretted having a wish come true, what happened?

As a mother of three children, not yet teen-agers, I often found myself complaining to anyone who would listen that I needed some peace and quiet. I longed for this often dreamed-about phenomenon. I would think about what I would do if only I had a couple of hours to do what I wanted, when I wanted, and for however long I wanted. However, three children who are active in school, sports, and social events curtail the amount of peace and quiet a mother can have. I always found myself taking someone somewhere, picking someone up, or baking for some function that someone was involved in. Throughout everything, I wished for some peace and quiet. Alas, my time came. A few days ago, for the first time, my kids all went on vacation for one glorious—or so I thought—week. I finally had my long-awaited peace and quiet. I could do whatever I wanted, whenever I wanted. The first hours were wonderful. I slept late; I didn't make breakfast; and it was certainly quiet. But to my amazement, I found there is such a thing as too much quiet. I now have only a couple of days to go before the kids come home, and I know one thing for sure. When my kids get home and I find myself longing for peace and quiet, I'll think back to this week and I'll gladly drive them, pick them up, and bake for them. Too soon, they will go again. And too soon they'll go for more than just a week's vacation.

Questions About the Reading

1. What are some of the words used to convey the writer's desire for peace and quiet?
2. What did the writer do with her first hours of peace and quiet?
3. What conclusions can you draw about the writer's character? Support your answer with statements from the paragraph.

Questions About the Writer's Strategies

1. Does the writer state the **main idea** (topic) of the paragraph? If so, in which sentence(s)?
2. What is the **point of view** of the paragraph? Could it be changed? If so, explain how, using sentences from the paragraph as examples.
3. The writer says, as she concludes, "When my kids get home . . . I'll think back to this week and I'll gladly drive them, pick them up, and bake for them." Could the sentence be made into more than one sentence? If so, how? If not, why not?
4. What is the **tone** of the paragraph? Identify words and expressions in the paragraph that support your answer.

Writing Assignments

1. Think of something you wanted very much and finally got. Were you pleased or disappointed? Write a paragraph in which you describe what you wanted and the way you reacted when you got it.
2. Think of some situation or condition you frequently complain about. Write a paragraph in which you describe the situation so that your readers will understand your feelings.
3. Write a paragraph in which you describe something that gives you great pleasure or happiness.

Dawn Watch

John Ciardi

How many things do we fail to see because we do not look? In this essay, poet and critic John Ciardi describes in rich detail exactly what happens when the sun comes up in the morning.

Words to Know

bedraggled wet and limp

braggarts people given to talking boastfully

buffet a meal at which guests serve themselves

grackles blackbirds

grate to make a rasping sound

inured accustomed to something undesirable

mulched covered with a protective covering of leaves, manure, and so on

phenomenon an unusual or unaccountable fact or occurrence

pincer to work together like a clawlike grasping tool

spectrum a broad sequence or range of colors

sprawl to spread out awkwardly

thickets dense growths of scrubs or underbrush

Getting Started

What time of day makes you feel most alive?

Unless a man is up for the dawn and for the half hour or so of first light, 1 he has missed the best of the day.

The traffic has just started, not yet a roar and a stink. One car at a time 2 goes by, the tires humming almost like the sound of a brook a half mile down in the crease of a mountain I know—a sound that carries not because it is loud but because everything else is still.

It isn't exactly a mist that hangs in the thickets but more nearly the 3 ghost of a mist—a phenomenon like side vision. Look hard and it isn't there, but glance without focusing and something registers, an exhalation that will be gone three minutes after the sun comes over the treetops.

The lawns shine with a dew not exactly dew. There is a rabbit bobbing 4 about on the lawn and then freezing. If it were truly a dew, his tracks would shine black on the grass, and he leaves no visible track. Yet, there is something on the grass that makes it glow a depth of green it will not show again all day. Or is that something in the dawn air?

Our cardinals know what time it is. They drop pure tones from the 5 hemlock tops. The black gang of grackles that makes a slum of the pin oak also knows the time but can only grate at it. They sound like a convention of broken universal joints grating uphill. The grackles creak and squeak, and the cardinals form tones that only occasionally sound through the noise. I scatter sunflower seeds by the birdbath for the cardinals and hope the grackles won't find them.

My neighbor's tomcat comes across the lawn, probably on his way 6 home from passion, or only acting as if he had had a big night. I suspect him of being one of those poolroom braggarts who can't get next to a girl but who likes to let on that he is a hot stud. This one is too can-fed and too lazy to hunt for anything. Here he comes now, ignoring the rabbit. And there he goes.

As soon as he has hopped the fence, I let my dog out. The dog charges 7 the rabbit, watches it jump the fence, shakes himself in a self-satisfied way, then trots dutifully into the thicket for his morning service, stopping to sniff everything on the way back.

There is an old mountain laurel on the island of the driveway turna- 8 round. From somewhere on the wind a white morning-glory rooted next to it and has climbed it. Now the laurel is woven full of white bells tinged pink by the first rays through the not quite mist. Only in earliest morning can they be seen. Come out two hours from now and there will be no morning-glories.

Dawn, too, is the hour of a weed I know only as day flower—a bright 9 blue button that closes in full sunlight. I have weeded bales of it out of my flower beds, its one daytime virtue being the shallowness of its root system that allows it to be pulled out effortlessly in great handfuls. Yet, now it shines. Had it a few more hours of such shining in its cycle, I would cultivate it as a ground cover, but dawn is its one hour, and a garden is for whole days.

There is another blue morning weed whose name I do not know. This 10 one grows from a bulb to pulpy stems and a bedraggled daytime sprawl. Only a shovel will dig it out. Try weeding it by hand and the stems will break off to be replaced by new ones and to sprawl over the chosen plants in the flower bed. Yet, now and for another hour it outshines its betters, its flowers about the size of a quarter and paler than those of the day flower but somehow more brilliant, perhaps because of the contrast of its paler foliage.

And now the sun is slanting in full. It is bright enough to make the 11 leaves of the Japanese red maple seem a transparent red bronze when the tree is between me and the light. There must be others, but this is the only tree I know whose leaves let the sun through in this way—except, that is, when the fall colors start. Aspen leaves, when they first yellow and before they dry, are transparent in this way. I tell myself it must have something to do with the red-yellow range of the spectrum. Green takes sunlight and holds it, but red and yellow let it through.

The damned crabgrass is wrestling with the zinnias, and I stop to 12 weed it out. The stuff weaves too close to the zinnias to make the iron claw usable. And it won't do to pull at the stalks. Crabgrass (at least in a mulched bed) can be weeded only with dirty fingers. Thumb and forefinger have to pincer into the dirt and grab the root-center. Weeding, of course, is an illusion of hope. Pulling out the root only stirs the soil and brings new crabgrass seeds into germinating position. Take a walk around the block and a new clump will have sprouted by the time you get back. But I am not ready to walk around the block. I fill a small basket with the plucked clumps, and for the instant I look at them, the zinnias are weedless.

Don't look back. I dump the weeds in the thicket where they will be 13 smothered by the grass clippings I will pile on at the next cutting. On the way back I see the cardinals come down for the sunflower seeds, and the jays join them, and then the grackles start ganging in, gatecrashing the buffet and clattering all over it. The dog stops chewing his rawhide and makes a dash into the puddle of birds, which splashes away from him.

I hear a brake-squeak I have been waiting for and know the paper has 14 arrived. As usual, the news turns out to be another disaster count. The function of the wire services is to bring us tragedies faster than we can pity. In the end we shall all be inured, numb, and ready for emotionless programming. I sit on the patio and read until the sun grows too bright on the page. The cardinals have stopped singing, and the grackles have flown off. It's the end of birdsong again.

Then suddenly—better than song for its instant—a hummingbird the 15 color of green crushed velvet hovers in the throat of my favorite lily, a lovely high-bloomer I got the bulbs for but not the name. The lily is a crest of white horns with red dots and red velvet tongues along the insides of the petals and with an odor that drowns the patio. The hummingbird darts in and out of each horn in turn, then hovers an instant, and disappears.

Even without the sun, I have had enough of the paper. I'll take that 16 hummingbird as my news for this dawn. It is over now. I smoke one more cigarette too many and decide that, if I go to bed now, no one in the family need know I have stayed up for it again. Why do they insist on shaking their heads when they find me still up for breakfast, after having scribbled through the dark hours? They always do. They seem compelled to express pity for an old loony who can't find his own way to bed. Why won't they understand that this is the one hour of any day that must not be missed, as it is the one hour I couldn't imagine getting up for, though I can still get to it by staying up? It makes sense to me. There comes a time when the windows lighten and the twittering starts. I look up and know it's time to leave the papers in their mess. I could slip quietly into bed and avoid the family's headshakes, but this stroll-around first hour is too good to miss. Even my dog, still sniffing and circling, knows what hour this is.

Come on, boy. It's time to go in. The rabbit won't come back till tomor- 17 row, and the birds have work to do. The dawn's over. It's time to call it a day.

Questions About the Reading

1. Why does the writer prefer the dawn to other hours of the day?
2. Why does the writer choose not to look back after he finishes weeding?
3. Although the writer is describing one specific day, which words indicate that every day is like this day?
4. How will his family react to finding out that he has stayed up to watch the sunrise again? Why?
5. In the last paragraph, why won't the rabbit come back until the next day?
6. What does the writer mean when he says, "It's time to call it a day"?

Questions About the Writer's Strategies

1. Which sentence states the **thesis** of the essay?
2. Even though the essay appears to ramble from one description to another, there is a deliberate **order** in the essay. What is the order the writer uses?
3. What **tone** does the writer use in his description? Is it formal or informal?
4. What are the topics of paragraphs 8, 9, and 10? Could the paragraphing be changed?

Writing Assignments

1. Write an essay describing a sunrise or sunset you have seen. Order your description **chronologically**.

2. Spend some time looking out a window and write an essay describing what you see, hear, and smell. Concentrate on concrete details, and try to order your description **spatially**.
3. Describe in great detail five minutes of your routine day and what you see during those five minutes. For example, describe what you see when you are waking up, leaving for work or school, finishing your lunch, or arriving home at the end of the day.

I Love Washington

David McCullough

Do you ever feel as though you like a place without knowing why? When you experience that feeling, try to think of this essay and the way David McCullough picks out individual details that explain his affection for the city of Washington as a whole.

Words to Know

adjourns   breaks for recess

the Mall   a large parklike area running from the Capitol building toward the Washington Monument and the Lincoln Memorial, lined with impressive buildings including the National Gallery and the Smithsonian Institution

Monet   a French Impressionist painter

Getting Started

What are your thoughts and feelings about our nation's capital?

Washington is a wonderful city. The scale seems right, more humane 1 than other places. I like all the white marble and green trees, the ideals celebrated by the great monuments and memorials. I like the climate, the slow shift of the seasons here. Spring, so Southern in feeling, comes early and the long, sweet autumns can last into December. Summers are murder, equatorial—no question; the compensation is that Congress adjourns, the city empties out, eases off. Winter evenings in Georgetown with the snow falling and the lights just coming on are as beautiful as any I've known.

I like the elegant old landmark hotels—the Willard, now restored to its 2 former glory, the Mayflower, with its long, glittering, palm-lined lobby, the Hay-Adams on Lafayette Square, overlooking the White House. And Massachusetts Avenue, as you drive down past the British Embassy and over Rock Creek Park, past the Mosque and around Sheridan Circle. This is an avenue in the grand tradition, befitting a world capital.

The presence of the National Gallery, it seems to me, would be reason 3 enough in itself to wish to live here.

In many ways it is our most civilized city. It accommodates its river, 4
accommodates trees and grass, makes room for nature as other cities
don't. There are parks everywhere and two great, unspoiled, green corri-
dors running beside the Potomac and out Rock Creek where Theodore
Roosevelt liked to take his rough cross-country walks. There is no more
beautiful entrance to any of our cities than the George Washington Park-
way which comes sweeping down the Virginia side of the Potomac. The
views of the river gorge are hardly changed from Jefferson's time. Across
the river, on the towpath of the old C&O Canal, you can start at Georgetown and walk for miles with never a sense of being in a city. You can
walk right out of town, ten, twenty, fifty miles if you like, more, all the
way to Harpers Ferry where you can pick up the Appalachian Trail going
north or south.

Some mornings along the towpath it is as if you are walking through 5
a Monet. Blue herons stalk the water. You see deer prints. Once, in Glover
Park, in the heart of the city, I saw a red fox. He stopped right in front of
me, not more than thirty feet down the path, and waited a count or two
before vanishing into the woods, as if giving me time to look him over, as
if he wanted me never to wonder whether my eyes had played tricks.

Even the famous National Zoo is a "zoological park," a place to walk, 6
as specifically intended in the original plan by Frederick Law Olmsted.

It was Olmsted also who did the magnificent Capitol grounds and 7
who had the nice idea of putting identifying tags on the trees, giving
their places of origin and Latin names. I like particularly the tulip trees
(*Liriodendron tulipifera*); the tulip is one of the common trees of Washington, and it lines the main drive to the east front of the Capitol. There are
red oak, white oak, silver linden, a tremendous spreading white ash,
sugar maples, five kinds of American magnolias, a huge Japanese pagoda
tree. A spectacular willow oak on the west side has a trunk three men
couldn't put their arms around. In spring the dogwood in bloom all
around the Capitol are enough to take your breath away.

There are trees and there is sky, the immense, blessed overarching sky 8
of the Mall. What city has anything to compare to the Mall? At first light
on a summer morning, before the rush hour, before the first jets come
roaring out of National, the dominant sound is of crows and the crunch
of your own feet along the gravel pathways. The air, still cool from the
night, smells of trees and damp grass, like a country town. Floodlights
are still on at the old red Smithsonian castle, bathing it in a soft theatrical
glow, like the backdrop for some nineteenth century Gothic fantasy. The
moon is up still, hanging in a pale, clear sky beyond the Monument,
which for the moment is a very pale pink.

Questions About the Reading

1. What does the writer mean when he says Washington "accommodates" its river, grass, and trees (paragraph 4)?
2. Who was Frederick Law Olmsted?
3. What makes Washington unlike other cities, according to the writer?
4. What type of audience do you think the essay is directed toward? People who know Washington? People who do not? Both? Cite **examples** from the essay to support your answer.

Questions About the Writer's Strategies

1. Why do you think the writer saved the description of the Mall for last? What purpose does it serve in the essay?
2. What is the **main idea** of the essay? Is there a **thesis statement**? If so, where is it located?
3. Besides the dominant mode, description, what other **modes of development** does the writer use in the essay? Cite one or two paragraphs in which other modes are used.
4. How do you suppose the writer went about choosing the **details** for his description? What criteria do you think he might have used? Cite examples from the essay to help explain your answer.

Writing Assignments

1. This writer identifies many details, but he doesn't give many "details about the details." Write an essay in which you describe an object of smaller scale, such as one of the types of trees the writer identifies, or a park or river that you know about. Describe your subject thoroughly, including some of its specific characteristics.
2. Write an essay describing your thoughts and feelings when you think of Washington. For example, does patriotism come to mind? Or do you think of corruption, architecture, or fancy clothes and limousines? Describe incidents and pictures that you have read about or seen in magazines or on TV that make you feel as you do.

The Monster

Deems Taylor

In this essay, Deems Taylor describes a totally unpleasant man. In each paragraph, he piles detail upon detail until we find ourselves wondering, "How bad can one man be?" Then we read the next paragraph and we find out—he gets worse. Near the end, though, Taylor identifies his subject and offers some possible explanations—some surprising ones—for the "monster's" bad nature.

Words to Know

arrogance   overbearing pride
Beethoven   a German composer
burlesquing   mocking
callous   unfeeling
delusions   false beliefs
harangue   a long, pompous speech
infidelities   unfaithful acts
libretto   the text of an opera
mania   an intense enthusiasm, a craze
monologue   a long speech by one person
Plato   a Greek philosopher
rajah   a prince in India
royalties   money paid to a composer out of the proceeds from a
   performance
scrupulous   conscientious, principled
synopsis   an outline of a story
trilogy   a group of three works
volubility   ready, fluent speech

Getting Started

Under what circumstances could extraordinary talent justify monstrous behavior?

He was an undersized little man, with a head too big for his body—a   1
sickly little man. His nerves were bad. He had skin trouble. It was agony

for him to wear anything next to his skin coarser than silk. And he had delusions of grandeur.

He was a monster of conceit. Never for one minute did he look at the 2 world or at people, except in relation to himself. He was not only the most important person in the world, for himself; in his own eyes he was the only person who existed. He believed himself to be one of the greatest dramatists in the world, one of the greatest thinkers, and one of the greatest composers. To hear him talk, he was Shakespeare, and Beethoven, and Plato, rolled into one. And you would have had no difficulty in hearing him talk. He was one of the most exhausting conversationalists that ever lived. An evening with him was an evening spent in listening to a monologue. Sometimes he was brilliant; sometimes he was maddeningly tiresome. But whether he was being brilliant or dull, he had one sole topic of conversation: himself. What *he* thought and what *he* did.

He had a mania for being in the right. The slightest hint of disagreement, from anyone, on the most trivial point, was enough to set him off on a harangue that might last for hours, in which he proved himself right in so many ways, and with such exhausting volubility, that in the end his hearer, stunned and deafened, would agree with him, for the sake of peace.

It never occurred to him that he and his doing were not of the most 4 intense and fascinating interest to anyone with whom he came in contact. He had theories about almost any subject under the sun, including vegetarianism, the drama, politics, and music; and in support of these theories he wrote pamphlets, letters, books . . . thousands upon thousands of words, hundreds and hundreds of pages. He not only wrote these things, and published them—usually at somebody else's expense—but he would sit and read them aloud, for hours, to his friends, and his family.

He wrote operas; and no sooner did he have the synopsis of a story, but 5 he would invite—or rather summon—a crowd of his friends to his house and read it aloud to them. Not for criticism. For applause. When the complete poem was written, the friends had to come again, and hear *that* read aloud. Then he would publish the poem, sometimes years before the music that went with it was written. He played the piano like a composer, in the worst sense of what that implies, and he would sit at the piano before parties that included some of the finest pianists of his time, and play for them, by the hour, his own music, needless to say. He had a composer's voice. And he would invite eminent vocalists to his house, and sing them his operas, taking all the parts.

He had the emotional stability of a six-year-old child. When he felt out 6 of sorts, he would rave and stamp, or sink into suicidal gloom and talk darkly of going to the East to end his days as a Buddhist monk. Ten minutes later, when something pleased him, he would rush out of doors and run around the garden, or jump up and down on the sofa, or stand on his head. He could be grief-stricken over the death of a pet dog, and he could be callous and heartless to a degree that would have made a Roman emperor shudder.

He was almost innocent of any sense of responsibility. Not only did he 7 seem incapable of supporting himself, but it never occurred to him that he was under any obligation to do so. He was convinced that the world owed him a living. In support to this belief, he borrowed money from everybody who was good for a loan—men, women, friends, or strangers. He wrote begging letters by the score, sometimes groveling without shame, at others loftily offering his intended benefactor the privilege of contributing to his support, and being mortally offended if the recipient declined the honor. I have found no record of his ever paying or repaying money to anyone who did not have a legal claim upon it.

What money he could lay his hand on he spent like an Indian rajah. 8 The mere prospect of a performance of one of his operas was enough to set him running up bills amounting to ten times the amount of his prospective royalties. On an income that would reduce a more scrupulous man to doing his own laundry, he would keep two servants. Without enough money in his pocket to pay his rent, he would have the walls and ceiling of his study lined with pink silk. No one will ever know—certainly he never knew—how much money he owed. We do know that his greatest benefactor gave him $6,000 to pay the most pressing of his debts in one city, and a year later had to give him $16,000 to enable him to live in another city without being thrown into jail for debt.

He was equally unscrupulous in other ways. An endless procession of 9 women marched through his life. His first wife spent twenty years enduring and forgiving his infidelities. His second wife had been the wife of his most devoted friend and admirer, from whom he stole her. And even while he was trying to persuade her to leave her first husband he was writing to a friend to inquire whether he could suggest some wealthy woman—*any* wealthy woman—whom he could marry for her money.

He was completely selfish in his other personal relationships. His lik- 10 ing for his friends was measured solely by the completeness of their devotion to him, or by their usefulness to him, whether financial or artistic. The minute they failed him—even by so much as refusing a dinner invitation—or began to lessen in usefulness, he cast them off without a second thought. At the end of his life he had exactly one friend left whom he had known even in middle age.

He had a genius for making enemies. He would insult a man who dis- 11 agreed with him about the weather. He would pull endless wires in order to meet some man who admired his work and was able and anxious to be of use to him—and would proceed to make a mortal enemy of him with some idiotic and wholly uncalled-for exhibition of arrogance and bad manners. A character in one of his operas was a caricature of one of the most powerful music critics of his day. Not content with burlesquing him, he invited the critic to his house and read him the libretto aloud in front of his friends.

The name of this monster was Richard Wagner. Everything I have said 12 about him you can find on record—in newspapers, in police reports, in the testimony of people who knew him, in his own letters, between the lines of his autobiography. And the curious thing about this record is that it doesn't matter in the least.

Because this undersized, sickly, disagreeable, fascinating little man 13 was right all the time. The joke was on us. He *was* one of the world's greatest dramatists; he *was* a great thinker; he *was* one of the most stupendous musical geniuses that, up to now, the world has ever seen. The world did owe him a living. People couldn't know those things at the time, 1 suppose; and yet to us, who know his music, it does seem as though they should have known. What if he did talk about himself all the time? If he talked about himself for twenty-four hours every day for the span of his life he would not have uttered half the number of words that other men have spoken and written about him since his death.

When you consider what he wrote—thirteen operas and music dra- 14 mas, eleven of them still holding the stage, eight of them unquestionably worth ranking among the world's great musico-dramatic masterpieces—when you listen to what he wrote, the debts and heartaches that people had to endure from him don't seem much of a price. Edward Hanslick, the critic whom he caricatured in *Die Meistersinger* and who hated him ever after, now lives only because he was caricatured in *Die Meistersinger*. The women whose hearts he broke are long since dead; and the man who could never love anyone but himself has made them deathless atonement, I think, with *Tristan und Isolde*. Think of the luxury with which for a time, at least, fate rewarded Napoleon, the man who ruined France and looted Europe; and then perhaps you will agree that a few thousand dollars' worth of debts were not too heavy a price to pay for the *Ring* trilogy.

What if he was faithless to his friends and to his wives? He had one 15 mistress to whom he was faithful to the day of his death: Music. Not for a single moment did he ever compromise with what he believed, with what he dreamed. There is not a line of his music that could have been conceived by a little mind. Even when he is dull, or downright bad, he is dull in the grand manner. There is a greatness about his worst mistakes. Listening to his music, one does not forgive him for what he may or may not have been. It is not a matter of forgiveness. It is a matter of being dumb with wonder that his poor brain and body didn't burst under the torment of the demon of creative energy that lived inside him, struggling, clawing, scratching to be released; tearing, shrieking at him to write the music that was in him. The miracle is that what he did in the little space of seventy years could have been done at all, even by a great genius. Is it any wonder he had no time to be a man?

Questions About the Reading

1. Was Wagner ever considerate of others? Give examples.
2. Why does the writer say that "the joke was on us"?
3. Does Wagner's great talent justify his behavior?
4. Would you like to have known Wagner? Would you like to have attended one of his parties?

Questions About the Writer's Strategies

1. What effect does the writer achieve by concealing the name of the composer until paragraph 12?
2. Is there any deliberate **order** to the presentation of examples?
3. What effect do the detailed, numerous **examples** have on the way you view Wagner? Are you led to think there is anything positive about his behavior?
4. In paragraphs 3 and 6, the writer uses colorful words to enliven his descriptive examples. Identify five particularly effective adjectives in those paragraphs, and five effective verbs.
5. Napoleon was a tyrant but also a military genius who changed the course of Western history. Why do you think the writer mentions him in paragraph 14?

Writing Assignments

1. Do you know someone who is extremely good at what he or she does but is impossible to live with? Describe that person in an essay.
2. Using **order of importance** to organize your essay, describe one of the following: your best friend, your worst enemy, your favorite (or most boring) professor, or the best pet you ever had.
3. Think of a movie, television, or sports personality whose personal behavior is disagreeable or in some way unacceptable. Write an essay using detailed examples to describe how that person's behavior influences your opinion of his or her professional achievements.

Marrying Absurd

Joan Didion

Las Vegas, Nevada: Depending on your point of view, it can symbolize the American dream or the American nightmare. If you have never visited that glittering city in the desert, Joan Didion's essay offers you a colorful action-packed tour.

Words to Know

allegorical   symbolic
bouvardia   tropical American shrubs with white or red flowers
en masse   all together, in one group
expendable   not worth keeping
facsimile   copy, reproduction
imperative   duty, authority to command control
implausibility   impossibility, unbelievability
jocularity   joking manner
liaisons   adulterous meetings or affairs
Panglossian   optimistic in a blind, naive manner
peau de soie   soft, satiny silk
venality   openness to bribery and corruption

Getting Started

Why does the idea of a dignified, traditional wedding seem out of place in the traditional image of Las Vegas?

T o be married in Las Vegas, Clark County, Nevada, a bride must swear   1
that she is eighteen or has parental permission and a bridegroom that he is twenty-one or has parental permission. Someone must put up five dollars for the license. (On Sundays and holidays, fifteen dollars. The Clark County Courthouse issues marriage licenses at any time of the day or night except between noon and one in the afternoon, between eight and nine in the evening, and between four and five in the morning.) Nothing else is required. The State of Nevada, alone among these United States, demands neither a premarital blood test nor a waiting period before or after the issuance of a marriage license. Driving in across the Mojave from Los Angeles, one sees the signs way out on the desert, looming up

from that moonscape of rattlesnakes and mesquite, even before the Las Vegas lights appear like a mirage on the horizon: "GETTING MARRIED? Free License Information First Strip Exit." Perhaps the Las Vegas wedding industry achieved its peak operational efficiency between 9:00 p.m. and midnight of August 26, 1965, an otherwise unremarkable Thursday which happened to be, by Presidential order, the last day on which anyone could improve his draft status merely by getting married. One hundred and seventy-one couples were pronounced man and wife in the name of Clark County and the State of Nevada that night, sixty-seven of them by a single justice of the peace, Mr. James A. Brennan. Mr. Brennan did one wedding at the Dunes and the other sixty-six in his office, and charged each couple eight dollars. One bride lent her veil to six others. "I got it down from five to three minutes," Mr. Brennan said later of his feat. "I could've married them *en masse,* but they're people, not cattle. People expect more when they get married."

What people who get married in Las Vegas actually do expect—what, 2 in the largest sense, their "expectations" are—strikes one as a curious and self-contradictory business. Las Vegas is the most extreme and allegorical of American settlements, bizarre and beautiful in its venality and in its devotion to immediate gratification, a place the tone of which is set by mobsters and call girls and ladies' room attendants with amyl nitrite poppers in their uniform pockets. Almost everyone notes that there is no "time" in Las Vegas, no night and no day and no past and no future (no Las Vegas casino, however, has taken the obliteration of the ordinary time sense quite so far as Harold's Club in Reno, which for a while issued, at odd intervals in the day and night, mimeographed "bulletins" carrying news from the world outside); neither is there any logical sense of where one is. One is standing on a highway in the middle of a vast hostile desert looking at an eighty-foot sign which blinks "STARDUST" or "CAESAR'S PALACE." Yes, but what does that explain? This geographical implausibility reinforces the sense that what happens there has no connection with "real" life; Nevada cities like Reno and Carson are ranch towns, Western towns, places behind which there is some historical imperative. But Las Vegas seems to exist only in the eye of the beholder. All of which makes it an extraordinarily stimulating and interesting place, but an odd one in which to want to wear a candlelight satin Priscilla of Boston wedding dress with Chantilly lace insets, tapered sleeves and a detachable modified train.

And yet the Las Vegas wedding business seems to appeal to precisely 3 that impulse. "Sincere and Dignified Since 1954," one wedding chapel advertises. There are nineteen such wedding chapels in Las Vegas, intensely competitive, each offering better, faster, and, by implication, more sincere services than the next: Our Photos Best Anywhere, Your

Wedding on A Phonograph Record, Candlelight with Your Ceremony, Honeymoon Accommodations, Free Transportation from Your Motel to Courthouse to Chapel and Return to Motel, Religious or Civil Ceremonies, Dressing Rooms, Flowers, Rings, Announcements, Witnesses Available, and Ample Parking. All of these services, like most others in Las Vegas (sauna baths, payroll-check cashing, chinchilla coats for sale or rent) are offered twenty-four hours a day, seven days a week, presumably on the premise that marriage, like craps, is a game to be played when the table seems hot.

But what strikes one most about the Strip chapels, with their wishing 4 wells and stained-glass paper windows and their artificial bouvardia, is that so much of their business is by no means a matter of simple convenience, of late-night liaisons between show girls and baby Crosbys. Of course there is some of that. (One night about eleven o'clock in Las Vegas I watched a bride in an orange minidress and masses of flame-colored hair stumble from a Strip chapel on the arm of her bridegroom, who looked the part of the expendable nephew in movies like *Miami Syndicate.* "I gotta get the kids," the bride whimpered. "I gotta pick up the sitter, I gotta get to the midnight show." "What you gotta get," the bridegroom said, opening the door of a Cadillac Coupe de Ville and watching her crumple on the seat, "is sober.") But Las Vegas seems to offer something other than "convenience"; it is merchandising "niceness," the facsimile of proper ritual, to children who do not know how else to find it, how to make the arrangements, how to do it "right." All day and evening long on the Strip, one sees actual wedding parties, waiting under the harsh lights at a crosswalk, standing uneasily in the parking lot of the Frontier while the photographer hired by The Little Church of the West ("Wedding Place of the Stars") certifies the occasion, takes the picture: the bride in a veil and white satin pumps, the bridegroom usually in a white dinner jacket, and even an attendant or two, a sister or a best friend in hot-pink *peau de soie*, a flirtation veil, a carnation nosegay. "When I Fall in Love It Will Be Forever," the organist plays, and then a few bars of Lohengrin. The mother cries; the stepfather, awkward in his role, invites the chapel hostess to join them for a drink at the Sands. The hostess declines with a professional smile; she has already transferred her interest to the group waiting outside. One bride out, another in, and again the sign goes up on the chapel door: "One moment please—Wedding."

I sat next to one such wedding party in a Strip restaurant the last time 5 I was in Las Vegas. The marriage had just taken place; the bride still wore her dress, the mother her corsage. A bored waiter poured out a few swallows of pink champagne ("on the house") for everyone but the bride, who was too young to be served. "You'll need something with more kick than that," the bride's father said with heavy jocularity to his new son-in-law; the ritual jokes about the wedding night had a certain Panglossian character, since the bride was clearly several months pregnant. Another round of pink champagne, this time not on the house, and the bride began to cry. "It was just as nice," she sobbed, "as I hoped and dreamed it would be."

Questions About the Reading

1. In Las Vegas's history, what is noteworthy about the date August 26, 1965?
2. According to Didion, why doesn't time exist in Las Vegas?
3. Why does Didion find it odd that the wedding business in Las Vegas advertises itself as "sincere and dignified"?
4. What is Didion's attitude toward Las Vegas? Does she like or dislike the city? Give specific **details** to support your opinion.
5. Why do you think Didion titled her essay "Marrying Absurd"?

Questions About the Writer's Strategies

1. What **impression** of Las Vegas does the writer offer her readers? List some descriptive words from the essay that create this impression.
2. Identify the **simile** that the writer uses in paragraph 1 to describe the lights of Las Vegas.
3. Is this essay written **subjectively** or **objectively**? Support your answer with details and examples from the essay.

Writing Assignments

1. Imagine that you have been a guest at a Las Vegas wedding. In a fictional essay, describe your experience there. Use your imagination to make up the details of your trip. Use **chronological order, spatial order**, or **order of importance** to organize your description.
2. Write a descriptive essay about a place that you love. Use specific **details** and **metaphors** or **similes** to provide your readers with a word picture of that special place.

This Man Has Expired

Robert Johnson

Do you favor the death penalty or oppose it? Do you think about it very much? Be warned that once you have read this sensitive and disturbing description of the final minutes before an execution, you may find it hard to stop thinking about it.

Words to Know

en route   on the way to

malice   ill will toward others

paradoxically   surprisingly contrary to common sense

Getting Started

Can you describe an experience so unpleasant that every detail was forever burned into your memory?

We entered the witness area, a room within the death chamber, and took our seats. A picture window covering the front wall of the witness room offered a clear view of the electric chair, which was about twelve feet away from us and well illuminated. The chair, a large, high-back solid oak structure with imposing black straps, dominated the death chamber. Behind it, on the back wall, was an open panel full of coils and lights. Peeling paint hung from the ceiling and walls; water stains from persistent leaks were everywhere in evidence.

Two officers, one a hulking figure weighing some 400 pounds, stood 6 alongside the electric chair. Each had his hands crossed at the lap and wore a forbidding, blank expression on his face. The witnesses gazed at them and the chair, most of us scribbling notes furiously. We did this, I suppose, as much to record the experience as to have a distraction from the growing tension. A correctional officer entered the witness room and announced that a trial run of the machinery would be undertaken. Seconds later, lights flashed on the control panel behind the chair indicating that the chair was in working order. A white curtain, opened for the test, separated the chair and the witness area. After the test, the curtain was

Chapter 3 / Description

drawn. More tests were performed behind the curtain. Afterwards, the curtain was reopened, and would be left open until the execution was over. Then it would be closed to allow the officers to remove the body.

A handful of high-level correctional officers were present in the death 7 chamber, standing just outside the witness area. There were two regional administrators, the director of the Department of Corrections, and the prison warden. The prisoner's chaplain and lawyer were also present. Other than the chaplain's black religious garb, subdued grey pinstripes and bland correctional uniforms prevailed. All parties were quite solemn.

At 10:58 the prisoner entered the death chamber. He was, I knew from 8 my research, a man with a checkered, tragic past. He had been grossly abused as a child, and went on to become grossly abusive of others. I was told he could not describe his life, from childhood on, without talking about confrontations in defense of a precarious sense of self—at home, in school, on the streets, in the prison yard. Belittled by life and choking with rage, he was hungry to be noticed. Paradoxically, he had found his moment in the spotlight, but it was a dim and unflattering light cast before a small and unappreciative audience. "He'd pose for cameras in the chair—for the attention," his counselor had told me earlier in the day. But the truth was that the prisoner wasn't smiling, and there were no cameras.

The prisoner walked quickly and silently toward the chair, an escort of 9 officers in tow. His eyes were turned downward, his expression a bit glazed. Like many before him, the prisoner had threatened to stage a last stand. But that was lifetimes ago, on death row. In the death house, he joined the humble bunch and kept to the executioner's schedule. He appeared to have given up on life before he died in the chair.

En route to the chair, the prisoner stumbled slightly, as if the momen- 10 tum of the event had overtaken him. Were he not held securely by two officers, one at each elbow, he might have fallen. Were the routine to be broken in this or indeed any other way, the officers believe, the prisoner might faint or panic or become violent, and have to be forcibly placed in the chair. Perhaps as a precaution, when the prisoner reached the chair he did not turn on his own but rather was turned, firmly but without malice, by the officers in his escort. These included the two men at his elbows, and four others who followed behind him. Once the prisoner was seated, again with help, the officers strapped him into the chair.

The execution team worked with machine precision. Like a disciplined 11 swarm, they enveloped him. Arms, legs, stomach, chest, and head were secured in a matter of seconds. Electrodes were attached to a cap holding his head and to the strap holding his exposed right leg. A leather mask was placed over his face. The last officer mopped the prisoner's brow, then touched his hand in a gesture of farewell.

During the brief procession to the electric chair, the prisoner was at- 12
tended by a chaplain. As the execution team worked feverishly to secure
the condemned man's body, the chaplain, who appeared to be upset,
leaned over him and placed his forehead in contact with the prisoner's,
whispering urgently. The priest might have been praying, but I had the
impression he was consoling the man, perhaps assuring him that a forgiving God awaited him in the next life. If he heard the chaplain, I doubt
the man comprehended his message. He didn't seem comforted. Rather,
he looked stricken and appeared to be in shock. Perhaps the priest's ur-
gent ministrations betrayed his doubts that the prisoner could hold himself together. The chaplain then withdrew at the warden's request, allowing the officers to affix the death mask.

The strapped and masked figure sat before us, utterly alone, waiting 13
to be killed. The cap and mask dominated his face. The cap was nothing
more than a sponge encased in a leather shell with a metal piece at the
top to accent an electrode. It looked decrepit and resembled a cheap,
ill-fitting toupee. The mask, made entirely of leather, appeared soiled
and worn. It had two parts. The bottom part covered the chin and
mouth, the top the eyes and lower forehead. Only the nose was exposed.
The effect of the rigidly restrained body, together with the bizarre cap
and the protruding nose, was nothing short of grotesque. A faceless
man breathed before us in a tragicomic trance, waiting for a blast of
electricity that would extinguish his life. Endless seconds passed. His
last act was to swallow, nervously, pathetically, with his Adam's apple
bobbing. I was struck by that simple movement then, and can't forget it
even now. It told me, as nothing else did, that in the prisoner's restrained body, behind that mask, lurked a fellow human being who, at
some level, however primitive, knew or sensed himself to be moments
from death.

Questions About the Reading

1. Why was the writer attending the execution?
2. If the curtain was open during the execution, why would it be closed
   "to allow the officers to remove the body"? Is there anything unexpected in this situation?
3. Explain the routine described in paragraph 6. What was the purpose
   of the officers' actions?
4. Do you think the writer is fully opposed to the death penalty or just
   did not like attending the execution? Or is he unsure? Cite **examples**
   from the essay to support your answer.

Questions About the Writer's Strategies

1. What is the writer's purpose in this essay? What method of development does this writer use? What **details** contribute to his purpose?
2. Which statements in the essay most clearly express the **main idea**? Why do you think the writer located them where they are?
3. What **order** does the writer use for his description?
4. Besides description, what is the main **mode of development** the writer uses?
5. This essay is **subjective** but also has **objective** elements. What techniques and details add objectivity to the description?

Writing Assignments

1. In an essay, describe an extremely unpleasant experience you have had. Use specific details to help your readers understand what was so disturbing about the situation.
2. Write an essay describing what you imagine jail to be like. Try to describe the actual effects you think being confined would have on you.

Aravaipa Canyon

Edward Abbey

A long tradition in American literature is one of finding solace in nature. Edward Abbey's descriptions of the American West have inspired many travelers to seek out the wilderness. This essay fulfills the two purposes common to much of his work: it pictures the beauty of Aravaipa Canyon and encourages us to preserve it.

Words to Know

apostate   one who abandons religious faith
comprehensible   understandable
endemic   native to a certain region, common
formidable   causing, or able to cause fear
Grendel   the name of the monster in the Old English epic, *Beowulf*
monolithic   massive, solid
obscure   not easily understood, unclear, ambiguous
omnivorous   eating both animal and vegetable substances
paradox   statement that seems to be contradictory, but actually may be true
pictographs   pictures representing a word or idea
riparian   on the bank of a natural course of water, or river
seeps   small pools formed by water oozing from underground
sylvan   typical of woods or forest regions
talus   slope formed by the buildup of debris
vesiculated   full of small cells or cavities
vigilante   enforcement of laws without authority
vivacity   liveliness, spirit, animation

Getting Started

Can you describe a time when you felt awed by the mystery and beauty of a particular natural setting?

Southeast of Phoenix and northeast of Tucson, in the Pinal Mountains,   1
is a short deep gorge called Aravaipa Canyon. It is among the few places

in Arizona with a permanent stream of water and in popular estimation one of the most beautiful. I am giving away no secrets here: Aravaipa Canyon has long been well known to hikers, campers, horsemen, and hunters from the nearby cities. The federal Bureau of Land Management (BLM), charged with administration of the canyon, recently decreed it an official Primitive Area, thus guaranteeing its fame. Demand for enjoyment of the canyon is so great that the BLM has been obliged to institute a rationing program: no one camps here without a permit and only a limited number of such permits are issued.

Two friends and I took a walk into Aravaipa Canyon a few days ago. 2 We walked because there is no road. There is hardly even a foot trail. Twelve miles long from end to end, the canyon is mostly occupied by the little river which gives it its name, and by stream banks piled with slabs of fallen rock from the cliffs above, the whole overgrown with cactus, trees, and riparian desert shrubbery.

Aravaipa is an Apache name (some say Pima, some say Papago) and 3 the commonly accepted meaning is "laughing waters." The name fits. The stream is brisk, clear, about a foot deep at normal flow levels, churning its way around boulders, rippling over gravelbars, plunging into pools with bright and noisy vivacity. Schools of loach minnow, roundtail chub, spike dace, and Gila mudsuckers—rare and endemic species—slip and slither past your ankles as you wade into the current. The water is too warm to support trout or other varieties of what are called game fish; the fish here live out their lives undisturbed by anything more than horses' hooves and the sneaker-shod feet of hikers. (PLEASE DO NOT MOLEST THE FISH.)

The Apaches who gave the name to this water and this canyon are not 4 around anymore. Most of that particular band—unarmed old men, women, children—huddled in a cave near the mouth of Aravaipa Canyon, were exterminated in the 1880s by a death squad of American pioneers, aided by Mexican and Papagos, from the nearby city of Tucson. The reason for this vigilante action is obscure (suspicion of murder and cattle stealing) but the results were clear. No more Apaches in Aravaipa Canyon. During pauses in the gunfire, as the pioneers reloaded their rifles, the surviving Indians could have heard the sound of laughing waters. One hundred and twenty-five were killed, the remainder relocated in the White Mountain Reservation to the northeast. Since then those people have given us no back talk at all.

Trudging upstream and over rocky little beaches, we are no more 5 troubled by ancient history than are the mudsuckers in the pools. We prefer to enjoy the scenery. The stone walls stand up on both sides, twelve hundred feet high in the heart of the canyon. The rock is of volcanic origin, rosy-colored andesites and buff, golden, consolidated tuff. Cleavages and fractures across the face of the walls form perfect stairways and sometimes sloping ramps, slick as sidewalks. On the beaches lie obsidian boulders streaked with veins of quartzite and pegmatite.

The walls bristle with spiky rock gardens of formidable desert vegeta- 6 tion. Most prominent is the giant saguaro cactus, growing five to fifty feet tall out of crevices in the 'stone you might think could barely lodge a flower. The barrel cactus, with its pink fishhook thorns, thrives here on the sunny side; and clusters of hedgehog cactus, and prickly pear with names like clockface and cows-tongue, have wedged roots into the rock. Since most of the wall is vertical, parallel to gravity, these plants grow first outward then upward, forming right-angled bends near the base. It looks difficult but they do it. They like it here.

Also present are tangles of buckhorn, staghorn, chainfruit, and teddy- 7 bear cholla; the teddybear cholla is a cactus so thick with spines it glistens under the sun as if covered with fur. From more comfortable niches in the rock grow plants like the sotol, a thing with sawtooth leaves and a flower stalk ten feet tall. The agave, a type of lily, is even bigger, and its leaves are long, rigid, pointed like bayonets. Near the summit of the cliffs, where the moisture is insufficient to support cactus, we see gray-green streaks of lichen clinging to the stone like a mold.

The prospect at streamside is conventionally sylvan, restful to desert- 8 weary eyes. Great cottonwoods and sycamores shade the creek's stony shores; when we're not wading in water we're wading through a crashing autumn debris of green-gold cottonwood and dusty-red sycamore leaves. Other trees flourish here—willow, salt cedar, alder, desert hackberry, and a kind of wild walnut. Cracked with stones, the nuts yield a sweet but frugal meat. At the water's edge is a nearly continuous growth of peppery-flavored watercress. The stagnant pools are full of algae; and small pale frogs, treefrogs, and leopard frogs leap from the bank at our approach and dive into the water; they swim for the deeps with kicking legs, quick breaststrokes.

We pass shadowy, intriguing side canyons with names like Painted 9 Cave (ancient pictographs), Iceberg (where the sun seldom shines), and Virgus (named in honor of himself by an early settler in the area). At midday we enter a further side canyon, one called Horsecamp, and linger here for a lunch of bread, cheese, and water. We contemplate what appears to be a bottomless pool.

The water in this pool has a dark clarity, like smoked glass, transparent 10 but obscure. We see a waterlogged branch six feet down resting on a ledge but cannot see to the bottom. The water feels intensely cold to hand and foot; a few tadpoles have attached themselves to the stony rim of the pool just beneath the surface of the water. They are sluggish, barely animate. One waterbug, the kind called boatman, propels itself with limp oars down toward darkness when I extend my hand toward it.

Above the pool is a thirty-foot bluff of sheer, vesiculated, fine-grained, 11 monolithic gray rock with a glossy chute carved down its face. Flash floods, pouring down that chute with driving force, must have drilled this basin in the rock below. The process would require a generous allowance of time—ten thousand, twenty thousand years—give or take a few thousand. Only a trickle of water from a ring of seeps enters the pool now, on this hot still blazing day in December. Feels like 80°F; a month from now it may be freezing; in June 110°. In the silence I hear the rasping chant of locusts—that universal lament for mortality and time—here in this canyon where winter seldom comes.

The black and bottomless pool gleams in the shining rock—a sinister 12 paradox, to a fanciful mind. To any man of natural piety this pool, this place, this silence, would suggest reverence, even fear. But I'm an apostate Presbyterian from a long-ago Pennsylvania: I shuck my clothes, jump in, and touch bottom only ten feet down. Bedrock bottom, as I'd expected, and if any Grendels dwell in this inky pool they're not inclined to reveal themselves today.

We return to the Aravaipa. Halfway back to camp and the canyon en- 13 trance we pause to inspect a sycamore that seems to be embracing a boulder. The trunk of the tree has grown around the rock. Feeling the tree for better understanding, I hear a clatter of loose stones, look up, and see six, seven, eight bighorn sheep perched on the rimrock a hundred feet above us. Three rams, five ewes. They are browsing at the local salad bar— brittlebush, desert holly, bursage, and jojoba—aware of us but not alarmed. We watch them for a long time as they move casually along the rim and up a talus slope beyond, eating as they go, halting now and then to stare back at the humans staring up at them.

Once, years before, I had glimpsed a mountain lion in this canyon, fol- 14 lowing me through the twilight. It was the only mountain lion I had ever seen, so far, in the wild. I stopped, the big cat stopped, we peered at each other through the gloom. Mutual curiosity: I felt more wonder than fear. After a minute, or perhaps it was five minutes, I made a move to turn. The lion leaped up into the rocks and melted away.

We see no mountain lions this evening. Nor any of the local deer, either 15 Sonoran whitetail or the desert mule deer, although the little heart-shaped tracks of the former are apparent in the sand. Javelina, or peccary, too, reside in this area; piglike animals with tusks, oversized heads, and tapering bodies, they roam the slopes and gulches in family bands (like the Apaches), living on roots, tubers, and innards of barrel cactus, on grubs, insects, and carrion. Omnivorous, like us, and equally playful, if not so dangerous. Any desert canyon with permanent water, like Aravaipa, will be as full of life as it is beautiful.

We stumble homeward over the stones and through the anklebone- 16 chilling water. The winter day seems alarmingly short; it is.

We reach the mouth of the canyon and the old trail uphill to the road- 17 head in time to see the first stars come out. Barely in time. Nightfall is quick in this arid climate and the air feels already cold. But we have earned enough memories, stored enough mental-emotional images in our heads, from one brief day in Aravaipa Canyon, to enrich the urban days to come. As Thoreau found a universe in the woods around Concord, any person whose senses are alive can make a world of any natural place, however limited it might seem, on this subtle planet of ours.

"The world is big but it is comprehensible," says R. Buckminster 18 Fuller. But it seems to me that the world is not nearly big enough and that any portion of its surface, left unpaved and alive, is infinitely rich in details and relationships, in wonder, beauty, mystery, comprehensible only in part. The very existence of existence is itself suggestive of the unknown—not a problem but a mystery.

We will never get to the end of it, never plumb the bottom of it, never 19 know the whole of even so small and trivial and useless and precious a place as Aravaipa. Therein lies our redemption.

Questions About the Reading

1. Why is Aravaipa Canyon so popular among Arizona hikers?
2. What is the author's attitude about the fate of the Apaches?
3. How do cacti manage to survive along the walls of the canyon?
4. Why do you think the writer jumped into the bottomless pool?
5. Why does Abbey find the world "comprehensible only in part"?

Questions About the Writer's Strategies

1. This essay is an **objective** description of a physical place, yet there is a **subjective** element, too. In what ways is the essay subjective?
2. What three **similes** does the writer use in paragraph 7?
3. Does the writer express the **main idea** in a **thesis statement**? If not, how is the main idea expressed?
4. Why do you think Abbey chose not to include **dialogue** in his essay even though he tells you that he is hiking with two friends?

5. Choose some particularly clear **details** the writer uses and analyze why they are effective. How do they help you visualize what the writer is describing?

Writing Assignments

1. Choose a natural place near your home and spend an hour or two there alone, observing. Write an essay that describes in detail the beauty and feel of the place.
2. Choose a destination you often walk to and describe the landmarks along the route in **chronological order**.
3. Write an essay about a stroll through a shopping mall. Describe the people you see in the same kind of detail Abbey uses to describe the plants and animals of Aravaipa Canyon.

Limbo

Rhonda S. Lucas (student)

A new experience, a change in our lives, can make us see familiar objects in a new light. And a new location can make an old possession—a piece of furniture, an article of clothing—look strange. Rhonda S. Lucas, a student at East Los Angeles College, discovered both these things one day as she sat in a garage full of packing boxes and old furniture. She describes what she saw in this essay.

Words to Know

cryptic   secret, mystifying

dilapidated   fallen into a state of disrepair

elegy   a mournful poem, often lamenting the dead

futility   a useless act or gesture

irony   the use of words to convey the opposite of their meaning

limbo   an intermediate place or state; a region or condition of oblivion or neglect

tubular   having the form of a tube

Getting Started

If you had to leave your house tomorrow, what would you miss most about it?

My parents' divorce was final. The house had been sold and the day 1 had come to move. Thirty years of the family's life was now crammed into the garage. The two-by-fours that ran the length of the walls were the only uniformity among the clutter of boxes, furniture, and memories. All was frozen in limbo between the life just passed and the one to come.

The sunlight pushing its way through the window splattered against 2 a barricade of boxes. Like a fluorescent river, it streamed down the sides and flooded the cracks of the cold, cement floor. I stood in the doorway between the house and garage and wondered if the sunlight would ever again penetrate the memories packed inside those boxes. For an instant, the cardboard boxes appeared as tombstones, monuments to those memories.

The furnace in the corner, with its huge tubular fingers reaching out 3
and disappearing into the wall, was unaware of the futility of trying to
warm the empty house. The rhythmical whir of its effort hummed the
elegy for the memories boxed in front of me. I closed the door, sat down
on the step, and listened reverently. The feeling of loss transformed the
bad memories into not-so-bad, the not-so-bad memories into good, and
committed the good ones to my mind. Still, I felt as vacant as the house
inside.

A workbench to my right stood disgustingly empty. Not so much as a 4
nail had been left behind. I noticed, for the first time, what a dull, lifeless
green it was. Lacking the disarray of tools that used to cover it, now it
seemed as out of place as a bathtub in the kitchen. In fact, as I scanned the
room, the only things that did seem to belong were the cobwebs in the
corners.

A group of boxes had been set aside from the others and stacked in 5
front of the workbench. Scrawled like graffiti on the walls of dilapidated
buildings were the words "Salvation Army." Those words caught my
eyes as effectively as a flashing neon sign. They reeked of irony. "Salvation—was a bit too late for this family," I mumbled sarcastically to myself.

The houseful of furniture that had once been so carefully chosen to com- 6
plement and blend with the color schemes of the various rooms was indis-
criminately crammed together against a single wall. The uncoordinated
colors combined in turmoil and lashed out in the greyness of the room.

I suddenly became aware of the coldness of the garage, but I didn't 7
want to go back inside the house, so I made my way through the boxes to
the couch. I cleared a space to lie down and curled up, covering myself
with my jacket. I hoped my father would return soon with the truck so
we could empty the garage and leave the cryptic silence of parting lives
behind.

Questions About the Reading

1. Why is the title of this essay "Limbo"? Between which two stages of
   life is the writer?
2. How does the writer feel about moving out of the house?
3. Why does the writer view the empty workbench as disgusting (paragraph 4)?
4. Why didn't she want to go back inside the house?
5. What does Lucas mean in the last line by the "cryptic silence" of the
   house?

Questions About the Writer's Strategies

1. Although she never says it, the writer is saddened by her parents' divorce and the subsequent need to move. What **details** does she use to convey this feeling?
2. In what ways is this an extremely **subjective** essay?
3. Give your **impression** of the writer's life before her parents' divorce. What methods does she use to suggest this impression?
4. What is the **thesis statement** in the essay? Which paragraphs are used to develop the thesis statement? Is there a concluding paragraph?
5. What is the purpose of the **metaphor** in the last sentence of paragraph 2? In which sentence of paragraph 3 is the metaphor repeated?

Writing Assignments

1. Write an essay describing your favorite room in the house where you live now or the one where you grew up. Try to use examples from your life to give meaning to the objects you describe.
2. Write an essay describing a walk through your neighborhood or another one with which you are familiar. Describe the things that most interest you or that you think you will remember best in the future.

4

Examples

WRITERS OFTEN USE one or more **examples** to explain or illustrate their main idea.

Topic sentence ⌐ In this century, the president is much more cut off from con-
                └ tact with the people than in earlier times. Ordinary citizens,
                ⌐ *for example,* could get to see Abraham Lincoln directly in the
Example   └ White House and make their requests to him in person.

Some writers announce their strategy outright by the words *for example* or *for instance*. Other writers may include several examples without announcing them directly, and thereby expect the reader to notice that they are indeed specific examples.

To make a clear case, the writer usually wants to give several examples, often to show several sides of an idea. The writer of the previous example might want to add an example about Jimmy Carter or Ronald Reagan and how they visited private citizens in their homes or invited them to special ceremonies. Or perhaps the writer might want to add an example of another type of president—how Nixon was hard to reach, even by his own staff.

As you learned in Chapter 1, the **topic sentence** states the **main idea** of a paragraph and the **thesis statement** states the main idea of an essay. Both are usually general statements that must be clarified through the writer's **mode of development**. Sometimes, without concrete examples, the reader will have only a vague idea of what the writer's topic sentence or thesis statement means. In the following paragraphs, notice how the examples illustrate and clarify the topic sentences.

Topic sentence	The American colonists used a variety of goods in place of money. These goods included <u>beaver pelts</u>, <u>grain</u>, <u>musket</u>
Examples	<u>balls</u>, and <u>nails</u>. Some colonists, especially in the tobacco-growing colonies of Maryland and Virginia, circulated <u>re-</u>
Examples	<u>ceipts for tobacco</u> stored in warehouses. <u>Indian wampum</u>, which consisted of beads made from shells, was mainly used for keeping records. But Indians and colonists also accepted it as money.
Topic sentence	The colonists also used any foreign coins they could get. <u>English shillings</u>, <u>Spanish dollars</u>, and <u>French and Dutch</u>
Examples	<u>coins</u> all circulated in the colonies. Probably the most common coins were large silver Spanish dollars called *pieces of*
Examples of Spanish dollars	*eight*. To make change, a person could chop the coin into eight pie-shaped pieces called *bits*. Two bits were worth a quarter of a dollar, four bits a half dollar, and so on. We still use the expression *two bits* to mean a quarter of a dollar.

World Book Encyclopedia, 1990

In essays, an example sometimes appears at the very beginning of the essay to introduce the thesis. The selection that follows illustrates the use of an introductory example—chosen to spark the reader's interest.

	The red-and-white pickup bounced along a gravel road in north-central Washington State. It was just past midnight on a summer Saturday last year. Two boys and two girls, recent graduates of Tonasket High School, had been "cruising" for a couple of hours, talking and laughing. At a sharp curve, the pickup somehow went off the road, rolled down the steep, rocky mountainside and twisted around a pine tree. All four	1
Example used to introduce essay	occupants—none wearing a seat belt—were tossed out of the cab.	
	Driver Joe McDaniel escaped with cuts on his face and arms. Josh Wheeler suffered bruises but was able to cradle Amy Burdick in his arms until help arrived. She died the next day. Katy Watson, a former cheerleader who had won a scholarship to college, was dead at the scene, with massive chest and back injuries.	2
Thesis statement	Motor-vehicle injury is the greatest threat to the lives of adolescents in America. During the 1980s, over 74,000 teenagers were killed in such accidents, more than died from all	3
	diseases combined. On average, every two or three weeks the equivalent of a senior class at a typical high school is wiped out on our streets and highways. The National Safety Council (NSC) estimates that the financial toll is at least $10 billion annually for medical and insurance costs, property damage and lost wages resulting from accidents involving teen drivers.	

Reader's Digest, June 1991

Examples in an essay can both illustrate and **support** the thesis. That is, if a writer makes a claim or a point in the thesis statement and then provides evidence in the form of actual situations that illustrate the thesis, it will help convince the reader that the thesis is valid. When you write, you should also search for examples as a way to test your thesis. For example, if you cannot think of a single specific example that supports your main idea, you will need to rethink it. Or if you think of several examples that support your thesis, but also of several that work against it, you might want to revise your thesis and develop an **objective** essay presenting both sides of the issue.

In addition to providing concrete support for the thesis, examples can be used in other ways to enliven and clarify writing. In a description, for instance, examples can give concrete details in a way that adds variety and interest. A single example may also be **extended** throughout an essay to illustrate the thesis, as in the following essay about the Kickapoo Indian Medicine Company. Notice, too, that minor examples are also used within the essay, as in paragraphs 2 and 3, for instance, to explain the topic sentences of some paragraphs.

Thesis

Major extended example—from here to end of essay

1 By 1880 several hundred medicine shows were traveling in the United States, giving performances varying from simple magic acts to elaborate "med-presentations." Among the largest of such operations from 1880 to 1910 was the Kickapoo Indian Medicine Company, "The King of Road Shows." Founded by two veteran troupers, John E. "Doc" Healy and Charles H. "Texas Charlie" Bigelow, the Kickapoo Company maintained a large headquarters building, "The Principal Wigwam," in New Haven, Connecticut, and from there sent out shows, as many as twenty-five at a time, to cities and villages throughout the country.

Minor examples of *performers* who were hired

2 Doc Healy hired performers, both Indian and white—dancers, singers, jugglers, fire-eaters, acrobats, comedians, fiddlers—and Texas Charlie managed the medicine business and trained the "Doctors" and "Professors" who gave "Medical Lectures."

Minor examples of *distinctively garbed* troupe members

3 All troupe members were distinctively garbed. The Indians—including Mohawks, Iroquois, Crees, Sioux, and Blackfeet—billed as "all pure-blooded Kickapoos, the most noted of all Indian Medical People," were adorned with colored beads and feathers and loaded down with primitive weapons; they trailed great strings of unidentified hairy objects. Some lecturers wore western-style leather clothes and boots with silver-capped toes, others fancy silk shirts, frock coats, and high silk hats. One of the most colorful Kickapoo figures was smooth-talking Ned T. Oliver—"Nevada Ned, the King of Gold"—who wore an enormous sombrero from

the brim of which dangled 100 gold coins, and a fancy suit loaded with buttons made of gold pieces.

The Kickapoo shows were presented under canvas at "Kickapoo Camps" during the summer and in opera houses and town halls in winter. On many nights the show was free to all, on others each adult was charged 10¢. The money poured in from medicine sales.   4

The wonder-working Kickapoo concoctions were "compounded according to secret ancient Kickapoo Indian tribal formulas" from "blood root, feverwort, spirit gum, wild poke berries, sassafras, slippery elm, wintergreen, white oak bark, yellow birch bark, dock root, sarsaparilla, and other Natural Products." The medicines were made in the Connecticut factory in vats so huge the "mixers" had to perch on ladders and wield long paddles. The leader of the Kickapoo line was Sagwa, which sold at 50¢ and $1 per bottle— "Sagwa, the wonderful remedy for catarrh, pulmonary consumption, and all ills that afflict the human body. It is made from roots, barks, gums, leaves, oils, and berries gathered by little Kickapoo children from God's great laboratory, the fertile fields and vast forests. Sagwa, Nature's own great secret cure, now available to all mankind!"   5

Long after the Kickapoo Company was dissolved, a woman who had worked in the medicine factory recalled that one of the ingredients of Kickapoo Cough Syrup was Jamaica rum. Could this "cure" have been the inspiration for the "Kickapoo Joy Juice" Al Capp featured in his popular comic strip?   6

Peggy Robbins,
"The Kickapoo Indian Medicine Company"

In this essay, the writer's use of concrete examples gives us a clear picture of the Kickapoo medicine show. In addition, the great number and variety of minor examples give us a good idea of the crazy-quilt nature of medicine shows in general.

When using examples in your own writing, **brainstorm** for possibilities (as described in Chapter 1) and select those that illustrate your idea most accurately. In choosing among possibilities, favor those that you sense your reader will respond to as convincing and colorful. Several well-chosen examples will often hold your reader's interest and add credibility to your main idea.

Naming Cows

Linda M. Hasselstrom

As every parent knows, naming a baby is a lengthy and sometimes controversial procedure. But what about our four-legged friends? Linda Hasselstrom's paragraph uses examples to illustrate just exactly how and why a cow by any other name would still be a cow.

Words to Know

brockle-faced scar-faced
temperament disposition

Getting Started

How do you suppose people choose names for their animals?

Most cows are named for their attributes or temperament, or because they resemble a relative or prominent person. Dolly Parton was not named for the reason that may spring to vulgar minds, but because her front legs were spangled with spots, like fancy western pants. Naming cows isn't too unusual, even among tough old ranchers. One friend used to name his bulls after the person who accompanied him to the sale ring when he bought the bull. The year I went with him, he reluctantly decided it would be too embarrassing to stand in the pasture calling a bull named "Linda," and settled on "Hazel," which seemed to him more masculine. Sometimes the name is merely a descriptive phrase, including "that old brockle-faced bitch," or "that damned cow with the short horns." Another nearby family faces facts from the beginning; calves raised for meat are always named for their destiny: Steak, Hamburger, Stew Meat.

Questions About the Reading

1. What are most cows named for?
2. Why was one type of cow named after Dolly Parton?
3. Why did the writer's friend decide to name his bull "Hazel"?

4. What does Hasselstrom mean when she writes that one family "faces facts from the beginning"?

Questions About the Writer's Strategies

1. What is the **main idea** in this paragraph? Is it stated in a **topic sentence** or does the writer **imply** it?
2. Does Hasselstrom use many examples, one extended example, or a combination of the two strategies to support her topic sentence?
3. Humor is a key element in this paragraph. Find two humorous **details** that help illustrate the main idea.
4. Identify the **simile** that helps the reader visualize one kind of cow. Is it effective? Why or why not?

Writing Assignments

1. Have you ever named, or helped to name, an animal? Write a paragraph about that procedure. Write a topic sentence and then include several examples, or one extended example, to illustrate and clarify your main idea.
2. Write a paragraph in which you use examples to explain how members of a fictional family, or animals on a farm or in a zoo, could be named. Be as imaginative and creative as possible.

The Pencil Rack

John Ciardi

In this paragraph, by poet John Ciardi, we see how an experienced writer can push himself to begin writing. This inventory of Ciardi's pencil rack, the little trough at the front of his desk drawer, gives the reader a colorful and amusing portrait of the ordinary litter of day-to-day living.

Words to Know

obscure   not easily seen or understood
unsubstantiated   unproven

Getting Started

Do you think the instinct to stockpile things is behavior common to all living beings? Why or why not?

Moved by what might be called an obscure impulse (to obscure my average reluctance to get to work), I recently fell to taking inventory of my average pencil rack and came up with the following itemization: two red pencils (unsharpened), one black grease pencil, one ball point and one fountain pen (both broken), one mailing sticker that had curled up into a small tube and which I unrolled to find that I had once printed on it with some care my social security number (032-10-1225), one purchaser's receipt for a money order in the amount of $7.15, one theater ticket stub (R 108) for the opening night of *The Rise of Arturo Ui*, one second-best (and therefore unused) letter opener, one spool of J. & P. Coats black thread (15¢, 125 yards, number 60, origin and purpose unknown), one dentist's tool (broken, but obviously useful for picking things out of things if I had anything of that sort to pick related things out of), two nail files, one pair of cuff links, one metal pill box (empty, origin and purpose unknown), one glass marble (probably a souvenir of a visit from Benn), one four-for-a-quarter-while-you-wait-press-the-button photo taken, as I recall, at, then, Idlewild Airport and showing Jonnel and me looking at one another in some sort of fond but unsubstantiated pride, one twenty-cent stamp (1938 Presidential issue, James A. Garfield), two rubber bands, one pocket comb, a litter of paper clips, one 1889 quarter (to give to the kids for their collection as soon as I am sure that they will not spend it on candy), one Canadian dime and one British halfpenny (to be given to them any time), one air-mail sticker, two six-penny nails, three thumb tacks, two match folders, one broken tie clip (probably repairable), one small screw driver (in case any small screws show up to be driven?), one pocket pack of Kleenex, one pair of paper scissors, one staple remover, assorted grit.

Questions About the Reading

1. Why do you think the writer saved all of these things? Is a reason **implied**?
2. Who do you think Benn and Jonnel are? Give reasons for your answer.
3. Does the writer ever use the dentist's tool? How do you know?
4. What thoughts did you have when you finished reading this paragraph? What do you think the writer wants you to conclude about the contents of his pencil rack?

Questions About the Writer's Strategies

1. Examine the arrangement of examples in this paragraph. See if you can detect any obvious or implied **order** in their arrangement.
2. Besides being a paragraph of examples, in what sense is this a **descriptive** paragraph?
3. One could say that this paragraph is just a list of junk. How does the writer hold your interest and keep you reading?

Writing Assignments

1. We all save some things we do not need or use, sometimes without even knowing why. Write a paragraph giving examples of such things—your own possessions or those of your friends—and try to describe some of the reasons for keeping them.
2. In a paragraph, use examples to describe the contents of the average refrigerator, garage, attic, or some other place where things tend to collect and be forgotten. Try to include examples that will interest or amuse your readers.

The Shoe as a Strategic Weapon

Alison Lurie

Clothing doesn't simply keep us warm and dry. What we wear and how we wear it can tell people a lot about who we are. In this selection taken from The Language of Clothes, *Alison Lurie gives examples of another use of clothing: to stop women from moving about quickly.*

Words to Know

gait   a way of moving on foot

hampering   making something difficult

lotus foot   a Chinese practice of binding women's feet to make them smaller

Getting Started

If you have ever worn something uncomfortable, simply out of vanity, was it worth it?

Attempts to limit female mobility by hampering locomotion are ancient and almost universal. The foot-binding of upper-class Chinese girls and the Nigerian custom of loading women's legs with pounds of heavy brass wire are extreme examples, but all over the world similar stratagems have been employed to make sure that once you have caught a woman she cannot run away, and even if she stays around she cannot keep up with you. What seems odd is that all these devices have been perceived as beautiful, not only by men but by women. The lotus foot, which seems to us a deformity, was passionately admired in China for centuries, and today most people in Western society see nothing ugly in the severely compressed toes produced by modern footwear. The high-heeled, narrow-toed shoes that for most of this century have been an essential part of woman's costume are considered sexually attractive, partly because they make the legs look longer—an extended leg is the biological sign of sexual availability in several animal species—and because they produce what anthropologists call a "courtship strut." They also make standing for any length of time painful, walking exhausting and running impossible. The halting, tiptoe gait they produce is thought provocative—perhaps because it guarantees that no woman wearing them can outrun a man who is chasing her. Worst of all, if they are worn continually from adolescence on, they deform the muscles of the feet and legs so that it becomes even more painful and difficult to walk in flat soles.

Questions About the Reading

1. Why have cultures attempted to limit female mobility?
2. What is the writer **implying** about modern Western society?
3. Do you agree with what Lurie says about high-heeled shoes? Why or why not?

Questions About the Writer's Strategies

1. What is the **topic sentence** of the paragraph? Where is it located?
2. Does the writer use many examples, one extended example, or a combination of the two strategies?
3. What **mode of development** does the writer use? Does she use more than one mode?

Writing Assignments

1. Do you own any clothing that limits mobility or is uncomfortable but that you wear anyway, like a formal suit or dress, a snug pair of jeans, or, as in Lurie's paragraph, an uncomfortable pair of shoes? In a paragraph, use examples to show how the article of clothing restricts you, and provide other examples to show why you wear it.
2. Write a paragraph giving several examples of customs or habits that are familiar to you but that someone from another country might find odd.

The Next Generation

Mary Paik Lee

People who succeed in life despite great hardships usually have help along the way. Family members, a coach, a teacher, a boss—these people provide invaluable support. Mary Paik Lee's paragraph describes one inspiring example of such a success story.

Getting Started

Why do you suppose some people succeed in life despite overwhelming hardships?

There is a good example among Koreans which makes me feel proud of what people can accomplish despite hardship. Mr. and Mrs. Lee (no relation to us) had a son named Sammy. The first time I saw him, he was only eleven months old. I watched his progress all the way through the University of Southern California School of Medicine, where he became a doctor, specializing in ear, nose, and throat ailments. He was always playing in the swimming pools and became interested in high diving. The coach at USC took an interest in him and helped him to develop into an expert high-platform diver. Sammy Lee won the Olympic Gold Medal for high-platform diving in 1948 and successfully defended his title in 1952. In 1953 he became the first non-Caucasian to win the James E. Sullivan Memorial Trophy. His parents helped with all his expenses by working in their chop suey restaurant for many years.

Questions About the Reading

1. How old was Sammy Lee when the writer first met him?
2. What did Lee study at USC?
3. Who helped Lee develop his diving talent?
4. How did Lee's parents support him?

Questions About the Writer's Strategies

1. Identify the **topic sentence** in this paragraph.
2. Does the writer use many examples, one extended example, or a combination of the two strategies to support her topic sentence?
3. What type of **order** does the writer use to organize the extended example? List the **details** that support this order.
4. Analyze the example in this paragraph. How does it support or illustrate the main idea of the paragraph?

Writing Assignments

1. Have you ever known or read about someone who succeeded in achieving his or her goals despite great hardship? Write a paragraph about that person. Use several examples, or one extended example, to illustrate and clarify your main idea about that person.
2. What are your goals in life? Write a paragraph in which you use examples to show how you hope to realize your personal and professional goals.

Wrappings

Andy Rooney

Andy Rooney, who appears on the television show "Sixty Minutes," is known for his opinions. Rooney has his own ideas—and gives them freely—on just about every topic, from women's handbags to the air force's use of glue. Here, he speaks his mind on our national mania for wrappings.

Words to Know

antimacassars   chair covers
silicone   a kind of water-resistant plastic

Getting Started

What do you think accounts for the American fascination with wrapping things?

Depending on what mood I'm in, I find it either irritating, funny or 1
civilized when I think about how we protect protective coverings in this country.

When I come home from the grocery store and start to unpack, I am 2
always unfavorably impressed with the layers of protective or decorative wrappings we cover our food with.

There is hardly anything we buy that doesn't come in at least two 3
wrappings, and then several of them are assembled by the cashier at the checkout counter and put into a small bag. Then several of the small bags are grouped together and put into a big bag. If you have several big bags with small bags in them, they give you a cardboard box to put the pack-ages-in-the-little-bags-in-the-big-bags in.

A lot of things we buy wouldn't really need any protective wrapping 4
at all. The skin of an orange protects an orange pretty well for most of its natural life, but we aren't satisfied with what nature has given it. We wrap ten of them in plastic or put them in a net bag, and we put the plas-tic bag in a paper bag. The orange inside the skin, inside the plastic which is in a paper bag, must wonder where it is.

A box of cookies or crackers often has waxed paper next to the cook- 5
ies, a cardboard box holding the cookies and then waxed paper and a

decorative wrapping around the cardboard box. What seems to be called for here is some stiff, decorative waxed paper.

We have always wrapped our cars in an incredible number of protec- 6 tive layers. We put fenders over the wheels to protect ourselves from flying dirt. Then we put bumpers front and back to protect the fenders. We proceed from there to put chrome on the bumpers to protect them from rust, and we undercoat the fenders to protect *them* from the dirt they're protecting us from.

We paint the car to protect the metal, wax the paint to protect that and 7 then we build a two-car garage to protect the whole thing. If it was a child, it would be spoiled.

I'm laughing, but I'm a protector of things myself. I use wood pre- 8 server before I paint lumber, and when I buy a raincoat I always spray it with Scotchgard or some other silicone water resister. Over the years, I'll bet I've spent more on Scotchgard than I have on raincoats.

A good book is designed with a hard cover to protect its contents. The 9 hard cover is protected from dirt and abuse by a dust jacket. A lot of people who are very careful with books cover the dust jacket with a plastic cover of its own.

A relative of ours bought a new couch recently because she liked the 10 fabric it was covered with. She liked it so much she didn't want it to get dirty, so she bought a slipcover to put over it and she laid little oblong pieces of cloth over the arms where the wear is heaviest to protect the slipcover. She called them antimacassars.

We may never again see the fabric she's protecting.   11

Questions About the Reading

1. In the first sentence the writer uses the word *civilized*. What types of protective wrappings might seem civilized? Does Rooney give any examples in the essay on wrappings that might be viewed that way?
2. Do you think the writer approves of all the wrappings and protective coverings Americans use? Support your answer with an example.
3. What does the writer mean by stating that if a car "was a child, it would be spoiled"?

Questions About the Writer's Strategies

1. What is the **tone** of this essay?
2. Is the **thesis** stated or implied? If it is stated, where is it stated? If it is implied, state it in your own words.

3. The writer uses a number of examples to make his point. Would the essay have been as effective if he had used one extended example?
4. How does Rooney use language to amuse the reader?

Writing Assignments

1. Are protective wrappings ever useful? Write an essay that gives examples of protective wrappings that are necessary.
2. Although Rooney presents it humorously, his topic also has a serious side: The use of too many protective wrappings can be wasteful and uses up scarce natural resources. Write an essay that gives examples of other ways in which our society is wasteful. Use a serious tone.
3. Think of another aspect of our society that is good or bad, right or wrong. Form a thesis statement to express your opinion and then write an essay using examples to support your thesis.

Down with the Forests

Charles Kuralt

Charles Kuralt roams the highways and byways of America in a mobile home, covering (and discovering) offbeat stories for his "Dateline America" series on CBS-TV and radio. In this one, he laments the disappearance of our great forests, all the while sneakily offering us examples of what we have done, what we have used, what we demand, that make the trees come down.

Word to Know

habitat   the place where something normally lives

Getting Started

What do you think about the relationship between your use of disposable paper goods and the destruction of the world's forests?

BALTIMORE, MARYLAND. I was waiting for breakfast in a coffee shop the 1 other morning and reading the paper. The paper had sixty-six pages. The waitress brought a paper place mat and a paper napkin and took my order, and I paged through the paper.

The headline said, "House Panel Studies a Bill Allowing Clear-Cutting 2 in U.S. Forests."

I put the paper napkin in my lap, spread the paper out on the paper 3 place mat, and read on: "The House Agriculture Committee," it said, "is looking over legislation that would once again open national forests to the clear-cutting of trees by private companies under government permits."

The waitress brought the coffee. I opened a paper sugar envelope and 4 tore open a little paper cup of cream and went on reading the paper: "The Senate voted without dissent yesterday to allow clear-cutting," the paper said. "Critics have said clear-cutting in the national forests can lead to erosion and destruction of wildlife habitats. Forest Service and industry spokesmen said a flat ban on clear-cutting would bring paralysis to the lumber industry." And to the paper industry, I thought. Clear-cutting a forest is one way to get a lot of paper, and we sure seem to need a lot of paper.

The waitress brought the toast. I looked for the butter. It came on a 5
little paper tray with a covering of paper. I opened a paper package of
marmalade and read on: "Senator Jennings Randolph, Democrat of West
Virginia, urged his colleagues to take a more restrictive view and permit
clear-cutting only under specific guidelines for certain types of forest.
But neither he nor anyone else voted against the bill, which was sent to
the House on a 90 to 0 vote."

The eggs came, with little paper packages of salt and pepper. I finished 6
breakfast, put the paper under my arm, and left the table with its used
and useless paper napkin, paper place mat, paper salt and pepper packages, paper butter and marmalade wrappings, paper sugar envelope,
and paper cream holder, and I walked out into the morning wondering
how our national forests can ever survive our breakfasts.

Questions About the Reading

1. Why does the writer describe his breakfast in so much detail?
2. Suggest some possible reasons why no one voted against the clear-
   cutting bill.
3. What does the writer want us to realize about our part in the destruction of the forests?

Questions About the Writer's Strategies

1. Is there a specific sentence in the essay that states the **thesis**, or is the
   thesis **implied**?
2. How do the quotes from the newspaper develop Kuralt's **main idea**?
3. Why does the writer use the word *paper* twenty-six times?
4. What is the **tone** of the essay? What would the tone have been if the
   lumber industry had written the article?

Writing Assignments

1. Each of us is to blame for the destruction of our forests. Write an essay
   illustrating with examples what individuals can do to reduce their
   consumption of paper.
2. Our society has become obsessed with the idea of throwaway packag-
   ing. Write an essay developing this idea through the use of examples.
3. Plastic has become a substitute for paper in many throwaway products, but we now know that the manufacture of many plastics is harmful to the earth's ozone layer. Write an essay using examples to illustrate other drawbacks to using disposable plastic products.

Of Shopping

Phyllis Rose

Whether we like it or not, shopping is an integral part of contemporary American life. From giant suburban malls to backyard garage sales, we are a nation of consumers. But once you have read Phyllis Rose's essay, "Of Shopping," you may never again set off for an afternoon at the mall in quite the same old way.

Words to Know

connoisseur   one with informed, discriminating taste
disparity   difference, inequality
egalitarianism   belief in equal political, economic, and legal rights for all human beings
émigré   someone who has left a country to settle in another
encumbrance   burden
Solzhenitsyn   Russian author, dissident
tahini   thick, smooth sauce made from sesame seeds

Getting Started

In what ways is shopping more than just the act of buying?

Last year a new Waldbaum's Food Mart opened in the shopping mall 1 on Route 66. It belongs to a new generation of superdupermarkets that have computerized checkouts and operate twenty-four hours a day. I went to see the place as soon as it opened and I was impressed. There was trail mix in Lucite bins. There was freshly made pasta. There were coffee beans, four kinds of tahini, ten kinds of herb teas, raw shrimp in shells and cooked shelled shrimp, fresh-squeezed orange juice. Every sophistication known to the big city, even goat's cheese covered with ash, was now available in Middletown, Connecticut. People raced from the warehouse aisle to the bagel bin to the coffee beans to the fresh fish market, exclaiming at all the new things. Many of us felt elevated, graced, complimented by the presence of this food palace in our town.

This is the wonderful egalitarianism of American business. Was it 2 Andy Warhol who said that the nice thing about Coke is, no can is any better or worse than any other? Some people may find it dull to cross the country and find the same chain stores with the same merchandise from coast to coast, but it means that my town is as good as yours, my shopping mall as important as yours, equally filled with wonders.

Imagine what people ate during the winter as little as seventy-five 3 years ago. They ate food that was local, long-lasting, and dull, like acorn squash, turnips, and cabbage. Walk into an American supermarket in February and the world lies before you: grapes, melons, artichokes, fennel, lettuce, peppers, pistachios, dates, even strawberries, to say nothing of ice cream. Have you ever considered what a triumph of civilization it is to be able to buy a pound of chicken livers? If you lived on a farm and had to kill a chicken when you wanted to eat one, you wouldn't ever accumulate a pound of chicken livers.

Another wonder of Middletown is Caldor, the discount department 4 store. Here is man's plenty: tennis racquets, pantyhose, luggage, glassware, records, toothpaste, Timex watches, Cadbury's chocolate, corn poppers, hair dryers, warm-up suits, car wax, light bulbs, television sets. All good quality at low prices with exchanges cheerfully made on defective goods. There are worse rules to live by. I feel good about America whenever I walk into this store, which is almost every midwinter Sunday afternoon, when life elsewhere has closed down. I go to Caldor the way English people go to pubs: out of sociability. To get away from my house. To widen my horizons. For culture's sake. Caldor provides me too with a welcome sense of seasonal change. When the first outdoor grills and lawn furniture appear there, it's as exciting a sign of spring as the first crocus or robin.

Someone told me about a Soviet émigré who practices English by declaiming, at random, sentences that catch his fancy. One of his favorites 5 is "Fifty percent off all items today only." Refugees from Communist countries appreciate our supermarkets and discount department stores for the wonders they are. An Eastern European scientist visiting Middletown wept when she first saw the meat counter at Waldbaum's. On the other hand, before her year in America was up, her pleasure turned sour. She wanted everything she saw. Her approach to consumer goods was insufficiently abstract, too materialistic. We Americans are beyond a simple, possessive materialism. We're used to abundance and the possibility of possessing things. The things, and the possibility of possessing them, will still be there next week, next year. So today we can walk the aisles calmly.

It is a misunderstanding of the American retail store to think we go 6 there necessarily to buy. Some of us shop. There's a difference. Shopping has many purposes, the least interesting of which is to acquire new articles. We shop to cheer ourselves up. We shop to practice decision making. We shop to be useful and productive members of our class and society. We shop to remind ourselves how much is available to us. We shop to remind ourselves how much is to be striven for. We shop to assert our superiority to the material objects that spread themselves before us.

Shopping's function as a form of therapy is widely appreciated. You 7 don't really need, let's say, another sweater. You need the feeling of power that comes with buying it or not buying it. You need the feeling that someone wants something you have—even if it's just your money. To get the benefit of shopping, you needn't actually purchase the sweater, any more than you have to marry every man you flirt with. In fact, window shopping, like flirting, can be more rewarding, the same high without the distressing commitment, the material encumbrance. The purest form of shopping is provided by garage sales. A connoisseur goes out with no goal in mind, open to whatever may come his way, secure that it will cost very little. Minimum expense, maximum experience. Perfect shopping.

I try to think of the opposite, a kind of shopping in which the object is 8 all-important, the pleasure of shopping at a minimum. For example, the purchase of blue jeans. I buy new blue jeans as seldom as possible because the experience is so humiliating. For every pair that looks good on me, fifteen look grotesque. But even shopping for blue jeans at Bob's Surplus on Main Street—no-frills, bare-bones shopping—is an event in the life of the spirit. Once again I have to come to terms with the fact that I will never look good in Levi's. Much as I want to be mainstream, I will never be.

In fact, I'm doubly an oddball, neither Misses nor Junior, but Misses 9 Petite. I look in the mirror, I acknowledge the disparity between myself and the ideal, I resign myself to making the best of it: I will buy the Lee's Misses Petite. Shopping is a time of reflection, assessment, spiritual self-discipline.

It is appropriate, I think, that Bob's has a communal dressing room. I 10 used to shop only in places where I could count on a private dressing room with a mirror inside. My impulse was to hide my weaknesses. Now I believe in sharing them. There are other women in the dressing room at Bob's trying on blue jeans who look as bad as I do. We take comfort in one another. Sometimes a woman will ask me which of two items looks better. I always give a definite answer. It's the least I can do. I figure we are all in this together, and I emerge from the dressing room not only with a new pair of jeans, but with a renewed sense of belonging to a human community.

When a Solzhenitsyn rants about American materialism, I have to look 11 at my digital Timex and check what year this is. Materialism? Like conformism, a hot moral issue of the 1950s, but not now. How to spread the goods, maybe. Whether the goods are the Good, no. Solzhenitsyn, like the visiting scientist who wept at the beauty of the Waldbaum's meat counter but came to covet everything she saw, takes American materialism too materialistically. He doesn't see its spiritual side. Caldor, Waldbaum's, Bob's—these, perhaps, are our cathedrals.

Questions About the Reading

1. According to the writer, what is a "superdupermarket"?
2. List some of the products Rose found in the new Waldbaum's on Route 66.
3. What does Rose mean when she writes that there is "a wonderful egalitarianism" in American business?
4. Why have America's eating habits changed in the last seventy-five years?
5. Why does the writer compare her trips to Caldor to visits to a British pub?
6. Why do you think Rose includes the story about the Eastern European scientist?
7. According to Rose, why is shopping a form of therapy?
8. How is window shopping like flirting? Do you agree or disagree?
9. What does Rose consider the purest form of shopping? Why?

Questions About the Writer's Strategies

1. What is the **thesis statement** in this essay? Is it stated directly or does the writer **imply** it?
2. Does Rose use many examples, one extended example, or a combination of the two strategies to support her thesis?
3. How does Phyllis Rose feel about shopping? Find details from the essay to support your answer.
4. The **tone** of this essay is humorous. Find several humorous details in the essay and explain how they support Rose's thesis.

Writing Assignments

1. Do you agree with the writer's ideas about the American experience of shopping? Is shopping therapy for you or is it simply a necessary evil? Write an essay using examples from your life that illustrate your ideas about shopping.
2. Are Americans too materialistic? Write an essay in which you use specific examples to illustrate your point of view on this topic.

Of Shopping / Phyllis Rose

What the Nose Knows

James Gorman

The connection between details that appeal to our senses and individual memories provides us with unexpected pleasure. Those magical threads of sound or smell or taste or sight instantly transport us back to a simpler time, a time that exists only in our memories. James Gorman's delightful essay reminds us of just how important these sensory details can be.

Words to Know

curmudgeon   a sour or ill-tempered person
inexhaustible   tireless
posterity   future generations

Getting Started

What odors stimulate your childhood memories?

Society is losing its odor integrity. Some enterprising souls are actually 1
marketing aerosol cans filled with the aromas of pizza, new cars, anything that might entice people to buy something they would otherwise not. From the inexhaustible engine of commerce have come Aroma Discs, which when warmed in a special container (only $22.50) emit such scents as Passion, Fireplace and After Dinner Mints. And, in what may be the odor crime of the century, a company in Ohio is selling a cherry-scented garden hose.

I may seem like a weird curmudgeon looking for something new to 2
complain about, but it's only the fake smells I don't like, the ones that are meant to fool you. This is a dangerous business because the human nose is emotional and not very bright. Inside the brain, smell seems snuggled right up to the centers for cooking, sex and memory.

I recently discovered a substance whose odor stimulates my memory 3
of childhood like nothing else: Crayola crayons.

I don't expect you to experience the effect of this odor memory just by 4
thinking about crayons, since most people can't recall smells the way they can recall pictures or sounds. But once you get a good whiff of waxy crayon odor, the bells of childhood will ring. Go out and buy a box. Get your nose right down on the crayons and inhale deeply. Pull that crayon

smell right up into the old reptile brain. You'll be flooded with a new-crayon, untouched-coloring-book feeling—you're young, the world is new, the next thing you know your parents may bring home a puppy.

The smell is part of our culture, in the same class as the Howdy Doody 5 song. Long after my daughters have stopped drawing with crayons, they will have in their brains, as I do now, the subconscious knowledge that if you smell stearic acid—the major component in the smell of Crayola crayons—you're about to have a good time.

Crayons have odor integrity. The Crayola people didn't stick stearic 6 acid into their product to make you buy it. Nobody in his right mind would buy something because it smelled like a fatty acid. If there were a national odor museum, I would give crayons pride of place in it. And I would surround them with other objects emitting the honest aromas that make up American odor culture.

I have a few ideas of what these other objects should be. I got them 7 from William Cain of Yale University and the John B. Pierce Foundation Laboratory in New Haven, Conn. Cain studies what he calls the smell game. He had people sniff 80 everyday things, and then he ranked the substances by how recognizable their odors were. His list is the place for the aroma preservationist to begin.

On it are Juicy Fruit gum and Vicks VapoRub (remember getting it 8 rubbed on your chest?), Ivory soap, Johnson's baby powder and Lysol. Cain also tested Band-Aids, nail-polish remover, shoe polish (which reminds me of church) and bleach.

Crayons are on the list, ranked eighteenth in recognizability. Coffee 9 was first, peanut butter second. Not on the list, but favorites of mine, are rubber cement (which I remember from my newspaper days) and Cutter Insect Repellent.

I know there will be judgment calls. Some people will want to preserve 10 Brut after shave and Herbal Essence shampoo, numbers 35 and 53 on Cain's list, while I will not. Others won't want fresh cow manure in the museum. I think it's a must.

Whatever the choices, it's time to start paying attention to our odor 11 culture. We're responsible for what posterity will smell, and like to smell. If we're not careful, we may end up with a country in which everyone thinks garden hoses are supposed to smell like cherries.

Questions About the Reading

1. What do you think the first sentence in this essay means?
2. What does Gorman consider the "odor crime of the century"?

3. Why is Gorman offended by the marketing of fake smells?
4. What odor stimulates the writer's childhood memories the most?
5. What other odors would Gorman place in a national odor museum?
6. Why does Gorman believe "we may end up with a country in which everyone thinks garden hoses are supposed to smell like cherries"?

Questions About the Writer's Strategies

1. What is the **thesis** in this essay? Where is it expressed?
2. Does the writer use many examples, one extended example, or a combination of the two strategies to support the thesis?
3. The **tone** of this essay is humorous and down-to-earth. Find two humorous **details** that help support Gorman's thesis.
4. Identify the examples Gorman uses in the first paragraph to help his readers understand his ideas more clearly.

Writing Assignments

1. Do you agree with Gorman about the relationship between Crayola crayons and childhood memories? Write an essay in which you discuss your own childhood memories and what kinds of sensory details stimulate them.
2. What smells would you place in a national odor museum? Write an essay discussing what "honest aromas" you think make up American odor culture. Feel free to include any of the products Gorman mentions, as well as your own personal favorites.

Living with Asymmetry

Deborah Tannen

From the moment of birth, human beings communicate. Without the ability to communicate, none of us would survive. But communication is not always as simple as a baby's first cry. Deborah Tannen's essay raises some important questions about this instinctive yet complicated human skill. At the same time it illustrates the disastrous consequences of miscommunication.

Word to Know

antiquity   relic

Getting Started

How often do you become frustrated by your inability to communicate effectively with another human being?

An American woman set out for a vacation cruise and landed in a   1
Turkish prison. Reading her book *Never Pass This Way Again*, I could see
that Gene LePere's ordeal was an extreme example of the disastrous consequences that can result from cross-cultural differences in what I term
conversational style—ways of framing how you mean what you say, and
what you think you are doing when you say it. LePere's experience also
illustrates, in an unusually dramatic way, the dangers of trying to avoid
conflict and say no in a polite way.

LePere left her cruise ship for a brief tour of ancient ruins in Turkey. At   2
an archeological site, she fell behind her group as she became absorbed in
admiring the ruins. Suddenly, her path was blocked by a man selling artifacts she had no interest in buying. Yet she found herself holding a stone
head, and when she told him politely that she did not want it, he would
not take it back. Instead, he thrust forward another one, which she also
automatically accepted. Since the man would not take either head back,
the only path to escape she could envision was offering to buy them. She
cut his price in half and hoped he'd refuse so she could move on. Instead,
he agreed to drop the price, and she dropped the two heads into her tote.
But as she handed him the money, he handed her a third head. Once

more she insisted she did not want it, but he just stepped back to avoid repossessing it. Seeing no alternative, she paid for the third head and stalked off—shaken and angry. When LePere tried to reboard her cruise ship, she showed her purchases to customs officials, who had her arrested and thrown into jail for trying to smuggle out a national treasure. The third head was a genuine antiquity.

Having lived in Greece and observed the verbal art of bargaining, I could see that talking to the vendor and saying she did not want the artifacts would mean to him that she might want them if the price were lower. If she really had no intention of buying, she would not have talked to him at all. She would have pushed her way past him and walked on, never establishing eye contact—and surely not taking possession of any heads, no matter how insistently he proffered them. Each time she accepted a head, he received evidence of her interest and encouragement to offer another. Each step in his increasingly aggressive sales pitch was a response to what likely appeared to him as her bargaining maneuvers. Refusing to look at or talk to him, or, as a last resort, placing the heads on the ground—these were unthinkable alternatives for a polite American woman.

Questions About the Reading

1. What does the writer mean by the term *conversational style?*
2. What was the frightening experience described in this essay?
3. Why was the tourist thrown in jail?
4. What is the "verbal art of bargaining," and why did the writer understand it?

Questions About the Writer's Strategies

1. Is the **thesis** directly stated or **implied**? If directly stated, in which sentence or sentences is it found?
2. Deborah Tannen uses one extended example to support her thesis. Would the essay have been as effective if she had used several different examples instead? Why or why not?
3. Does Tannen use other **modes of development** in addition to the extended example? Give **details** from the essay to support your answer.
4. What do you think the title of this essay means? Translate it into your own words.

Writing Assignments

1. How many times have you felt that miscommunication was the cause of a problem you were having with another person—perhaps a boss, a friend, or a parent? Write an essay in which you use one extended example, or several short examples, to illustrate miscommunication.
2. How do you think people can learn to communicate more effectively? Write an essay using examples that illustrate different ways of bridging the communication gap between cultures or sexes.

Back to the Dump

Russell Baker

*When our society changes, we often have to change our personal beliefs
and habits as well. In this humorous essay, noted essayist Russell Baker
gives examples of beliefs he has had to discard.*

Words to Know

contemplated   considered

interrogator   questioner

Svengalis   people with irresistible hypnotic powers (from a
 character in the novel *Trilby* by George du Maurier)

swinish   like a pig

Getting Started

Can you describe a time when you had to unlearn something you
had learned earlier?

When I was a boy everybody urged me to get plenty of sunshine, so I   1
got plenty of sunshine for a long time. One day while I was absorbing
July sun as fast as I could, a doctor asked what I thought I was doing.

"Getting plenty of sunshine," I said.   2

"Are you mad?" he replied.   3

No, I was not mad, just slow to catch up with life's revisions. Getting   4
plenty of sunshine had been declared dangerous while I was out to lunch.
I revised my store of knowledge. Now I get only small droppers of sunshine extracted from the half hour just before sunset.

When I was old enough to notice that girls were pleasantly different   5
from boys, my mother told me the fact of life. "You must always treat a
woman like a lady," she said. So for a long time I went through life treating women like ladies.

One day while I was helping a woman into her coat, another woman   6
asked me what I thought I was doing.

"Treating a woman like a lady," I said.   7

"Are you mad?" she replied.   8

No, I was not mad, but my interrogator was furious. I had been out to   9
lunch during one of life's revisions and missed the announcement that it

was swinish to treat a woman like a lady. I discarded another piece of my childhood education. Now I treat women like ticking bombs.

When I was 17 and for many years afterward, I admired Franklin and 10 Eleanor Roosevelt as the ideal couple. One evening I had an encounter with a ticking bomb, and contemplated behaving like a fool, but rejected the impulse because we weren't married.

"What do you think you're doing?" she asked as I fled. I told her that 11 someday I wanted to be half of a couple as ideal as Franklin and Eleanor Roosevelt.

"Are you mad?" she replied.   12

No, not mad. I had been out to lunch during another of life's revisions 13 and, so, had missed the disclosure that Eleanor didn't get along well with Franklin and that Franklin fooled around when she was out of town. Another part of my youthful education went to the dump, but too late. By then, age had brought its inevitable energy crisis and I had begun to prefer napping to behaving like a fool.

Perhaps it was not age that defeated me, though. Maybe it was fatigue 14 caused by the constant trips to the dump to discard everything I'd learned in the first half of my life. Life seemed to be an educator's practical joke in which you spent the first half learning and the second half learning that everything you learned in the first half was wrong.

The trips to the dump became more and more frequent. There I lugged 15 the old precept that a hearty breakfast of bacon and eggs was good for me.

I also hauled away the old lesson that it was racist to refer to people of 16 African ancestry as "black." One windy night, I hoisted up the cherished teaching that every American had a duty to drive a two-ton, eight-cylinder automobile with room enough inside for a steamer trunk and the whole darn family, and staggered off to the dump. That was a heavy night's work and left me bent in spine and spirit.

At about this time, movie actors began running for President, astro- 17 nauts began flying around the planet to get from one desert to another, and people began renting one-bedroom apartments for $2,000 a month. Out to the dump went important fragments of my education which had made me believe that movie actors existed to be browbeaten by Congressional investigators, that if you've seen one cactus you've seen them all, and that $2,000 a month ought to buy you a controlling interest in the Gritti Palace Hotel.

No wonder I was tired. And then, a terrible fear seized me. If everything 18 I'd learned in life's first half had to go to the dump, wasn't it inevitable that everything I was learning in the second half would also have to go?

A crushing thought. I'm not getting any younger. I've had the stamina 19 so far to heave out everything I learned in youth, but if everything I've learned since has to go in the next 25 years I'll be too feeble for the job.

I'm sitting here right now wondering what present certainties might 20 have to be junked before the century is out. My conviction that President Reagan is a nice guy, for instance. Will some whippersnapper someday say, "If you hadn't been out to lunch again, old-timer, you'd have read the recent book reporting that Reagan had to be dosed on jolly pills to control his passion for kicking orphans"?

And there's my present fear that the nuclear weapons race could kill 21 us all. Some people already say I wouldn't have that fear if the Russians hadn't manipulated my brain. I think that's silly right now. Considering all the other people I know are manipulating my brain, I don't see how the Russians could get a crack at it. But you never know. Someday I might have to learn that I wasn't really afraid of nuclear war at all, but only under the sway of Moscow Svengalis.

It wouldn't surprise me. Live long enough and you'll eventually be 22 wrong about everything.

Questions About the Reading

1. What does the writer mean when he states, "I had an encounter with a ticking bomb"?
2. What was Baker afraid would eventually happen?
3. In what way is the writer's brain being "manipulated"?

Questions About the Writer's Strategies

1. What is the **tone** of this essay?
2. Is there a direct **thesis statement** in this essay? If not, state the thesis in your own words. How well do the examples support the thesis?
3. "The dump" is a **metaphor**. Interpret what it refers to.
4. In the first half of the essay, the writer repeats the question, "Are you mad?" and the statement, "No, I was not mad," several times. What is the effect of this strategy?

Writing Assignments

1. Think of a popular or highly publicized idea that you do not agree with—say, that success is more important than being considerate, that hunting is inhumane, that nuclear power plants are (or are not) dangerous, or that students entering college today are (or are not) poorly educated. Write an essay in which you use examples to persuade your readers that you are right.

2. Imagine what your city will be like in the year 2010, and write an essay that describes it, using examples to show how it will differ from the way it is now.
3. Write an essay giving examples of beliefs you have had to discard as you have grown older.

My Mother Never Worked

Bonnie Smith-Yackel

Bonnie Smith-Yackel's family survived on a farm during the Great De-
pression, a time when both the weather and the economy made the hard-
ships of farm life nearly overwhelming. In this personal essay,
Smith-Yackel uses the example of her mother's life to reveal the unfairness
in American society's attitudes toward women and the work they do to
keep their families going.

Words to Know

cholera   a contagious, often fatal disease, usually restricted to
   farm animals in this country

reciprocated   returned

sustenance   nourishment, support for life

widow's pension   the Social Security payments given to a
   widow, based on her deceased husband's eligibility, who is not
   eligible herself for Social Security

Getting Started

What do you think about our government's attitude that home-
makers are not legally workers?

"**S**ocial Security Office." (The voice answering the telephone sounds   1
very self-assured.)

"I'm calling about . . . I . . . my mother just died . . . I was told to call you   2
and see about a . . . death-benefit check, I think they call it. . . ."

"I see. Was your mother on Social Security? How old was she?"   3

"Yes . . . she was seventy-eight. . . ."   4

"Do you know her number?"   5

"No . . . I, ah . . . don't you have a record?"   6

"Certainly. I'll look it up. Her name?"   7

"Smith. Martha Smith. Or maybe she used Martha Ruth Smith. . . .   8
Sometimes she used her maiden name . . . Martha Jerabek Smith."

"If you'd care to hold on, I'll check our records—it'll be a few min-   9
utes."

"Yes. . . ."   10

Her love letters—to and from Daddy—were in an old box, tied with 11
ribbons and stiff, rigid-with-age leather thongs: 1918 through 1920; hers
written on stationery from the general store she had worked in full-time
and managed, single-handed, after her graduation from high school in
1913; and his, at first, on YMCA or Soldiers and Sailors Club stationery
dispensed to the fighting men of World War I. He wooed her thoroughly
and persistently by mail, and though she reciprocated all his feelings for
her, she dreaded marriage. . . .

"It's so hard for me to decide when to have my wedding day—that's 12
all I've thought about these last two days. I have told you dozens of times
that I won't be afraid of married life, but when it comes down to setting
the date and then picturing myself a married woman with half a dozen or
more kids to look after, it just makes me sick. . . . I am weeping right
now—I hope that some day I can look back and say how foolish I was to
dread it all."

They married in February, 1921, and began farming. Their first baby, a 13
daughter, was born in January, 1922, when my mother was 26 years old.
The second baby, a son, was born in March, 1923. They were renting
farms; my father, besides working his own fields, also was a hired man
for two other farmers. They had no capital initially, and had to gain it
slowly, working from dawn until midnight every day. My town-bred
mother learned to set hens and raise chickens, feed pigs, milk cows, plant
and harvest a garden, and can every fruit and vegetable she could
scrounge. She carried water nearly a quarter of a mile from the well to fill
her wash boilers in order to do her laundry on a scrub board. She learned
to shuck grain, feed threshers, shock and husk corn, feed corn pickers. In
September, 1925, the third baby came, and in June, 1927, the fourth
child—both daughters. In 1930, my parents had enough money to buy
their own farm, and that March they moved all their livestock and be-
longings themselves, 55 miles over rutted, muddy roads.

In the summer of 1930 my mother and her two eldest children re- 14
claimed a 40-acre field from Canadian thistles, by chopping them all out
with a hoe. In the other fields, when the oats and flax began to head out,
the green and blue of the crops were hidden by the bright yellow of wild
mustard. My mother walked the fields day after day, pulling each mustard plant. She raised a new flock of baby chicks—500—and she spaded
up, planted, hoed, and harvested a half-acre garden.

During the next spring their hogs caught cholera and died. No cash 15
that fall.

And in the next year the drought hit. My mother and father trudged 16
from the well to the chickens, the well to the calf pasture, the well to the
barn, and from the well to the garden. The sun came out hot and bright,
endlessly, day after day. The crops shriveled and died. They harvested

half the corn, and ground the other half, stalks and all, and fed it to the cattle as fodder. With the price at four cents a bushel for the harvested crop, they couldn't afford to haul it into town. They burned it in the furnace for fuel that winter.

In 1934, in February, when the dust was still so thick in the Minnesota 17 air that my parents couldn't always see from the house to the barn, their fifth child—a fourth daughter—was born. My father hunted rabbits daily, and my mother stewed them, fried them, canned them, and wished out loud that she could taste hamburger once more. In the fall the shotgun brought prairie chickens, ducks, pheasant, and grouse. My mother plucked each bird, carefully reserving the breast feathers for pillows.

In the winter she sewed night after night, endlessly, begging cast-off 18 clothing from relatives, ripping apart coats, dresses, blouses, and trousers to remake them to fit her four daughters and son. Every morning and every evening she milked cows, fed pigs and calves, cared for chickens, picked eggs, cooked meals, washed dishes, scrubbed floors, and tended and loved her children. In the spring she planted a garden once more, dragging pails of water to nourish and sustain the vegetables for the family. In 1936 she lost a baby in her sixth month.

In 1937 her fifth daughter was born. She was 42 years old. In 1939 a 19 second son, and in 1941 her eighth child—and third son.

But the war had come, and prosperity of a sort. The herd of cattle had 20 grown to 30 head; she still milked morning and evening. Her garden was more than a half acre—the rains had come, and by now the Rural Electricity Administration and indoor plumbing. Still she sewed—dresses and jackets for the children, housedresses and aprons for herself, weekly patching of jeans, overalls, and denim shirts. Still she made pillows, using the feathers she had plucked, and quilts every year—intricate patterns as well as patchwork, stitched as well as tied—all necessary bedding for her family. Every scrap of cloth too small to be used in quilts was carefully saved and painstakingly sewed together in strips to make rugs. She still went out in the fields to help with the haying whenever there was a threat of rain.

In 1959 my mother's last child graduated from high school. A year 21 later the cows were sold. She still raised chickens and ducks, plucked feathers, made pillows, baked her own bread, and every year made a new quilt—now for a married child or for a grandchild. And her garden, that huge, undying symbol of sustenance, was as large and cared for as in all the years before. The canning, and now freezing, continued.

In 1969, on a June afternoon, mother and father started out for town so 22 that she could buy sugar to make rhubarb jam for a daughter who lived in Texas. The car crashed into a ditch. She was paralyzed from the waist down.

In 1970 her husband, my father, died. My mother struggled to regain 23
some competence and dignity and order in her life. At the rehabilitation
institute, where they gave her physical therapy and trained her to live
usefully in a wheelchair, the therapist told me: "She did fifteen pushups
today—fifteen! She's almost seventy-five years old! I've never known a
woman so strong!"

From her wheelchair she canned pickles, baked bread, ironed clothes, 24
wrote dozens of letters weekly to her friends and her "half dozen or more
kids," and made three patchwork housecoats and one quilt. She made
balls and balls of carpet rags—enough for five rugs. And kept all her love
letters.

"I think I've found your mother's records—Martha Ruth Smith; mar- 25
ried to Ben F. Smith?"

"Yes, that's right."   26

"Well, I see that she was getting a widow's pension. . . ."   27

"Yes, that's right."   28

"Well, your mother isn't entitled to our $255 death benefit."   29

"Not entitled! But why?"   30

The voice on the telephone explains patiently: 31

"Well, you see—your mother never worked."   32

Questions About the Reading

1. Why didn't the writer's mother want to get married?
2. How old was the writer's mother when she had her eighth child? How
   old was she when she was paralyzed?
3. In her later years, how do you think Mrs. Smith's attitude had changed
   from the one she expressed in the letter quoted in paragraph 12? What
   had become of her fears of marriage?
4. Why did Mrs. Smith do the pushups, and why did she continue to
   work in her final years, when she really didn't have to?
5. Speculate about why Mrs. Smith kept her love letters. Why do you
   think the writer mentions the fact in paragraph 24?

Questions About the Writer's Strategies

1. What is the **thesis** in this essay? Where is it expressed?
2. How well do the writer's examples support her thesis?
3. Aside from the extended example of her mother's life, what other
   mode of development does the writer use in the essay?

4. Describe the writer's **point of view** in the essay. How does she use time? Does her **tone** change during the essay?
5. Why does the writer give so few **details** about her father and the family's children?

Writing Assignments

1. Write an essay giving examples of the obstacles women have to overcome in today's society.
2. Think of an extraordinary person you know, and write an essay using examples to show what makes that person extraordinary and why he or she is important to others.
3. Write an essay using examples, or one extended example, to show what the term *sacrifice* means.

5

Classification
and Division

SUPPOSE YOU ARE looking over the clothing in your closet, trying to sort out the confusion. You decide to classify your clothing into several categories: good clothes for looking your best on the job; older clothes for weekends and informal occasions; and very old clothes that have some stains and holes (but that you can still use when you wash the car or the dog). You have now classified all your clothes into three orderly categories, according to their various uses. You may even want to expand your classification by adding a fourth category, clothes that are no longer useful and should be thrown away. You may have washed the dog in them once too often.

The purpose of **classification** is to take many of the same type of thing—clothing, school papers, presidents, recipes, music—and organize this large, unsorted group into categories. You may decide to classify your group of similar things, such as music, into such categories as classical, jazz, and rock and roll, or classify recipes into main dishes, salads, and desserts.

You should organize your categories by some quality or characteristic that the items share in common. In each case, you will have to search for the categories that will help you classify an unsorted group of items.

In the following example, which is from a textbook, the writer classifies mothers of handicapped children according to categories marked by three attitudes.

Classification | Researchers note three frequent attitudes among mothers of handicapped children. The first attitude is reflected by those | 1

Category 1:
rejection

mothers who reject their child or are unable to accept the child as a handicapped person. Complex love-hate and acceptance-rejection relationships are found within this group. Rejected children not only have problems in adjusting to themselves and their disabilities, but they also have to contend with disturbed family relationships and emotional insecurity. Unfortunately, such children receive even less encouragement than the normal child and have to absorb more criticism of their behavior.

Category 2:
overcompensation

A second relationship involves mothers who overcompensate in their reactions to their child and the disorder. They tend to be unrealistic, rigid, and overprotective. Often, such parents try to compensate by being overzealous and giving continuous instruction and training in the hope of establishing superior ability.

2

Category 3:
acceptance

The third group consists of mothers who accept their children along with their disorders. These mothers have gained the ability to provide for the special needs of their handicapped children while continuing to live a normal life and tending to family and home as well as civic and social obligations. The child's chances are best with parents who have accepted both their child and the defects.

3

Janet W. Lerner,
Learning Disabilities, Fifth Edition

Writing a **classification** paragraph or essay requires sorting a group of similar things—such as clothing, music, recipes, or even students—according to some quality or characteristic that they share in common. A **division** paper requires taking one thing—a dress or suit, a piece of music, a recipe, or even a student—and dividing it into its component parts or characteristics.

Classification and division are often used together. For example, you might want to divide a group into its subgroups and then evaluate the subgroups. You might take your neighborhood and first *divide* it into sections (north, south, west). You might then *classify* the sections by how much noise and traffic are present in each—noisy, relatively quiet, and quiet. The purpose of classification and division is to categorize a complex whole into simple, useful categories or subdivisions.

In the following example, the writer establishes two general types of wood sill construction and then divides each class into its components.

Classification

The two general types of wood sill construction used over the foundation wall conform either to platform or balloon framing. The box sill is commonly used in platform construction.

Category 1:
components

It consists of a 2-inch or thicker wooden board, called a plate, anchored to the top of the foundation wall over a sill sealer. The plate provides support and fastening for the joists, the large boards that support the floor, and the header at the ends of the joists into which they are nailed. . . .

Category 2: components

> Balloon-frame construction uses a 2-inch or thicker wood sill upon which the joists rest. The studs, which form the interior of the walls, also rest on this sill and are nailed both into the floor joists and the sill. The subfloor is laid diagonally or at right angles to the joists, and a firestop, a wood block that restricts air flow within the wall, is added between the studs at the floorline. When diagonal subfloor is used, an extra board for nailing is normally required between joists and studs at the wall lines.

Adapted from L. O. Anderson,
Wood-Frame House Construction

Whether using classification or division, the writer has to give some thought to making the categories logical and appropriate, with as little overlap between categories as possible. If you are classifying chocolate desserts, you do not want to add vanilla custard to your list. You will also want to make your categories reasonably complete. You would not want to leave out chocolate cake in your classification of chocolate desserts.

If you are groping for a method of classification, you may want to try *several* ways of categorizing the same information. You will want to find the most efficient or productive category. In our first example of organizing the closet, you may have tried to classify your clothes according to color (red clothes, brown clothes, blue clothes). Or you may have decided to arrange them by type: all pants together; all jackets together; all shirts together—and so forth.

Experienced writers often use classification or division or both to organize a composition. In the following paragraph, the writer uses classification to discuss the different kinds (categories) of book owners.

Topic sentence: classification

Category 1: nonreaders

Category 2: occasional readers

Category 3: devoted readers

> There are three kinds of book owners. The first has all the standard sets and best-sellers—unread, untouched. (This deluded individual owns woodpulp and ink, not books.) The second has a great many books—a few of them read through, most of them dipped into, but all of them as clean and shiny as the day they were bought. (This person would probably like to make books his own, but is restrained by a false respect for their physical appearance.) The third has a few books or many—every one of them dog-eared and dilapidated, shaken and loosened by continual use, marked and scribbled in from front to back. (This man owns books.)

Mortimer J. Adler,
"How to Mark a Book"

Notice, too, in the previous paragraph that the topic sentence clearly tells the reader to expect to read about *three* kinds of book owners and that the words *first, second,* and *third* are used to identify them according to how much they read their books. The words *first, second,* and *third* also help move the reader from one point to another and, when used in this way, are called **transitional words**. Some other transitional words and phrases that are often used in classification and division are *one, two, three;* and *for one thing, for another thing, finally.* As you write and revise your paragraphs and essays, you will want to think about using transitions to help maintain the **unity** and logical flow, or **coherence**, of your writing.

Like Adler, author of the paragraph on book owners, writers often use topic sentences such as "A safe city street has three main qualities" or "The treatment prescribed for the disease was aspirin, bed rest, and fluids" to indicate the categories that will follow in the body of a paragraph or essay. Following "A safe city street has three main qualities," the writer would explain the three specific qualities that make a city street safe. Following "The treatment prescribed for the disease was aspirin, bed rest, and fluids," the writer would probably explain the reasons for prescribing aspirin, bed rest, and fluids.

Usually, too, writers will *follow the same order* in discussing the divisions (or categories) that they used in first introducing them. For instance, suppose the topic is "Four methods can be used to cook fish: broiling, baking, poaching, and frying." Ordinarily the writer would explain (1) broiling, then (2) baking, (3) poaching, and (4) frying. Listing the categories and explaining them in order can make the composition easier for the reader to follow. Notice, for example, that in the student essay that follows, the three students who collaborated in writing the essay classified students as "unconcerned," "ambitious," and "inconsistent." Although they did not follow this order in their first draft, in revising the essay the students could change the order in which they listed the types of students, the order of their explanation of the types, or the order of both the list and the paragraphs. After revising the order of the list, reorganizing the paragraphing, and doing some initial editing of grammar and punctuation—which your instructor may want to go over in class—the essay could read as follows:

Thesis statement: classification

Students come in all ages, races, and genders. You can find the unconcerned, inconsistent, and ambitious in any group of students.

Category 1: unconcerned students

First, Ralph, a student in my English class, is an example of a student who has an unconcerned attitude. He has a negative outlook on life, and at times his attitude is downright hostile. He enters the classroom late and disrupts the class by slamming the door or by talking to other students while the teacher is giving a lecture. He does not care at all about the importance of an education. Ralph is more interested in watching sports, enjoying some form of entertainment, or going to parties.

Second, an inconsistent student can be described as a person whose attitude toward education changes or varies. For example, a first grader's grades have gone up and down. She has been in school for only two semesters, but she has shown a big change in her grades. The first semester she received an E (Excellent) in reading and an S (Satisfactory) in math. The second semester she received an N (Not satisfactory) in reading and an E in math. When asked why her reading grade dropped, she said because she no longer liked reading. After her teacher taught her how to have fun doing her math, she no longer concentrated on reading. As a result, she would only take her math homework out of her book bag when it came time to do her homework.

Category 3:
ambitious
students

Last, there are many ambitious students who are eager to do well in their studies and to achieve degrees. Their priorities have been set, and they have made plans for reaching their goals. Their sole ambition is to excel and succeed. Many students can be classified as ambitious. Valerie, who is pursuing a degree in nursing, is a classic example. She attends class eagerly and regularly, even though she has two children and a home to care for. Recently, she had an illness that caused her to be absent for two weeks and to fall behind in her assignments. She returned and, with her usual ambition, soon caught up with her overdue assignments and achieved Bs or better grades in her courses.

Conclusion:
restatement
of thesis

In conclusion, the attitudes exemplified above can be found in students of any age, race, or gender. Whether they are attending grade school, high school, or college, students can be found who are unconcerned, inconsistent, or ambitious.

As with any piece of writing, a useful practice is to jot down many ideas and make rough lists as part of your brainstorming and prewriting. Do not skimp on your planning, and do expect to revise—perhaps several times—and, finally, to thoroughly edit the grammar and punctuation of your work before you turn it in.

A Matter of Perspective

A. Zee

A well-written paragraph can sometimes clarify even the most difficult ideas. A. Zee's paragraph, from the book Swallowing Clouds, *does just that. In approximately two hundred words, Zee clearly and succinctly illustrates the differences between the three major philosophical-religious-ethical systems practiced in China: Buddhism, Confucianism, and Taoism.*

Words to Know

benevolent   kind, humane
Nirvana   an ideal state of rest, harmony, stability, joy
pragmatic   practical
reincarnation   cycle of rebirth in another body
virtuously   righteously, morally

Getting Started

What do you know about the philosophies of Buddha, Confucius, and Lao-tze?

Buddha, Confucius, and Lao-tze were each given a sip of vinegar and asked about its taste. Buddha sighed, "Ah, bitter, so bitter, all is bitter in the sea of bitterness as we seek passage toward Nirvana." The rather matter-of-fact Confucius replied, "Why, vinegar tastes sour, of course." Finally, Lao-tze grinned and said with a wink, "How sweet!" . . . A Buddhist sees life as suffering and strives to break out of the reincarnation cycle by living each life more virtuously than the previous one. A Confucian is positive about life and seeks to live it as an upright, benevolent person. The ever pragmatic Confucius (he was a police commissioner early in life) would indeed be puzzled if anybody ever asked him about the taste of vinegar. Lao-tze, on the other hand, gives the impression that he is saying everything with a twinkle in his eyes. Much more than Buddha, and certainly more than Confucius, he is attracted by the unknowable.

Questions About the Reading

1. Why does the writer begin the paragraph with the story about vinegar?
2. According to the writer, how does a Buddhist see life?
3. How might a Buddhist break out of the reincarnation cycle?
4. How does a Confucian's attitude about life differ from that of his Buddhist neighbor?
5. What job did Confucius hold early in his life?
6. How does the writer describe Lao-tze?
7. What do you think the writer means when he states that Lao-tze was "attracted by the unknowable"?

Questions About the Writer's Strategies

1. Is there a **topic sentence** in this paragraph? If so, where is it? If not, state the **main idea** in a sentence of your own.
2. Is this a paragraph of classification, division, or both? Support your answer.
3. Does the writer use any other **modes of development** in this paragraph? If so, what are they and where in the paragraph are they used?
4. What does the title of this paragraph mean? How does it summarize the main idea of the paragraph?

Writing Assignments

1. Do you have your own philosophy of life? Are you an optimist, a pessimist, or a realist about life? Write a paragraph about several of your friends, classifying them according to their outlooks on life.
2. Choose a controversial topic that can be seen from many different viewpoints. Write a paragraph in which you classify at least three of the different points of view about the topic.

The Three New Yorks

E. B. White

*There is, of course, only one New York. But our largest city presents a
different face to each person who experiences it. E. B. White, who died in
1985, was a student of the city. In this paragraph, he finds that there are
three ways of looking at New York, and that these are also, in a way, three
ways of using New York—to live, to work, and to dream.*

Words to Know

Consolidated Edison Company   the electric power company
   serving New York City
continuity   existence over a long period
deportment   behavior, conduct
solidarity   wholeness
turbulence   agitation, disturbance

Getting Started

What are your thoughts about the different groups of people who
inhabit your hometown?

There are roughly three New Yorks. There is, first, the New York of the
man or woman who was born here, who takes the city for granted and
accepts its size and its turbulence as natural and inevitable. Second, there
is the New York of the commuter—the city that is devoured by locusts
each day and spat out each night. Third, there is the New York of the person who was born somewhere else and came to New York in quest of
something. Of these three trembling cities the greatest is the last—the city
of final destination, the city that is a goal. It is this third city that accounts
for New York's high-strung disposition, its poetical deportment, its dedi-
cation to the arts, and its incomparable achievements. Commuters give
the city its tidal restlessness, natives give it solidarity and continuity, but
the settlers give it passion. And whether it is a farmer arriving from Italy
to set up a small grocery store in a slum, or a young girl arriving from a
small town in Mississippi to escape the indignity of being observed by
her neighbors, or a boy arriving from the Corn Belt with a manuscript in
his suitcase and a pain in his heart, it makes no difference: each embraces

New York with the intense excitement of first love, each absorbs New York with the fresh eyes of an adventurer, each generates heat and light to dwarf the Consolidated Edison Company.

Questions About the Reading

1. Which of the New Yorks does White think is the greatest? Why? Support your answer with statements from the paragraph.
2. What do the people who make up the first New York contribute to it? Which statements tell you?
3. What is the meaning of the essay's final clause ("each generates heat")?

Questions About the Writer's Strategies

1. Does the paragraph have a **topic sentence**? If so, identify it. If not, state the topic in a sentence of your own.
2. What **transitions** does White use to help the reader identify the relation of ideas?
3. Identify the **metaphor** in the essay's third sentence and interpret what it means.
4. Is the paragraph developed by classification, division, or both?

Writing Assignments

1. Write a paragraph in which you classify the different groups of people in the town where you grew up.
2. Write a paragraph in which you identify and classify at least three groups of people in your school or place of work.
3. Suppose you are getting ready to do your laundry. Write a paragraph in which you explain how you sort the clothes for washing.

Where I Come from
Is Like This

Paula Gunn Allen

The extraordinary, sometimes bewildering, process of growing up is a journey we all share. Lessons about life—from parents, teachers, or even from books—help us along the way. Paula Gunn Allen's paragraph, from her book entitled The Sacred Hoop, *focuses on her mother's stories and the significant role they played in teaching Allen about the circle of life and her own place within it.*

Words to Know

Laguna   Native American people of the Southwest
mesa   flat-topped elevation with one or more clifflike sides

Getting Started

In what ways can stories teach young people about life?

M y mother told me stories all the time, though I often did not recognize them as that. My mother told me stories about cooking and childbearing; she told me stories about menstruation and pregnancy; she told me stories about gods and heroes, about fairies and elves, about goddesses and spirits; she told me stories about the land and the sky, about cats and dogs, about snakes and spiders; she told me stories about climbing trees and exploring the mesas; she told me stories about going to dances and getting married; she told me stories about dressing and undressing, about sleeping and waking; she told me stories about herself, about her mother, about her grandmother. She told me stories about grieving and laughing, about thinking and doing; she told me stories about school and about people; about darning and mending; she told me stories about turquoise and about gold; she told me European stories and Laguna stories; she told me Catholic stories and Presbyterian stories; she told me city stories and country stories; she told me political stories and religious stories. She told me stories about living and stories about dying. And in all of those stories she told me who I was, who I was supposed to be, who I came from, and who would follow me. In this way she taught me the meaning of the words she said, that all life is a circle and everything has a place within it. That's what she said and what she showed me in the things she did and the way she lives.

Questions About the Reading

1. Why do you think Paula Gunn Allen's mother told her daughter stories?
2. Why do you think Allen often didn't recognize the stories as stories?
3. What kinds of stories did the writer's mother tell? List the different categories.
4. What part did Allen play in all of her mother's stories?
5. According to the writer, what was the meaning of her mother's stories?

Questions About the Writer's Strategies

1. Is the **main idea** of this paragraph directly stated or implied? Write the main idea in your own words.
2. Does the writer use classification, division, or both? Support your answer with details from the paragraph.
3. Besides classification/division, what is another **mode of development** the writer uses in this paragraph? List details that support your answer.
4. Is this paragraph written **subjectively, objectively**, or both? Find examples to support your answer.
5. How does the writer feel about her mother and her mother's stories?

Writing Assignments

1. As you were growing up, what lessons did you learn about life? Write a paragraph in which you classify and divide the important lessons you learned and where you learned them.
2. Paula Gunn Allen's mother was an important role model for her daughter. What role models have you had in your life? Think of people such as parents, teachers, coaches, and others who have helped you learn how to be a better person. Write a paragraph in which you classify these people and explain how they have served as role models for you.

No More Bad Bugs

Colin McEnroe

Colin McEnroe writes humorous columns for the Hartford Courant. *In this passage, he uses classification and division to mock our tendency to classify and divide things.*

Words to Know

exude   ooze forth
panoply   a huge collection
serrated   saw-toothed

Getting Started

How many categories of bugs can you name?

You may remember reading, as a child, in the *Golden Wonder Book of the* 1
Living World of Exciting and Fun Bugs, about the thrilling panoply of
roughly 9 jillion species of insect, each as marvelously different from one
another as snowflakes.

Don't believe it.   2

Bugs would like nothing better than for us humans to waste enormous 3
bundles of time classifying them. A much more useful way of understanding bugs involves breaking them down into four easy-to-remember
categories.

1. Bugus horrificus: bugs with massive, serrated, flesh-tearing jaws   4
2. Bugus terribilis: bugs with massive, hooked, flesh-puncturing stingers 5
   full of disease-causing venom
3. Bugus disgustibus: bugs which exude toxic, germ-infested, nauseating   6
   rabid purple slime
4. Bugus invisibilis: bugs so tiny you can't see them at all but which can 7
   bite the bejabbers out of you

That's it. Anyone tells you there are other kinds of bugs, chances are 8
he's on their payroll. Look into it.

Questions About the Reading

1. Why do bugs want us to waste our time classifying them?
2. What is the writer's overall attitude toward bugs?
3. Is the writer making fun of science? What does he **imply** about the usefulness of science in our everyday encounters with insects?

Questions About the Writer's Strategies

1. In the descriptions of his four classes, the writer uses exaggeration to create humor. Analyze his method.
2. In the first sentence the writer implies a comparison between bugs and snowflakes. What is the effect of this suggestion? What term could be used to describe it?
3. What is the **main idea** of the passage? Is the main idea directly stated or **implied?**

Writing Assignments

1. In an essay, choose one of McEnroe's categories and classify it further, identifying the different classes of biting bugs, stinging bugs, or whatever. Make this essay humorous or informative (or both), whichever you prefer.
2. Write a paragraph classifying people into two or three categories according to the way they behave when they are attacked by bugs. For example, some people try to sneak a hand up quietly to swat, some just shoo the bug away, and so on.

The Plot Against People

Russell Baker

Russell Baker's humorous and lighthearted columns appear regularly in the Sunday magazine section of the New York Times. *Here he claims that objects we depend on in everyday life frustrate us intentionally by not working, breaking down, or getting lost.*

Words to Know

attain   achieve, reach
conciliatory   tending to make peace
cunning   shrewdness, slyness
inanimate   not living
plausible   believable

Getting Started

How would you categorize your everyday frustrations?

WASHINGTON, JUNE 17—Inanimate objects are classified scientifically 1
into three major categories—those that don't work, those that break
down and those that get lost.

The goal of all inanimate objects is to resist man and ultimately to de- 2
feat him, and the three major classifications are based on the method
each object uses to achieve its purpose. As a general rule, any object capable of breaking down at the moment when it is most needed will do so.
The automobile is typical of the category.

With the cunning typical of its breed, the automobile never breaks 3
down while entering a filling station with a large staff of idle mechanics.
It waits until it reaches a downtown intersection in the middle of the rush
hour, or until it is fully loaded with family and luggage on the Ohio turn-
pike.

Thus it creates maximum misery, inconvenience, frustration and irrita- 4
bility among its human cargo, thereby reducing its owner's life span.

Washing machines, garbage disposals, lawn mowers, light bulbs, auto- 5
matic laundry dryers, water pipes, furnaces, electrical fuses, television
tubes, hose nozzles, tape recorders, slide projectors—all are in league

with the automobile to take their turn at breaking down whenever life threatens to flow smoothly for their human enemies.

Many inanimate objects, of course, find it extremely difficult to break down. Pliers, for example, and gloves and keys are almost totally incapable of breaking down. Therefore, they have had to evolve a different technique for resisting man. 6

They get lost. Science has still not solved the mystery of how they do it, and no man has ever caught one of them in the act of getting lost. The most plausible theory is that they have developed a secret method of locomotion which they are able to conceal the instant a human eye falls upon them. 7

It is not uncommon for a pair of pliers to climb all the way from the cellar to the attic in its single-minded determination to raise its owner's blood pressure. Keys have been known to burrow three feet under mattresses. Women's purses, despite their great weight, frequently travel through six or seven rooms to find hiding space under a couch. 8

Scientists have been struck by the fact that things that break down virtually never get lost, while things that get lost hardly ever break down. 9

A furnace, for example, will invariably break down at the depth of the first winter cold wave, but it will never get lost. A woman's purse, which after all does have some inherent capacity for breaking down, hardly ever does; it almost invariably chooses to get lost. 10

Some persons believe this constitutes evidence that inanimate objects are not entirely hostile to man, and that a negotiated peace is possible. After all, they point out, a furnace could infuriate a man even more thoroughly by getting lost than by breaking down, just as a glove could upset him far more by breaking down than by getting lost. 11

Not everyone agrees, however, that this indicates a conciliatory attitude among inanimate objects. Many say it merely proves that furnaces, gloves and pliers are incredibly stupid. 12

The third class of objects—those that don't work—is the most curious of all. These include such objects as barometers, car clocks, cigarette lighters, flashlights and toy-train locomotives. It is inaccurate, of course, to say that they never work. They work once, usually for the first few hours after being brought home, and then quit. Thereafter, they never work again. 13

In fact, it is widely assumed that they are built for the purpose of not working. Some people have reached advanced ages without ever seeing some of these objects—barometers, for example—in working order. 14

Science is utterly baffled by the entire category. There are many theories about it. The most interesting holds that the things that don't work have attained the highest state possible for an inanimate object, the state 15

The Plot Against People / Russell Baker

to which things that break down and things that get lost can still only aspire.

They have truly defeated man by conditioning him never to expect 16 anything of them, and in return they have given man the only peace he receives from inanimate society. He does not expect his barometer to work, his electric locomotive to run, his cigarette lighter to light or his flashlight to illuminate, and when they don't it does not raise his blood pressure.

He cannot attain that peace with furnaces and keys, and cars and 17 women's purses as long as he demands that they work for their keep.

Questions About the Reading

1. What contradictory qualities does the writer ascribe to inanimate objects?
2. According to the writer, when is an object most likely to break down? Why?
3. What is the "highest state possible for inanimate objects"?

Questions About the Writer's Strategies

1. What is the function of paragraph 6?
2. Do scientists really study the problems described in the essay? Why does the writer refer to science and scientists?
3. What is the **tone** of the essay? How does the clear classification structure contribute to the tone?
4. Although the writer uses structure and wording that make his ideas seem logical and **objective**, the essay really just expresses his own imaginative opinion. How does he let the reader know, early in the essay, that he is presenting a **subjective** interpretation of reality?

Writing Assignments

1. Write an essay in which you classify household tasks according to the amount of work or trouble they are to you.
2. Write an essay in which you classify household appliances according to their work-saving qualities. If you prefer, classify tools or yard equipment according to their work-saving or efficiency qualities.
3. Write your own humorous essay in which you use classification as your **mode of development**. Try to be absurd. Possible topics might include dorm food, dogs or cats, winter weather, housekeeping styles, or types of laziness.

Friends, Good Friends—
and Such Good Friends

Judith Viorst

*Friendship is not a subject we give a lot of thought to. As the saying goes,
we know who our friends are. But we've probably never considered the
difference between, say, "convenience friends" and "crossroads friends."
Judith Viorst has, and the classification of friends she outlines here will
probably ring true to you.*

Words to Know

ardor   intensity, emotion, passion
calibrated   checked, adjusted, standardized
Ingmar Bergman   Swedish screenwriter and director
nonchalant   casual, offhand
sufficient   enough, adequate

Getting Started

How could you think about your friends in terms of categories?

W omen are friends, I once would have said, when they totally love 1
and support and trust each other, and bare to each other the secrets of
their souls, and run—no questions asked—to help each other, and tell
harsh truths to each other (no, you can't wear that dress unless you lose
ten pounds first) when harsh truths must be told.

Women are friends, I once would have said, when they share the same 2
affection for Ingmar Bergman, plus train rides, cats, warm rain, charades,
Camus, and hate with equal ardor Newark and Brussels sprouts and
Lawrence Welk and camping.

In other words, I once would have said that a friend is a friend all the 3
way, but now I believe that's a narrow point of view. For the friendships
I have and the friendships I see are conducted at many levels of intensity,
serve many different functions, meet different needs and range from
those as all-the-way as the friendship of the soul sisters mentioned above
to that of the most nonchalant and casual playmates.

Consider these varieties of friendship: 4

1. Convenience friends. These are the women with whom, if our paths 5 weren't crossing all the time, we'd have no particular reason to be friends: a next-door neighbor, a woman in our car pool, the mother of one of our children's closest friends or maybe some mommy with whom we serve juice and cookies each week at the Glenwood Co-op Nursery.

Convenience friends are convenient indeed. They'll lend us their cups 6 and silverware for a party. They'll drive our kids to soccer when we're sick. They'll take us to pick up our car when we need a lift to the garage. They'll even take our cats when we go on vacation. As we will for them.

But we don't, with convenience friends, ever come too close or tell too 7 much; we maintain our public face and emotional distance. "Which means," says Elaine, "that I'll talk about being overweight but not about being depressed. Which means I'll admit being mad but not blind with rage. Which means I might say that we're pinched this month but never that I'm worried sick over money."

But which doesn't mean that there isn't sufficient value to be found in 8 these friendships of mutual aid, in convenience friends.

2. Special-interest friends. These friendships aren't intimate, and they 9 needn't involve kids or silverware or cats. Their value lies in some interest jointly shared. And so we may have an office friend or a yoga friend or a tennis friend or a friend from the Women's Democratic Club.

"I've got one woman friend," says Joyce, "who likes, as I do, to take 10 psychology courses. Which makes it nice for me—and nice for her. It's fun to go with someone you know and it's fun to discuss what you've learned, driving back from the classes." And for the most part, she says, that's all they discuss.

"I'd say that what we're *doing* is *doing* together, not being together," 11 Suzanne says of her Tuesday-doubles friends. "It's mainly a tennis relationship, but we play together well. And I guess we all need to have a couple of playmates."

I agree. 12

My playmate is a shopping friend, a woman of marvelous taste, a 13 woman who knows exactly *where* to buy *what*, and furthermore is a woman who always knows beyond a doubt what one ought to be buying. I don't have the time to keep up with what's new in eyeshadow, hemlines and shoes and whether the smock look is in or finished already. But since (oh shame!) I care a lot about eyeshadow, hemlines and shoes, and since I don't *want* to wear smocks if the smock look is finished, I'm very glad to have a shopping friend.

3. Historical friends. We all have a friend who knew us when . . . 14 maybe way back in Miss Meltzer's second grade, when our family lived in that three-room flat in Brooklyn, when our dad was out of work for seven months, when our brother Allie got in that fight where they had to

call the police, when our sister married the endodontist from Yonkers and when, the morning after we lost our virginity, she was the first, the only friend we told.

The years have gone by and we've gone separate ways and we've little 15 in common now, but we're still an intimate part of each other's past. And so whenever we go to Detroit we always go to visit this friend of our girl-hood. Who knows how we looked before our teeth were straightened. Who knows how we talked before our voice got unBrooklyned. Who knows what we ate before we learned about artichokes. And who, by her presence, puts us in touch with an earlier part of ourself, a part of ourself it's important never to lose.

"What this friend means to me and what I mean to her," says Grace, "is 16 having a sister without sibling rivalry. We know the texture of each oth-er's lives. She remembers my grandmother's cabbage soup. I remember the way her uncle played the piano. There's simply no other friend who remembers those things."

4. Crossroads friends. Like historical friends, our crossroads friends 17 are important for *what was*—for the friendship we shared at a crucial, now past, time of life. A time, perhaps, when we roomed in college to-gether; or worked as eager young singles in the Big City together; or went together, as my friend Elizabeth and I did through pregnancy, birth and that scary first year of new motherhood.

Crossroads friends forge powerful links, links strong enough to en- 18 dure with not much more contact than once-a-year letters at Christmas. And out of respect for those crossroads years, for those dramas and dreams we once shared, we will always be friends.

5. Cross-generational friends. Historical friends and crossroads 19 friends seem to maintain a special kind of intimacy—dormant but always ready to be revived—and though we may rarely meet, whenever we do connect, it's personal and intense. Another kind of intimacy exists in the friendships that form across generations in what one woman calls her daughter-mother and her mother-daughter relationships.

Evelyn's friend is her mother's age—"but I share so much more than 20 I ever could with my mother"—a woman she talks to of music, of books and of life. "What I get from her is the benefit of her experience. What she gets—and enjoys—from me is a youthful perspective. It's a pleasure for both of us."

I have in my own life a precious friend, a woman of 65 who has lived 21 very hard, who is wise, who listens well; who has been where I am and can help me understand it; and who represents not only an ultimate ideal mother to me but also the person I'd like to be when I grow up.

In our daughter role we tend to do more than our share of self-revela- 22 tion; in our mother role we tend to receive what's revealed. It's another kind of pleasure—playing wise mother to a questing younger person. It's another very lovely kind of friendship.

6. Part-of-a-couple friends. Some of the women we call our friends we 23 never see alone—we see them as part of a couple at couples' parties. And though we share interests in many things and respect each other's views, we aren't moved to deepen the relationship. Whatever the reason, a lack of time or—and this is more likely—a lack of chemistry, our friendship remains in the context of a group. But the fact that our feeling on seeing each other is always, "I'm *so* glad she's here" and the fact that we spend half the evening talking together says that this too, in its own way, counts as a friendship.

(Other part-of-a-couple friends are the friends that came with the mar- 24 riage, and some of these are friends we could live without. But sometimes, alas, she married our husband's best friend; and sometimes, alas, she *is* our husband's best friend. And so we find ourself dealing with her, somewhat against our will, in a spirit of what I'll call *reluctant* friendship.)

7. Men who are friends. I wanted to write just of women friends, but 25 the women I've talked to won't let me—they say I must mention man-woman friendships too. For these friendships can be just as close and as dear as those that we form with women. Listen to Lucy's description of one such friendship:

"We've found we have things to talk about that are different from 26 what he talks about with my husband and different from what I talk about with his wife. So sometimes we call on the phone or meet for lunch. There are similar intellectual interests—we always pass on to each other the books that we love—but there's also something tender and caring too."

In a couple of crises, Lucy says, "he offered himself, for talking and for 27 helping. And when someone died in his family he wanted me there. The sexual, flirty part of our friendship is very small, but *some*—just enough to make it fun and different." She thinks—and I agree—that the sexual part, though small is always *some*, is always there when a man and a woman are friends.

It's only in the past few years that I've made friends with men, in the 28 sense of a friendship that's *mine*, not just part of two couples. And achieving with them the ease and the trust I've found with women friends has value indeed. Under the dryer at home last week, putting on mascara and rouge, I comfortably sat and talked with a fellow named Peter. Peter, I finally decided, could handle the shock of me minus mascara under the dryer. Because we care for each other. Because we're friends.

8. There are medium friends, and pretty good friends, and very good 29 friends, indeed, and these friendships are defined by their level of inti-

macy. And what we'll reveal at each of these levels of intimacy is calibrated with care. We might tell a medium friend, for example, that yesterday we had a fight with our husband. And we might tell a pretty good friend that this fight with our husband made us so mad that we slept on the couch. And we might tell a very good friend that the reason we got so mad in that fight that we slept on the couch had something to do with that girl who works in his office. But it's only to our very best friends that we're willing to tell all, to tell what's going on with that girl in his office.

The best of friends, I still believe, totally love and support and trust 30 each other, and bare to each other the secrets of their souls, and run—no questions asked—to help each other, and tell harsh truths to each other when they must be told.

But we needn't agree about everything (only 12-year-old girl friends 31 agree about *everything*) to tolerate each other's point of view. To accept without judgment. To give and to take without ever keeping score. And to *be* there, as I am for them and as they are for me, to comfort our sorrows, to celebrate, our joys.

Questions About the Reading

1. What was Viorst's original idea of what made women friends? How does her explanation within the essay differ from her original idea?
2. How many kinds of friends does Viorst identify? Support your answer with statements from the reading.
3. Why does the writer refer to special-interest friends as playmates?
4. Explain in your own words what the writer means in her description of the importance of historical friends.
5. How are special-interest friends like part-of-a-couple friends?

Questions About the Writer's Strategies

1. What purpose do the quotations in the essay serve?
2. How does the writer indicate that her dominant **mode of development** will be classification? How does she introduce the classifications she will use?
3. Are the last three statements of the last paragraph complete sentences? Why or why not?
4. Why do you think Viorst uses the **order** she does in discussing different kinds of friends? What is the order that she uses—time, space, or importance?
5. Does the writer use other modes of development in addition to classification? If so, give examples from the essay.

Writing Assignments

1. Classify some of the people you know based on some category—perhaps study methods, sense of humor (or lack of it), taste in clothes, or levels of physical fitness. Use **examples** to clarify your classifications.
2. Classify the kinds of Christmas gifts you received when you were little or that you receive now. Again, use examples to clarify your classifications.
3. Classify at least three types of music that you and your friends listen to. Use **description** to explain your classifications.

Doublespeak

William Lutz

If you have ever tried to read a loan agreement or understand an insurance policy, you have undoubtedly encountered jargon, gobbledygook, or inflated language. But take heart. Once you have read the following essay by William Lutz, you will never again be deceived by the fine art of doublespeak.

Words to Know

esoteric understood by a particular group, confined

euphemism substitution of an inoffensive term for an offensive one

jargon specialized language of a particular profession or group

obscure unclear, remote

pretentious pompous, affected

profundity depth, wisdom

Getting Started

How often do you encounter—or use—doublespeak in your everyday world?

How to Spot Doublespeak

How can you spot doublespeak? Most of the time you will recognize 1
doublespeak when you see or hear it. But, if you have any doubts, you can identify doublespeak just by answering these questions: Who is saying what to whom, under what conditions and circumstances, with what intent, and with what results? Answering these questions will usually help you identify as doublespeak language that appears to be legitimate or that at first glance doesn't even appear to be doublespeak.

First Kind of Doublespeak

There are at least four kinds of doublespeak. The first is the euphemism, 2
an inoffensive or positive word or phrase used to avoid a harsh, unpleas-

ant, or distasteful reality. But a euphemism can also be a tactful word or phrase which avoids directly mentioning a painful reality, or it can be an expression used out of concern for the feelings of someone else, or to avoid directly discussing a topic subject to a social or cultural taboo.

When you use a euphemism because of your sensitivity for someone's 3 feelings or out of concern for a recognized social or cultural taboo, it is not doublespeak. For example, you express your condolences that someone has "passed away" because you do not want to say to a grieving person, "I'm sorry your father is dead." When you use the euphemism "passed away," no one is misled. Moreover, the euphemism functions here not just to protect the feelings of another person, but to communicate also your concern for that person's feelings during a period of mourning. When you excuse yourself to go to the "restroom," or you mention that someone is "sleeping with" or "involved with" someone else, you do not mislead anyone about your meaning, but you do respect the social taboos about discussing bodily functions and sex in direct terms. You also indicate your sensitivity to the feelings of your audience, which is usually considered a mark of courtesy and good manners.

However, when a euphemism is used to mislead or deceive, it becomes 4 doublespeak. For example, in 1984 the U.S. State Department announced that it would no longer use the word "killing" in its annual report on the status of human rights in countries around the world. Instead, it would use the phrase "unlawful or arbitrary deprivation of life," which the department claimed was more accurate. Its real purpose for using this phrase was simply to avoid discussing the embarrassing situation of government-sanctioned killings in countries that are supported by the United States and have been certified by the United States as respecting the human rights of their citizens. This use of a euphemism constitutes doublespeak, since it is designed to mislead, to cover up the unpleasant. Its real intent is at variance with its apparent intent. It is language designed to alter our perception of reality.

The Pentagon, too, avoids discussing unpleasant realities when it re- 5 fers to bombs and artillery shells that fall on civilian targets as "incontinent ordnance." And in 1977 the Pentagon tried to slip funding for the neutron bomb unnoticed into an appropriations bill by calling it a "radiation enhancement device."

Second Kind of Doublespeak

A second kind of doublespeak is jargon, the specialized language of a 6 trade, profession, or similar group, such as that used by doctors, lawyers, engineers, educators, or car mechanics. Jargon can serve an important and useful function. Within a group, jargon functions as a kind of verbal shorthand that allows members of the group to communicate with each other clearly, efficiently, and quickly. Indeed, it is a mark of membership in the group to be able to use and understand the group's jargon.

But jargon, like the euphemism, can also be doublespeak. It can be— 7 and often is—pretentious, obscure, and esoteric terminology used to give an air of profundity, authority, and prestige to speakers and their subject matter. Jargon as doublespeak often makes the simple appear complex, the ordinary profound, the obvious insightful. In this sense it is used not to express but impress. With such doublespeak, the act of smelling something becomes "organoleptic analysis," glass becomes "fused silicate," a crack in a metal support beam becomes a "discontinuity," conservative economic policies become "distributionally conservative notions."

Lawyers, for example, speak of an "involuntary conversion" of prop- 8 erty when discussing the loss or destruction of property through theft, accident, or condemnation. If your house burns down or if your car is stolen, you have suffered an involuntary conversion of your property. When used by lawyers in a legal situation, such jargon is a legitimate use of language, since lawyers can be expected to understand the term.

However, when a member of a specialized group uses its jargon to 9 communicate with a person outside the group, and uses it knowing that the nonmember does not understand such language, then there is doublespeak. For example, on May 9, 1978, a National Airlines 727 airplane crashed while attempting to land at the Pensacola, Florida, airport. Three of the fifty-two passengers aboard the airplane were killed. As a result of the crash, National made an after-tax insurance benefit of $1.7 million, or an extra 18¢ a share dividend for its stockholders. Now National Airlines had two problems: It did not want to talk about one of its airplanes crashing, and it had to account for the $1.7 million when it issued its annual report to its stockholders. National solved the problem by inserting a footnote in its annual report which explained that the $1.7 million income was due to "the involuntary conversion of a 727." National thus acknowledged the crash of its airplane and the subsequent profit it made from the crash, without once mentioning the accident or the deaths. However, because airline officials knew that most stockholders in the company, and indeed most of the general public, were not familiar with legal jargon, the use of such jargon constituted doublespeak.

Third Kind of Doublespeak

A third kind of doublespeak is gobbledygook or bureaucratese. Basically, 10 such doublespeak is simply a matter of piling on words, of overwhelming the audience with words, the bigger the words and the longer the sentences the better. Alan Greenspan, then chair of President Nixon's Council of Economic Advisors, was quoted in *The Philadelphia Inquirer* in 1974 as having testified before a Senate committee that "It is a tricky problem to find the particular calibration in timing that would be appropriate to stem the acceleration in risk premiums created by falling incomes without prematurely aborting the decline in the inflation-generated risk premiums."

Nor has Mr. Greenspan's language changed since then. Speaking to 11 the meeting of the Economic Club of New York in 1988, Mr. Greenspan, now Federal Reserve chair, said, "I guess I should warn you, if I turn out to be particularly clear, you've probably misunderstood what I've said." Mr. Greenspan's doublespeak doesn't seem to have held back his career.

Sometimes gobbledygook may sound impressive, but when the quote 12 is later examined in print it doesn't even make sense. During the 1988 presidential campaign, vice-presidential candidate Senator Dan Quayle explained the need for a strategic-defense initiative by saying, "Why wouldn't an enhanced deterrent, a more stable peace, a better prospect to denying the ones who enter conflict in the first place to have a reduction of offensive systems and an introduction to defense capability? I believe this is the route the country will eventually go."

The investigation into the Challenger disaster in 1986 revealed the 13 doublespeak of gobbledygook and bureaucratese used by too many involved in the shuttle program. When Jesse Moore, NASA's associate administrator, was asked if the performance of the shuttle program had improved with each launch or if it had remained the same, he answered, "I think our performance in terms of the liftoff performance and in terms of the orbital performance, we knew more about the envelope we were operating under, and we have been pretty accurately staying in that. And so I would say the performance has not by design drastically improved. I think we have been able to characterize the performance more as a function of our launch experience as opposed to it improving as a function of time." While this language may appear to be jargon, a close look will reveal that it is really just gobbledygook laced with jargon. But you really have to wonder if Mr. Moore had any idea what he was saying.

Fourth Kind of Doublespeak

The fourth kind of doublespeak is inflated language that is designed to 14 make the ordinary seem extraordinary; to make everyday things seem impressive; to give an air of importance to people, situations, or things that would not normally be considered important; to make the simple seem complex. Often this kind of doublespeak isn't hard to spot, and it is usually pretty funny. While car mechanics may be called "automotive internists," elevator operators members of the "vertical transportation corps," used cars "pre-owned" or "experienced cars," and black-and-white television sets described as having "non-multicolor capability," you really aren't misled all that much by such language.

However, you may have trouble figuring out that, when Chrysler "initiates a career alternative enhancement program," it is really laying off five thousand workers; or that "negative patient care outcome" means the patient died; or that "rapid oxidation" means a fire in a nuclear power plant.

The doublespeak of inflated language can have serious consequences. In Pentagon doublespeak, "pre-emptive counterattack" means that American forces attacked first; "engaged the enemy on all sides" means American troops were ambushed; "backloading of augmentation personnel" means a retreat by American troops. In the doublespeak of the military, the 1983 invasion of Grenada was conducted not by the U.S. Army, Navy, Air Force, and Marines, but by the "Caribbean Peace Keeping Forces." But then, according to the Pentagon, it wasn't an invasion, it was a "predawn vertical insertion."

Questions About the Reading

1. According to William Lutz, what is "doublespeak"?
2. What questions help you identify doublespeak?
3. How many kinds of doublespeak does William Lutz discuss? List each type and an accompanying example.
4. Why does Lutz believe that an expression like "passed away" is not doublespeak?
5. What kind of useful function can jargon serve?
6. Translate into plain English the following phrase, taken from a National Airlines annual report: "the involuntary conversion of a 727."
7. According to the writer, what is "gobbledygook"?
8. Give three **examples** of inflated language mentioned in the final section of the essay.

Questions About the Writer's Strategies

1. Is the **thesis** of this essay directly stated or implied? State the thesis in your own words.
2. Does Lutz use classification, division, or both? Support your answer with **details** from the essay.
3. Besides classification and division, what is another **mode of development** the writer uses in this essay? List details from the text that support your answer.

4. In what ways is the essay **subjective**? In what ways is it **objective**?
5. How does the writer feel about his subject matter? Use examples from the essay to support your answer.

Writing Assignments

1. Do you use different language with your friends, your boss, and your professors? Write an essay in which you classify your different audiences and how your language changes to suit each group.
2. Choose one kind of doublespeak and use it in an essay on the topic of your choice. For example, you could use sports jargon to write about a game or use inflated language to write about buying a used car. Use classification and division as your essay's mode of development. Be imaginative and creative. Feel free to make up any new doublespeak words or categories.

The Womanly Art of Beast Feeding

Alice Kahn

As a contemporary parent, Alice Kahn is confronted by the many theories being publicized today about health and child care. This essay from her book My Life as a Gal *introduces us to her notions about how parents can influence what their children eat or, to look at it another way, how children can influence their parents to give them what they want to eat.*

Words to Know

conscientious   governed by conscience
empirical   gained through experiment or observation
fomented   proposed, supported
indistinguishable   without distinctive qualities
La Leche   Spanish for milk
morphology   structure
nonadulterated   uncontaminated—free of preservatives, for
   example

Getting Started

How could you classify food into what you eat and how you eat it?

Us parents, we have a hell of a time feeding our kids these days. How   1
simple it was in the olden days when people knew nothing of the science of nutrition and the little darlings had to eat their porridge, swallow their spinach, and lap up their stew with its juices while keeping their yaps shut.

Today, it's not untypical to sit down to dinner and hear, "Oh, no, not   2
steak again" or "I hate quiche Lorraine" or "Yuck—homemade tortellini with pesto." In my family, two girls, *tyrannicus girlus*, have divided up the known food world so that dining is virtually impossible. One hates Chinese, the other hates Mexican. One won't eat chicken, the other won't eat meat. They have achieved unity on fish and French cuisine—neither will eat either.

Concern about what the children eat naturally follows the returned 3 importance of breast-feeding as fomented by those Friends of the Breast, the La Leche League. The League, which I always suspected grew out of the French obsession with the mammary gland (so evident in their art and their postcards), wrote a pamphlet, "The Womanly Art of Breast Feeding," which urged women not only to nurse their babies but to do it in public. They were aided in this effort by a male support group, the Le Lechers League.

It became gospel that a child who got off to a good start by consuming 4 nothing but healthy breast milk would be hooked for life on simple natural foods. But has a truly scientific study ever shown that any child (or adult, for that matter) who spends long hours at the breast is any more intelligent for the experience?

Nevertheless, a generation of well-educated, busy women devoted 5 themselves to breast-feeding. We nursed them in offices, we nursed them on buses, we nursed them at tax accountants except when the trauma made our milk dry up. Once I actually saw a bride coming down the aisle nursing her baby. We pumped our milk and saved it lest we deprive our child while on the job. We bared our breasts as well-meaning fathers-in-law self-consciously shouted, "Chow bag!"

And what did we get for our effort? Offspring who, as soon as they 6 could talk, demanded "Jell-O Pudding Pops—*now*."

Well, we tried. Maybe we tried too hard. Maybe it's hopeless, in this 7 crazy Ronald McDonald world, to think you can do something as simple as feed children well. Christ, I hardly know what to feed myself between low-fat, high-fiber, calcium-rich, iron-rich, nonadulterated foods. Vitamin pills, that's what most adults take to feel wholesome these days— pills.

There are several theories on how to handle the unmistakable lust 8 for consuming junk that seems to be epidemic in our youth. There is the hard-line approach: Eat it and weep. Most of us parents are simply too wimpy for that. There is the bribery approach: Eat the chicken and vegetable and then you can have the cookies and ice cream and bubble gum. And finally there is the Little Bo-peep approach: Leave them alone and they will come home wagging their tails behind them.

The Bo-peep Plan or the non-nutrisystems approach allows the child 9 to self-select foods. There have been scientific studies showing that if allowed to pick at random, a baby will eventually select all it needs to satisfy its nutritional needs. A similar approach can be taken with older children, but it is best done if the parent provides some structure. Here, some education is necessary so that the child can choose from the Seven

Chapter 5 / Classification and Division

Basic Junk Food Groups. A well-balanced meal would include something from each of the following:

The Seven Basic Junk Food Groups

1. The Chip Group. Like any conscientious parent, I try to steer my 10 little heifers toward the healthier chips—the pure, natural potato chip as opposed to cheese puffs or sour cream and onion. I skip barbecued anything. The children will enjoy exercising choice concerning the morphology of the chip—ruffled versus flat—as well as selecting among corn, potato, and the newer nacho chips that provide an opportunity to become acquainted with a different culture.

2. The Nitrate/Nitrite Group. There is a growing body of empirical 11 evidence that children are born with an innate need for nitrates and nitrites. Whether it is due to a missing gene or a result of mutation is unclear. But no child's lunch is complete without the protein portion consisting of salami, bologna, bacon, hot dog, and so on. Further evidence of the biological need for nitrates is seen in the child's refusal to eat nitrate-free versions of these products amid claims that these adulterated foods taste "gross." Even children's normal intolerance of ambiguity in food is held in check as they select mysterious items like "luncheon meat."

3. The Grainless Bread Group. Thanks to modern marketing, a wide 12 variety of grainless breads are now available, from the traditional Wonder to the historic San Francisco sourdough. And because of improved food technology one can even purchase a variety of whole wheat bread that is indistinguishable in flavor and texture from white. Don't ask me how they do it. No doubt some truth-in-labeling law requires that for every ton of processed flour one actual whole grain must be dropped in the mix. At any rate, either bread will do very nicely to hold the catsup, mustard, or mayo that accompanies the nitrite filler.

4. The Fruitoid Group. Children quickly learn that there's a whole 13 world of fruit-related products that are much sweeter and more interestingly packaged than actual fruit. These range from canned fruits that save wear and tear on teeth and jaws to fruit rolls in which the uninteresting pulp portion of the fruit is removed, leaving only the important sugar portion. This is arranged in a leathery substance that sticks to the teeth as well as the ribs. Since the addition of artificial fluorides have rendered much of modern dentistry unnecessary, these products are useful for restoring the natural balance between the tooth enamel and Mr. Cavity.

5. The Cake and Cookie Group. Although a balanced meal, one that 14 includes all the basic junk food groups, makes it less difficult to get

through the rest of the crap so one can come to the finale, the addition of a treat is always welcome. Most children prefer a sandwich-style cookie so the filling can be scraped off and the remaining cookie can still be traded with a friend for something else.

6. The Health Food Group. Most supermarkets now include a health 15 food section where delicious snacks are displayed in large old-fashioned wooden bins to which you help yourself. Here one can find a variety of treats from plain carob chips to honey-soaked granola cereal (said to have nine times more sweetener than a Hershey bar). Some traditional foods here include the yogurt-covered nuts, and some stores even have mint-flavored yogurt-covered nuts. Those little bright green balls are my favorite natural food. To find out which ones your child likes, just have him reach in the bins, squeeze a few pieces, and eat a bunch of each one right out of his hands.

7. The Drink Group. Choosing a drink used to be a battle. Children 16 always wanted Coke or Pepsi. But today's sophisticated kid is reaching out for natural-flavored soft drinks or oddities like cola-flavored Calistoga water. Exciting developments in fruit drinks go beyond the traditional teeth-rotting apple juice to a whole range of drinks that boast of being fruit-flavored. One orange drink label brags "20% Real Fruit Flavoring!"

The wise parent will simply stand back and let the child choose among 17 these groups. In fact, this is a process that may already be occurring in your house, but it's nice to read about it from an expert like myself so you can tell a friend that you saw an article saying it was okay to do this.

Questions About the Reading

1. Why does the writer call her children *tyrannicus girlus*?
2. In paragraph 12, the writer says, "Don't ask me how they do it." Who are "they"?
3. How does the writer feel about so-called health food?
4. How does the writer feel about contemporary child-rearing advice?

Questions About the Writer's Strategies

1. What is the **main idea** in this essay? Is there a **thesis statement**? If so, where is it? If not, how does the writer express the main idea?
2. In addition to classification and division, what are some other **modes of development** that the writer uses in the essay?

3. What is the humor in the writer's classification of "basic junk food groups"? Identify some specific **examples** of the writer's use of exaggeration to achieve a humorous effect.

Writing Assignments

1. In an essay, classify the ways people behave at the table when they eat. For example, your categories might be "wolfers," "pickers," and "chewers." To illustrate each category, use an example, either of someone you know or of a **fictional** person eating the way you are describing.
2. Write an essay dividing the human body into three or more parts. Explain how each part works and some of the important things it does. (Or, if you like, take one part of the body and divide that into its components.)

Three Disciplines for Children

John Holt

Classification or division can be useful in helping us understand how life works. In reading this essay, try to think back to your own childhood. Can you apply the writer's categories to what you experienced as you grew up?

Word to Know

impotent   powerless, weak

Getting Started

What is your definition of the word *discipline?*

A child, in growing up, may meet and learn from three different kinds 1 of disciplines. The first and the most important is what we might call the Discipline of Nature or of Reality. When he is trying to do something real, if he does the wrong thing or doesn't do the right one, he doesn't get the result he wants. If he doesn't pile one block right on top of another, or tries to build on a slanting surface, his tower falls down. If he hits the wrong key, he hears the wrong note. If he doesn't hit the nail squarely on the head, it bends, and he has to pull it out and start with another. If he doesn't measure properly what he is trying to build, it won't open, close, fit, stand up, fly, float, whistle, or do whatever he wants it to do. If he closes his eyes when he swings, he doesn't hit the ball. A child meets this kind of discipline every time he tries to *do* something, which is why it is so important in school to give children more chances to do things, instead of just reading or listening to someone talk (or pretending to). This discipline is a great teacher. The learner never has to wait long for his answer; it usually comes quickly, often instantly. Also it is clear, and very often points toward the needed correction; from what happened he cannot only see what he did was wrong, but also why, and what he needs to do instead. Finally, and most important, the giver of the answer, call it Nature, is impersonal, impartial, and indifferent. She does not give opinions, or make judgments; she cannot be wheedled, bullied, or fooled; she does not get angry or disappointed; she does not praise or blame; she does not remember past failures or hold grudges; with her one always gets a fresh start, this time is the one that counts.

The next discipline we might call the Discipline of Culture, of Society, 2 of What People Really Do. Man is a social, a cultural animal. Children sense around them this culture, this network of agreements, customs, habits, and rules binding the adults together. They want to understand it and be a part of it. They watch very carefully what people around them are doing and want to do the same. They want to do right, unless they become convinced they can't do right. Thus children rarely misbehave seriously in church, but sit as quietly as they can. The example of all those grownups is contagious. Some mysterious ritual is going on, and children, who like rituals, want to be part of it. In the same way, the little children that I see at concerts or operas, though they may fidget a little, or perhaps take a nap now and then, rarely make any disturbance. With all those grownups sitting there, neither moving nor talking, it is the most natural thing in the world to imitate them. Children who live among adults who are habitually courteous to each other, and to them, will soon learn to be courteous. Children who live surrounded by people who speak a certain way will speak that way, however much we may try to tell them that speaking that way is bad or wrong.

The third discipline is the one most people mean when they speak of 3 discipline—the Discipline of Superior Force, of sergeant to private, of "you do what I tell you or I'll make you wish you had." There is bound to be some of this in a child's life. Living as we do surrounded by things that can hurt children, or that children can hurt, we cannot avoid it. We can't afford to let a small child find out from experience the danger of playing in a busy street, or of fooling with the pots on the top of a stove, or of eating up the pills in the medicine cabinet. So, along with other precautions, we say to him, "Don't play in the street, or touch things on the stove, or go into the medicine cabinet, or I'll punish you." Between him and the danger too great for him to imagine we put a lesser danger, but one he can imagine and maybe therefore want to avoid. He can have no idea of what it would be like to be hit by a car, but he can imagine being shouted at, or spanked, or sent to his room. He avoids these substitutes for the greater danger until he can understand it and avoid it for its own sake. But we ought to use this discipline only when it is necessary to protect the life, health, safety, or well-being of people or other living creatures, or to prevent destruction of things that people care about. We ought not to assume too long, as we usually do, that a child cannot understand the real nature of the danger from which we want to protect him. The sooner he avoids the danger, not to escape our punishment, but as a matter of good sense, the better. He can learn that faster than we think. In Mexico, for example, where people drive their cars with a good deal of spirit, I saw many children no older than five or four walking un-attended on the streets. They understood about cars, they knew what to do. A child whose life is full of the threat and fear of punishment is locked into babyhood. There is no way for him to grow up, to learn to take responsibility for his life and acts. Most important of all, we should not assume that having to yield to the threat of our superior force is good for the child's character. It is never good for anyone's character. To bow to superior force makes us feel impotent and cowardly for not having had the strength or courage to resist. Worse, it makes us resentful and vengeful. We can hardly wait to make someone pay for our humiliation, yield to us as we were once made to yield. No, if we cannot always avoid using the Discipline of Superior Force, we should at least use it as seldom as we can.

Questions About the Reading

1. What makes the Discipline of Nature a "great teacher"?
2. In paragraph 2, the writer says children "want to do right, unless they become convinced they can't do right." What are the **implications** of this statement? What happens to the children who are convinced they can't do right?
3. What is wrong with the Discipline of Superior Force? Why should we use it as seldom as possible? Why must we use it sometimes?
4. As a young adult, you probably remember experiencing many kinds of discipline while you were growing up. Can you think of any classes besides the ones the writer identifies? Try to describe some different types of discipline.

Questions About the Writer's Strategies

1. What primary **mode of development** does the writer use for each paragraph of the essay?
2. This essay is clearly structured, with one paragraph for each class of discipline. In what **order** are the paragraphs presented? Explain your answer.
3. What is the **thesis statement** in the essay? What is the **topic sentence** of each paragraph? How is the **main idea** expressed?
4. Reread the writer's description of Nature at the end of paragraph 1. In a few words, describe the method he uses, and explain why it is or is not effective.
5. Why is paragraph 3 the longest one in the essay?

Writing Assignments

1. *Discipline* means many things. It isn't just a way to teach or to control misbehavior. Write an essay classifying different meanings of discipline. Use **examples**, or one extended example, to illustrate each class. Your categories might include things like academic discipline (study habits); the discipline needed for athletics, drama, or dance; moral discipline; the discipline needed to do your part in your family; and so on.

2. Write an essay in which you identify different classes of parental style, such as stern, friendly, playful, immature, supportive, or aloof. Create a single **fictional** example to illustrate each category, but base it on parents you know, if you like.

The Big Five Popular Fears of Our Time

Stephanie Brush

Franklin D. Roosevelt once said, "The only thing we have to fear is fear itself." It is true that fear can paralyze us if we let it. In the following essay, Stephanie Brush uses a touch of humor to help us see our fears in a new light.

Words to Know

bereft   deprived, lacking

cumulative   increasing

frescoes   paintings on moist plaster done in earth colors

inestimable   not able to be determined or calculated

nebbish   timid person

netherworld   underworld, hell

obsequious   excessively eager to serve, comply, or obey

paradoxically   seemingly contradictory

REM cycle   period of sleep time during which dreaming
   occurs

venerate   adore, honor

virulent   destructive, harmful

waffling   speaking or writing evasively

Getting Started

What is your greatest fear?

In a recent survey, 1,000 Americans were asked to name the fear that   1
torments them the most. They're listed here in no particular order-of-fearsomeness, but most everyone has a personal favorite on this list.

1. Fear of Gradual Hysteria

Gradual hysteria is what happens when you feel your life is completely   2
out of control.

Many of us attempt to exert control by redecorating our homes, for ex- 3 ample. We move a picture and find that there is a rectangular spot on the wall where the picture used to be. Then we move the TV stand and find that there are four identical indentations in the rug. Then we move the TV stand back and find that there are now eight identical indentations in the rug. Then someone starts drilling into the pavement outside the window, and the phone rings exactly once, and stops, and we run to answer it, and hear only a metallic click and start to scream, very quietly. We feel that God is talking to us. "Just try it," He is saying. "Just try and make something out of your life."

Gradual hysteria happens in this way to just about everybody. It is 4 usually triggered by loud noises, helplessness, and cumulative stress, and yes, it has the power to destroy everything in its path. But you'd rather have that happening to you than to someone else, wouldn't you?

2. Fear of People Who Have Had Too Much Assertiveness Training

There was a movement back in the seventies in which thousands of inef- 5 fectual nebbishes decided that they were not standing firm where it counted in life, and they went out and shelled out $300 at adult-education classes around the country, so that they could Learn to Say No! To Get Their Needs Met! To Not Take a Lot of BS From the Guy at the Auto Body Shop!

They walk among us now, and the threat they pose is inestimable. 6

Have they become, in fact, "assertive" people? Let's be serious. Asser- 7 tiveness comes from being *born* knowing you're going to get the goods in life, whatever they may be. You don't have to take *courses* in this stuff, okay? And the reason an assertiveness-trained nebbish is a dangerous commodity is that he suspects he is still a nebbish but he's not sure whether it shows or not. *It shows*, all right?

He starts to breathe heavily at the cleaners' because he's just found a 8 spot on his jacket that wasn't there before, and now he is trying to remember his "lines" for the big confrontation to come.

Sometimes, Assertiveness-Trained Nebbishes get the heady feeling of 9 "being honest" and "owning their feelings"—and they do embarrassing things like embrace you and say, "I hate your rug, but the honesty of this moment feels beautiful."

Whatever we do, it is essential for us to impress on our friends that we 10 liked them better when they were obsequious, waffling little toadies. At least then we knew what we were dealing with. At least life had some kind of structure.

There is some work being done to "de-program" these people, sort of 11
like former members of cults. But it is too soon to tell whether this technique is going to have any effect.

3. Insomnia: Fear of Consciousness

"Consciousness" is a state of awareness of all the realities of life. If we 12
had to live in a state of total awareness all the time, if we had to dwell on
realities like crime and war and what happens to the members of "Menudo" after they turn fifteen, then we should all surely become mad and
highly depressed.

So sleep was invented to spare us from total consciousness. But 13
the more we can't sleep, the more conscious—and therefore *anxious*—
we become. The same scientists who have clocked things like REM
cycles and muscle-activity cycles have also clocked pre-sleep anxiety
cycles.

- Cycle I usually involves WORK ANXIETY: Did I remember to turn off
  my office light? Does my boss like me? Would my boss recognize
  me if he saw me in a small crowd?
- Cycle II involves CURRENT-EVENTS ANXIETY: Is there plutonium in
  my drinking water? Will the world be safe for my children? With
  street crime in the state it's in, would it be all right if I asked my
  dog to walk himself at night?
- Cycle III occurs when the mind drifts off to a netherworld of half-
  formed dreads and sinister potentialities. What if my family got
  sick and died? What if they were tied to a stake in the Amazon
  rain forest and eaten by termites? What if I were on a quiz show
  and had to know the Gross National Product of Burma?

Some of these fears, unfortunately, have more than a little merit (al- 14
though for what it's worth, the GNP of Burma is 657,000 Bwenzii a year,
and there are no termites in the Amazon rain forest. Then again, there's
nothing to stop them from being flown in.)

It is estimated that over 45 percent of the population suffers from 15
insomnia on any given night; which means that on any given night
YOU ARE ALONE WITH 150 MILLION OTHER AMERICANS. So when you think
about it, it would make sense if you were given these people's phone
numbers, so you'd at least have someone to talk to. (And yet, paradoxically, if you called them, they would scream into the receiver, "What are
you, *crazy*? It's *three o'clock in the morning!*" And they would call the
police.)

4. Fear of Amnesia

There are really three varieties of amnesia we need to talk about here: 16

"Random" amnesia strikes about 5 million Americans a year, includ- 17
ing an undisclosed number of dental patients who "forget" to floss between meals, and a number of hotel guests who "forget" to return the
towels, stationery, and light fixtures to the rooms where they found them.
Also every year, twelve or thirteen natives of Florence, Oregon, fall victim to *group* amnesia and awaken and imagine themselves to be natives
of Florence, Italy. They immediately start painting frescoes all over the
sides of municipal buildings, and each year the frescoes have to be sand-
blasted off, at the expense of thousands to the taxpayers, since no one in
Oregon is known to have any artistic talent.

By far the most virulent form of amnesia is SOAPSTAR amnesia, which 18
occurs relentlessly in daytime television. Hardly a day goes by when
someone on one of the major networks is not suffering from a complete
memory loss—"*What do you mean 'Nicki Matuszak?' I've never heard of a
'Nicki Matuszak' in my life! I'm a beekeeper! Stay away from me!*"

These poor doomed sufferers are destined to wander around strange 19
towns in brunette wigs and unattractive clothing, marry people they
have never met before, and ignore the pleas of their husbands and wives
on television ("Nicki! It's me, Stefano! I never meant to shoot you in the
brain! Please come home!").

Naturally, if we watch a lot of daytime TV, we are afraid that this fate 20
could befall us (although we secretly wonder how TV amnesiacs can use
their American Express cards for months at a time, pay the finance
charge, and still not have a clue to their identity).

5. Fear of Major Brain-Loss

Many people are afraid of appearing helpless, foolish, and "brainless." 21
For example, of being in serious car crashes and becoming "vegetables."
(Although if you get incinerated in a *plane* crash, you get to become a
"mineral," which is probably much, much worse.)

A far greater threat than this, however, is that of having a song you 22
really hate running through your head that you just can't get rid of.
It certainly happens more frequently. NO ONE EVER HAS A SONG THEY
LIKE RUNNING THROUGH THEIR HEAD. Large numbers of college grad-
uates still hear "Yummy, Yummy, Yummy," by the Ohio Express, and
some people have gone nearly insane with a continual rendition of
"Hey! You! Get Offa My Cloud!" as performed by the Ray Conniff
Singers.

Add to the dangers of brain-loss the persistent lure of religious cults, 23
lurking tantalizingly with "all the answers" around every corner. Beyond
even the Hare Krishnas and the Unification Church lies the "Pepsi Generation," a dangerous cult headed by singer LIONEL RICHIE. Instead of
working regular hours and contributing to the Gross National Product,
the Pepsi Generation spends hours taking dancing lessons and having
their teeth professionally polished. They venerate organized volleyball
and drive dune buggies to all their major appointments. Fortunately, they
are closely watched and monitored by a number of federal agencies.

Questions About the Reading

1. According to Stephanie Brush, what is "gradual hysteria" and why do
   people fear it?
2. Who are the "ineffectual nebbishes" and why do they pose a threat to
   us?
3. According to the writer, what is "consciousness" and how are we
   spared from it?
4. Identify the presleep anxiety cycles that the author discusses.
5. What percentage of the population suffers from insomnia on any
   given night?
6. What are the three varieties of amnesia mentioned in the essay?
7. According to the writer, what is "brain-loss"?

Questions About the Writer's Strategies

1. Is the **thesis** of this essay directly stated or **implied?** If it is implied,
   state the thesis in your own words. If it is stated directly, where is it
   found?
2. Besides classification and division, what is another **mode of development** the writer uses in this essay? List **details** from the essay to support your answer.
3. Is the essay written **subjectively, objectively,** or a combination of
   both? Cite **examples** from the essay to support your answer.
4. Why do you think Brush uses a **humorous** tone in this essay? Identify
   examples in which humor masks serious ideas.

Writing Assignments

1. What are your biggest fears? Do they concern your own life or the future of the world? Are they about school, work, or even the environ-

ment? Write an essay in which you classify your different fears and give examples of each.

2. What things make you happy? Using classification and division as your mode of development, write an essay in which you describe your favorite things or activities. Include details and examples to support your statements.

6

Comparison
and Contrast

To COMPARE IS to show how items are alike. To **contrast** is to show how items are different. Thus comparison and contrast involve pointing out the similarities or differences between two (or more) items. Birdwatchers, for instance, may compare bird A with bird B by certain distinguishing marks, colors, and features.

In the preceding chapter, you learned about the **mode of development** called **classification and division**, and the comparison and contrast mode is related. In deciding what to compare or contrast, you will want to make sure that the items share points in common. Thus, the items compared are usually the same kind or **class** of things, and in comparing or contrasting them, you essentially establish two or more categories, showing the differences or similarities between or among them. For instance, you can compare two passenger cars—a Ford and a Chevrolet— with more precision than you can compare a Ford and a helicopter. Fords are compared with Chevrolets because they share many features in common—features that you can pinpoint. Similarly, you can usually compare two paintings more precisely than you can compare a novel and a painting.

Once you have picked out the closely related items, you will want to explain as clearly as possible the ways in which the items are alike or different. In any given piece of writing, you may want to use comparison only—or contrast only. Or you may decide to use some of both in the same essay. These three possibilities are illustrated in the following paragraphs. Notice, in each case, how the writer compares or contrasts *specific* points.

Comparison

A Buick and a Cadillac, both built by General Motors, are alike in many ways. A Buick, which measures over 200 inches in length and weighs over 3,000 pounds, is large and holds the road well. A Cadillac is similar in length and weight. Like a Buick, a Cadillac gets relatively low gas mileage compared with smaller economy cars made by the same manufacturer. The Buick provides an unusually comfortable ride, especially on cross-country trips on the highway, as does a Cadillac. And both cars enjoy a certain status as a luxury automobile.

Contrast

The twins are as different as two people can be. Sally, who is always hoping someone will have a party, has black hair, brown eyes, and an outgoing personality. She wants to be an actress or a popular singer. Susan, more serious and studious, has blonde hair, blue eyes, and a somewhat shy manner. Since she has done well in all her classes in graphic arts and math, she plans to become an architect or an engineer.

Mixed Comparison and Contrast

Most Americans would say it is not really possible to establish an ideal society. But time after time, a small dedicated group of people will drop out of the mainstream of American society to try, once more, to live according to the group's concept of an ideal society. Most of these groups have believed in holding their property in common. Most have used the word *family* to refer to all members of the group. Many of these groups, however, have differed widely in their attitudes toward sex and marriage.

Notice that all three of these paragraphs supply information but do not try to claim that one of the compared items is better or worse than the other. Notice, too, the **objective** tone of these paragraphs. However, writers also use comparison and contrast to support their opinions about subjects or to show how a certain thing or idea is superior to others in the same class. The writer of the second previous paragraph, for instance, could have used her information to support an opinion, as in the following revised paragraph.

The twins are as different as two people can be. Sally, who has black hair, brown eyes, and an outgoing, flighty personality, is always hoping someone will have a party. She fritters away her time and money shopping for the latest clothes, and she dreams of being an actress or a popular singer. But

Opinion

until she settles down and applies her energy to something useful, she will probably not be successful at anything. Susan, more serious and studious, has blonde hair, blue eyes, and a somewhat shy manner. Since she works hard and makes good use of her time, she has done well in all her

Opinion   classes in graphic arts and math. She plans to become an architect or an engineer and will no doubt be a good one.

As you plan a comparison-and-contrast composition, it is again very useful to **brainstorm** for items of comparison. That is, as described in Chapter 1, think about the subjects of your composition and jot down briefly whatever comes to mind about them. You can then pick and choose from your list in deciding on the contents of your comparison.

Organization

You should organize your comparison (or contrast) by whichever method suits your material best. One simple method is to explain one characteristic of item A, perhaps its cost, and then compare it immediately with the cost of item B—and then go on to compare the two items point by point. For example, in contrasting two chocolate cakes, you may first want to say cake A is more expensive to prepare than cake B. Second, you may say that cake A, requiring more steps and ingredients, takes more time than cake B. Third, cake A is richer—almost too rich—and sweeter than cake B. You may conclude by saying you recommend cake B. In this manner, the writer moves back and forth, mentioning the specific differences between cake A and cake B in an orderly manner.

When the writer compares (or contrasts) two objects item by item, it is called the *alternating* or *point-by-point* method. The following diagram shows how this method works in the earlier paragraph comparing Buicks and Cadillacs (page 190).

Alternating (or point-by-point) method

Topic sentence: "A Buick and a Cadillac . . . are alike in many ways."

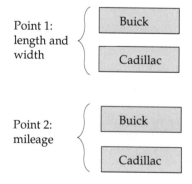

Point 1:
length and
width
   Buick
   Cadillac

Point 2:
mileage
   Buick
   Cadillac

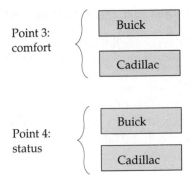

Point 3: comfort
- Buick
- Cadillac

Point 4: status
- Buick
- Cadillac

If the writer prefers a second type of organization, the *block* method, he or she explains all the characteristics of the first item together in a block and then explains all the characteristics of the second item in a corresponding block. The paragraph contrasting the twins Sally and Susan (page 190) is organized in this block method.

Block method

Topic sentence: "The twins are as different as two people can be."

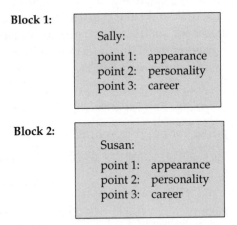

Block 1:

Sally:

point 1: appearance
point 2: personality
point 3: career

Block 2:

Susan:

point 1: appearance
point 2: personality
point 3: career

A third, *mixed* method is useful when the writer wants both to compare and contrast in the same paragraph. All the similarities of the two items may be explained first and then all the differences. (If the writer chooses, the differences may be explained first and then the similarities.) The following diagram shows this third method of organization, which was used in the paragraph on ideal societies (page 190).

Mixed comparison-and-contrast method

Topic sentence: "[P]eople . . . drop out of the mainstream of American society . . . to live according to the group's concept of an ideal society."

Block 1: comparisons

> Comparison
> * common property
> * group as "family"

Block 2: contrast

> Contrast
> * attitudes toward sex and marriage

You will want to use these same three methods—alternating, block, and mixed—in writing longer essays. In the following essay, the writer uses the alternating method of organization to contrast types of people.

There are only two types of people in the world, Type A and Type Z. It isn't hard to tell which type you are. How long before the plane leaves do you arrive at the airport?

Point 1: catching a plane

Early plane-catchers, Type A, pack their bags at least a day in advance, and they pack neatly. If they're booked on a flight that leaves at four in the afternoon, they get up at 5:30 that morning. If they haven't left the house by noon, they're worried about missing the plane.

Late plane-catchers, Type Z, pack hastily at the last minute and arrive at the airport too late to buy a newspaper.

Point 2: reading a book

What do you do with a new book? Type A reads more carefully and finishes every book, even though it isn't any good.

Type Z skims through a lot of books and is more apt to write in the margins with a pencil.

Point 3: eating breakfast

Type A eats a good breakfast; Type Z grabs a cup of coffee.

Point 4: turning off lights

Type As turn off the lights when leaving a room and lock the doors when leaving a house. They go back to make sure they've locked it, and they worry later about whether they left the iron on or not. They didn't.

Type Zs leave the lights burning and if they lock the door at all when they leave the house, they're apt to have forgotten their keys.

Point 5: seeing the dentist

Type A sees the dentist twice a year, has an annual physical checkup and thinks he may have something.

Type Z has been meaning to see a doctor.

Point 6: using toothpaste	Type A squeezes a tube of toothpaste from the bottom, rolls it very carefully as he uses it and puts the top back on every time. Type Z squeezes the tube from the middle, and he's lost the cap under the radiator.
Point 7: other characteristics	Type Zs are more apt to have some Type A characteristics than Type As are apt to have any Type Z characteristics.
Point 8: marriage	Type As always marry Type Zs. Type Zs always marry Type As.

Andy Rooney,
"Types"

The comparison and contrast mode of development gives Rooney a framework for making use of **irony**. Irony is a device used by writers to imply something different or the opposite from what is actually stated. Here, Rooney uses irony for its humorous effect, with the ultimate irony being that Type As and Type Zs always marry their opposites.

Comparison and contrast, like classification and division, is a useful mode of development for writing on the academic subjects you will study in college courses. You will encounter it in textbooks and, again, if you become comfortable with this mode, it will come in handy in your writing for other courses. Be alert, for example, to essay assignments and exam questions that begin "Compare and contrast. . . ."

In the readings that follow, you will find the alternating, block, and mixed methods of organizing comparison-and-contrast development. You will also see the variety of ideas that writers express through comparison and contrast.

Good Girl, Bad Girl

Anna Quindlen

Understanding why two people become friends is sometimes difficult. In this paragraph, essayist Anna Quindlen provides a candid assessment of an unbalanced friendship from her days at a boarding school for girls.

Words to Know

dialectical   contradiction between two conflicting forces
naïve   innocent
refectory   cafeteria, dining hall

Getting Started

What is it that attracts two friends to each other?

She was my best friend, and hard as it may have been to figure by the looks of us, she was the good girl, I the bad. I suppose everyone has at least one friendship like this in their lives. We were dialectical, she the thesis, I the antithesis. She was direct, trustworthy, kind, and naïve; I was manipulative, selfish, and clever. She laughed at all my jokes, took part in all my schemes, told everyone that I was the smartest and the funniest and the best. Like a B movie of boarding school life, we stole peanut butter from the refectory, short-sheeted beds, called drugstores and asked them if they had Prince Albert in a can. Whenever I hear a mother say, "If so-and-so told you to jump off the Brooklyn Bridge, would you do it?" I think of her. On my order, she would have jumped.

Questions About the Reading

1. How do you imagine the author and her friend looked? Reread the first sentence before you describe the two girls.
2. What does the writer mean when she says her exploits were "like a B movie of boarding school life"?

3. Does the writer believe she and her friend had a healthy relationship? Why or why not?

Questions About the Writer's Strategies

1. Is the writer's **mode of development** comparison, contrast, or a combination of the two?
2. What other mode of development does the writer use?
3. What words does the writer use to describe herself? What words does she use to describe how her friend thought of her?
4. What **simile** does the author use to describe the friendship?

Writing Assignments

1. Write a **narrative** paragraph that compares your personality with that of one of your closest friends.
2. Write a paragraph in which you compare and contrast a childhood friendship with a current friendship.
3. In a paragraph, compare and contrast a relationship between friends with one between brothers and sisters. Use examples from your own experience to show similarities and differences.

Two Views of Time

Robert Grudin

Is time a single entity, always having the same meaning? Hardly, says Robert Grudin in this passage. Time, he indicates, can be viewed in sharply contrasting ways, suggesting quite different realities.

Word to Know

cosmos   the universe

Getting Started

How does your personal concept of time affect your perceptions?

Imagine that you spent your whole life at a single house. Each day at the   1
same hour you entered an artificially-lit room, undressed and took up the same position in front of a motion picture camera. It photographed one frame of you per day, every day of your life. On your seventy-second birthday, the reel of film was shown. You saw yourself growing and aging over seventy-two years in less than half an hour (27.4 minutes at sixteen frames per second). Images of this sort, though terrifying, are helpful in suggesting unfamiliar but useful perspectives of time. They may, for example, symbolize the telescoped, almost momentary character of the past as seen through the eyes of an anxious or disaffected individual. Or they may suggest the remarkable brevity of our lives in the cosmic scale of time. If the estimated age of the cosmos were shortened to seventy-two years, a human life would take about ten seconds.

But look at time the other way. Each day is a minor eternity of over   2
86,000 seconds. During each second, the number of distinct molecular functions going on within the human body is comparable to the number of seconds in the estimated age of the cosmos. A few seconds are long enough for a revolutionary idea, a startling communication, a baby's conception, a wounding insult, a sudden death. Depending on how we think of them, our lives can be infinitely long or infinitely short.

Questions About the Reading

1. Which view of time do you prefer? Why?
2. What does the writer **imply** is useful about each view of time?
3. How old is the cosmos? (Don't grab your calculator. Just give a rough estimate in your own words.)

Questions About the Writer's Strategies

1. What method did the writer use to organize the passage?
2. What primary **mode of development** does the writer use for his contrast? Does he use more than one?
3. What is the **main idea** of this contrast? Where is the **thesis statement**?

Writing Assignments

1. Write a paragraph contrasting the amount of time it takes to do two different things; for example, writing a paragraph versus reading a paragraph, jogging a mile in the rain versus walking home from class on a pleasant day. Try to give a sense of how time *feels* in each situation.
2. In a paragraph, compare and contrast your views of time now with those you remember having as a child. Think, for instance, about the value you attach to time now versus the value you attached then, or about how quickly time seems to pass now versus then.

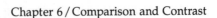

Jungle and Desert

Joseph Wood Krutch

In the study of the natural world, one could learn a great deal by comparing environments as dissimilar as deserts and jungles. After all, as Joseph Wood Krutch explains in this paragraph, every living thing, no matter where it lives, is engaged in a basic life-and-death struggle to survive.

Words to Know

mitigated   moderated, made less severe
proliferation   rapid growth
scant   bare, meager

Getting Started

How do you suppose plants and animals survive in extreme climates?

The way of the desert and the way of the jungle represent the two opposite methods of reaching stability at two extremes of density. In the jungle there is plenty of everything life needs except mere space, and it is not for the want of anything else that individuals die or that races have any limit set to their proliferation. Everything is on top of everything else; there is no cranny which is not both occupied and disputed. At every moment, war to the death rages fiercely. The place left vacant by any creature that dies is seized almost instantly by another, and life seems to suffer from nothing except too favorable an environment. In the desert, on the other hand, it is the environment itself which serves as the limiting factor. To some extent the struggle of creature against creature is mitigated, though it is of course not abolished even in the vegetable kingdom. For the plant which in the one place would be strangled to death by its neighbor dies a thirsty seedling in the desert because that same neighbor has drawn the scant moisture from the spot of earth out of which it was attempting to spring.

Questions About the Reading

1. What are the "two extremes of density" the writer refers to in the first sentence?
2. What does the writer mean when he says that life in the jungle suffers from "too favorable an environment"?
3. What is the difference in the way plants are killed by other plants in the two environments?

Questions About the Writer's Strategies

1. Is the **main idea** of the paragraph directly stated? If so, in which sentence(s)? If not, state the main idea in a sentence of your own.
2. Is the writer's **mode of development** comparison, contrast, or both?
3. Draw a diagram of the organizational method the writer uses (see pages 191–193).
4. Would you label this paragraph **subjective** or **objective**?

Writing Assignments

1. Write a paragraph that contrasts how a robin lives in a rural area to how it lives in an urban area.
2. Large cities are often referred to as jungles. In a paragraph, use comparison as your **mode of development** to compare life in a crowded city to life in a tropical jungle.
3. In a paragraph, compare and contrast your learning experiences in small discussion classes with learning experiences in large lecture classes. Use **examples** to show similarities and differences.

That Lean
and Hungry Look

Suzanne Britt

In this paragraph, taken from a humorous, sarcastic essay about being overweight, Suzanne Britt uses broad generalizations to contrast thin people and fat people.

Words to Know

chortling   chuckling joyfully

neurotic   a person suffering from anxiety or phobia, abnormal behavior

surly   domineering, gruff

wizened   withered

Getting Started

What are some of your preconceived notions about thin people and overweight people?

———

Some people say the business about the jolly fat person is a myth, that all of us chubbies are neurotic, sick, sad people. I disagree. Fat people may not be chortling all day long, but they're a hell of a lot *nicer* than the wizened and shriveled. Thin people turn surly, mean, and hard at a young age because they never learn the value of a hot-fudge sundae for easing tension. Thin people don't like gooey soft things because they themselves are neither gooey nor soft. They are crunchy and dull, like carrots. They go straight to the heart of the matter while fat people let things stay all blurry and hazy and vague, the way things actually are. Thin people want to face the truth. Fat people know there is no truth. One of my thin friends is always staring at complex, unsolvable problems and saying, "The key thing is. . . ." Fat people never say that. They know there isn't any such thing as the key thing about anything.

———

Questions About the Reading

1. Is the writer fat or thin? How do you know?
2. What does the writer imply about thin people's eating habits?
3. What is it that fat people know that thin people can't seem to grasp?

Questions About the Writer's Strategies

1. In your own words, state the **main idea** of this paragraph.
2. What **examples** does the writer use to clarify her contrast?
3. What words does the writer use to describe thin people? What is the meaning that is **implied** by these words?
4. What is **subjective** about this paragraph? How does this contribute to the humor of the selection?

Writing Assignments

1. Choose a facet of your personality or looks that could be described in a negative way and write a humorous paragraph that describes that trait in a positive light.
2. Write a paragraph in which you compare and contrast cats and dogs (or fish and birds) to explain which animal makes the best pet.
3. In an **objective** paragraph, compare and contrast thin and overweight people from a health perspective.

Eating American-style

Henry Petroski

Sometimes the most common of habits, such as how one greets an old friend or how one holds a knife and fork, can reveal a great deal about where one comes from. In this essay, Henry Petroski contrasts American diners with their counterparts in Europe and finds differences in style and history.

Getting Started

How do you suppose different methods of eating developed?

To most Europeans, the American way of using a knife and fork 1 involves a lot of wasted motion, with the fork being passed back and forth between left hand and right, the knife alternatively being set down on the edge of the plate and being picked up to slice off another piece of meat. As if the American style weren't confusing enough, the fork is turned upside down with each pass, so the tines curve downward when holding a piece of meat to be cut, and curve up when carrying food to the mouth.

To Americans, the European style of keeping a firm grasp on knife and 2 fork, each in its respective hand throughout the meal, is equally confusing. And the European manner of using the fork upside down, sometimes with food plastered high upon the back of its tines, is beyond comment.

The origins of these table manners may never be fully explained, but 3 one theory attributes their differences to the gradual emergence of the fork in Western culture. Of the common eating implements, the fork was the last to develop. Spoons can be traced back to prehistoric times, when shells were an improvement over cupped hands for holding water and other liquids. Fingers had long served to convey solid food to the mouth. The first knifelike objects were fashioned 8,000 years ago from sharp pieces of chipped flint and obsidian and were used as weapons and butchering tools. By the Middle Ages they had achieved a recognizably modern form, with pointy-ended blades and handles of wood, bone, brass, or horn. They were the only eating utensils for solid food.

Such methods of eating served people well until early in the 17th century, when a desire to eat foods that didn't cut easily under a single knife caused a second pointed knife to appear at well-set tables, or to be brought to the table by the sophisticated traveler. One knife held the food steady while the other cut it, and then the cut-off piece of food could be speared and carried to the mouth. Eventually the knife that held the food steady became blunt and broader at the tip so that it might be more effective for conveying to the mouth food that couldn't easily be speared. The use of two knives remained the custom of well-mannered diners until a new implement became available. 4

The earliest European table forks appeared in Italy a thousand years ago but fell out of use until the 14th century. They moved westward to France in 1533 and to England nearly a hundred years later. During this time, forks had two straight (rather than several curved) tines, and were grasped in the left hand. They were a great convenience for eating meat because the separate tines held the meat much more securely than a single knife point could. 5

By the end of the 17th century, forks had come into such widespread use in England that the point on the knife had lost its spearing function at the table. 6

In the American colonies, however, a different situation prevailed. Forks were harder to produce than knives, and so they didn't really become available here until the middle of the 18th century, when they were manufactured for export from England. The customary way of eating in the colonies was the old way, with a pair of pointed knives. When the new, blunt-ended knives began arriving from across the ocean—unaccompanied by forks—colonists, who had never used a knife blade to scoop up food, had to adopt the spoon as the utensil that conveyed food from plate to mouth. Since a colonist was also in the habit of holding a spoon in his right hand when conveying soup to his mouth, the knife was laid down after being used for cutting and the spoon in his left hand was passed to his right hand in order to scoop up the food. By the time forks finally became available in America, the manner of using the knife and spoon had become so customary that the fork merely replaced the spoon in the left hand and was used as the spoon had been. 7

Questions About the Reading

1. What was the inspiration for the development of the spoon?
2. How did people eat before forks were invented? Why did forks come to America so long after they were commonplace in Europe?

3. Based on how the writer compares European and American table manners, which do you think are the most efficient?

Questions About the Writer's Strategies

1. What is the **main idea** of the essay? Is it stated in a **thesis statement**? If so, in which sentence(s)? If not, state the main idea in a sentence of your own.
2. What kind of **order** did the writer use to organize the essay?
3. If you had never seen someone eat in the European style, what **details** in the essay would help you picture this method?
4. Has the writer written a **subjective** or **objective** essay? Support your answer.

Writing Assignments

1. Write an essay that compares how children eat ice-cream cones with how adults eat them. Keep a subjective tone throughout the essay.
2. In some cultures picking up food with your fingers is considered rude. Write a subjective essay from the point of view of someone who always uses a knife and fork, comparing his or her table manners with an American eating a hamburger, corn on the cob, and watermelon at a picnic.
3. In an essay, compare and contrast how people traveled before the invention of the automobile with how they travel now. Use point-by-point organization.
4. In Asia, rice has always been more of a dietary staple than meat. Write an essay that compares the use of knives and forks with chopsticks. Contrast the utensils and the traditional foods that are eaten with them.

Nursing Practices—England and America

Mary Madden

Mary Madden contrasts the way the important profession of nursing is practiced in England and in the United States. Her approach is a generous one. Until the last paragraph, she concentrates on the positive features of a nurse's life and work in each country. She leaves the drawbacks of working in each country unstated—though she implies them clearly.

Words to Know

restrictions limitations
vocation a regular occupation or profession

Getting Started

What accounts for there being very different approaches to the same job or problem?

I left my native Ireland after I had completed a high school education. 1
I studied to become a nurse and midwife in England, and I eventually came to the United States of America. Because I have worked five years in hospitals in England and the U.S.A., my friends frequently ask about differences, as I see them, in the practice of nursing on both sides of the Atlantic.

Until I realized how different the licensing laws of Great Britain are 2
from those in the United States, I was surprised at the number of restrictions placed on a nurse's actions in this country. A nurse licensed in Britain may practice anywhere in the British Isles and in some countries abroad; in the United States, the nurse must apply in every state in which she hopes to work.

In Britain, a nurse is a deeply respected, devoted woman, entrusted 3
with a vast amount of responsibility. The patients place unquestioned confidence in her judgment and advice. The doctor relies on her report of her observations, and he seldom interferes in what is considered a nursing duty.

The nurse decides when the patient is allowed out of bed or what type 4 of bath he may have. I do not recall ever seeing an order on a physician's chart such as "OOR in 24 hours" or "may take a shower." The nurse judges when a wound is healed and when sutures may be removed. She is always consulted about the patient's requirements and his progress. And because of the structure of most hospitals in England, the nurse is in view of the patient constantly. Whenever he needs attention, the nurse is there in the ward, and she may observe him, too, unobtrusively.

Furthermore, the nurse is a member of the health team who sees the 5 patient most frequently. To the patient she is the most familiar person in the strange hospital world.

In the United States, the patient is likely to be under the care of the 6 same doctor in and out of the hospital, so the doctor is the person the patient knows best and the one in whom he confides most easily. But though the patient's treatment and care are discussed with the nursing staff, a nurse is not allowed much freedom to advise a patient. Also, I have seen doctors visit patients without a word of communication to the nurse. Personally I think it difficult to be ignored when a patient's care is concerned and I think it prevents full utilization of the nurse's knowledge and skills.

I myself found nursing practice easier, in a way, under the so-called 7 "socialized medicine" of Great Britain than the more individual type of medical care found in the United States. It involved much less writing and left me at the patient's bedside, where I am happiest. There was no need to write several charges and requests for the needs of the patient. Stocks of drugs and other medicines were kept on each ward, so that when medication was ordered, it was at hand. All charges were met by "National Health"—including all supplies and equipment used on the ward. The nurse tends a person who is free from much anxiety and hence more easily cared for while he is an inpatient.

On the other hand, I found that my introduction to an American hospi- 8 tal was a happy experience. As a new nurse, I was guided by an orientation program given by another nurse and quickly found my place on the patient care team. I had never experienced such an orientation in England.

Policy, drug reference, and procedure books at the nurses' station pro- 9 vide a ready reference where a nurse may check facts when she is in doubt, and she can instruct a new nurse on the staff without confusion. The active U.S. nurse, while working, can keep informed about new trends, discoveries, and inventions in a rapidly changing world of medicine.

Here in the United States the nurse is regarded as an individual person 10 and her personal life outside the hospital is given consideration. She develops interests in arts, sport or a creative hobby; she is encouraged to further her education. Time and means are available to her to expand her horizons and to enrich her personality. Many nurses combine marriage and a career very ably in this country, but not in England or Ireland. All this tends to involve her more with people other than the sick. She is an interesting, informed, and happy person and at the bedside she can show understanding and perception.

In Britain, like most nurses, I lived in a nurses' home on the hospital 11 grounds and was thus isolated in a special hospital community. Theoretically I worked eight hours each day that I was on duty. But these hours were so arranged that one went to work twice in one day. One might work four hours in the morning, have a few hours free, and then go back to the ward for the evening. This schedule demands most of one's waking hours, and so mingling in the larger community outside the hospital was quite limited. The nurse was expected to find full satisfaction in her vocation, and thoughts of increases in salary were considered unworthy. Now, such attitudes are beginning to change and the winds of unrest are blowing through nursing in England, ruffling many a well-placed cap.

Questions About the Reading

1. What is the relationship between nurse and patient in the United States? How does this relationship differ from that found in Great Britain?
2. Does the writer suggest that nurses in the United States are not respected by doctors? Cite statements in the essay to support your answer.
3. How does Great Britain's "socialized" health-care system affect nursing practice?
4. Based on what the essay says about the nursing profession in the two countries, in which do you think patients would receive better care? Why do you feel this way?

Questions About the Writer's Strategies

1. Does the writer express opinions on whether it is better to work as a nurse in the United States or in England? Are the writer's opinions directly stated or **implied**?
2. Is the essay as a whole organized according to the point-by-point method, the block method, or the mixed comparison-and-contrast method?

3. Do you think the writer's main **purpose** in the essay is to supply information or to judge the quality of English nursing care versus care in the United States?
4. In your own words, state the **thesis** of this essay.

Writing Assignments

1. Write an essay comparing and contrasting the teaching styles of two college instructors. Use the point-by-point method to organize your essay.
2. Using the block method of organization, write an essay comparing and contrasting one of the following pairs: older brothers/older sisters, houses/dormitories, riding the bus/walking, or high school classes/college classes.

The Difference Between a Brain and a Computer

Isaac Asimov

Most scientists and knowledgeable observers agree that computers will change our lives more completely than the automobile did, than television did, or than any technological innovation has so far. How far can computers go? Science writer Isaac Asimov here compares the computer with the human brain. His conclusions may frighten you. They're sure to make you stop and think.

Words to Know

components   individual parts

conceiving   forming an idea

mammal   the class of animals, including human beings, that have backbones and controlled body temperature and nurse their young

neurons   nerve cells

program   a set of directions, instructions, or rules

Getting Started

Do you believe a computer will ever be built that is as complex as the human brain?

$\mathbf{T}$he difference between a brain and a computer can be expressed in a single word: complexity.

The large mammalian brain is the most complicated thing, for its size, known to us. The human brain weighs three pounds, but in that three pounds are ten billion neurons and a hundred billion smaller cells. These many billions of cells are interconnected in a vastly complicated network that we can't begin to unravel as yet.

Even the most complicated computer man has yet built can't compare in intricacy with the brain. Computer switches and components number in the thousands rather than in the billions. What's more, the computer switch is just an on-off device, whereas the brain cell is itself possessed of a tremendously complex inner structure.

Can a computer think? That depends on what you mean by "think." If 4
solving a mathematical problem is "thinking," then a computer can
"think" and do so much faster than a man. Of course, most mathematical
problems can be solved quite mechanically by repeating certain straightforward processes over and over again. Even the simple computers of
today can be geared for that.

It is frequently said that computers solve problems only because they 5
are "programmed" to do so. They can only do what men have them do.
One must remember that human beings also can only do what they are
"programmed" to do. Our genes "program" us the instant the fertilized
ovum is formed, and our potentialities are limited by that "program."

Our "program" is so much more enormously complex, though, that we 6
might like to define "thinking" in terms of the creativity that goes into
writing a great play or composing a great symphony, in conceiving a brilliant scientific theory or a profound ethical judgment. In that sense, computers certainly can't think and neither can most humans.

Surely, though, if a computer can be made complex enough, it can be 7
as creative as we. If it could be made as complex as a human brain, it
could be the equivalent of a human brain and do whatever a human brain
can do.

To suppose anything else is to suppose that there is more to the human 8
brain than the matter that composes it. The brain is made up of cells in a
certain arrangement and the cells are made up of atoms and molecules in
certain arrangements. If anything else is there, no signs of it have ever
been detected. To duplicate the material complexity of the brain is therefore to duplicate everything about it.

But how long will it take to build a computer complex enough to du- 9
plicate the human brain? Perhaps not as long as some think. Long before
we approach a computer as complex as our brain, we will perhaps build
a computer that is at least complex enough to design another computer
more complex than itself. This more complex computer could design one
still more complex and so on and so on and so on.

In other words, once we pass a certain critical point, the computers 10
take over and there is a "complexity explosion." In a very short time
thereafter, computers may exist that not only duplicate the human
brain—but far surpass it.

Then what? Well, mankind is not doing a very good job of running the 11
earth right now. Maybe, when the time comes, we ought to step grace-
fully aside and hand over the job to someone who can do it better. And if
we don't step aside, perhaps Supercomputer will simply move in and
push us aside.

Questions About the Reading

1. What makes the human brain more complex than a computer?
2. Can a computer be built that would duplicate the human brain? Explain your answer.
3. What processes of the human brain can be duplicated by a computer?
4. Can a computer be creative? Explain your answer.
5. What might happen to humanity if a computer were built that could surpass the human brain?

Questions About the Writer's Strategies

1. In your own words, explain the **thesis** of this essay.
2. What does the writer think of human beings? Which sentences express his attitude?
3. Which paragraphs provide information primarily on the computer? Which paragraphs deal mainly with the human brain? Which does Asimov spend more time describing? Why?
4. Besides comparison and contrast, what primary **mode of development** does the writer use in forming his paragraphs?

Writing Assignments

1. Write an essay in which you compare and contrast the human memory with the memory of a computer. Do you think each can remember the same kinds of things? Is each equally capable of remembering things?
2. At the end of the essay, Asimov suggests that a supercomputer could one day move in and push people aside. Write an essay comparing a person's everyday life with life in a supercomputer society.
3. Asimov maintains that there is nothing more to the human brain than its material substance—that the brain is just "atoms and molecules in certain arrangements. If anything else is there, no signs of it have ever been detected." Do you agree? Write an essay in which you compare and contrast Asimov's description of the brain with your own views.

Aria

Richard Rodriguez

Language is what connects us to other people. In the beginning that connection is to our family, and then we learn to communicate with the outside world. For bilingual children in America, the first language is the one associated with home. The second language is learned later, to be used in public with strangers. In this essay, Richard Rodriguez recalls how life for a native Spanish speaker in an English-speaking world begins—with the first discernment of how different the two languages actually sound.

Words to Know

gaudy   tasteless, tacky
guttural   produced in the throat
polysyllabic   words with more than three syllables
syntax   grammar, formation of sentences

Getting Started

How do unfamiliar foreign languages sound to you?

———————

I grew up in a house where the only regular guests were my relations. 1 For one day, enormous families of relatives would visit and there would be so many people that the noise and the bodies would spill out to the backyard and front porch. Then, for weeks, no one came by. (It was usually a salesman who rang the doorbell.) Our house stood apart. A gaudy yellow in a row of white bungalows. We were the people with the noisy dog. The people who raised pigeons and chickens. We were the foreigners on the block. A few neighbors smiled and waved. We waved back. But no one in the family knew the names of the old couple who lived next door; until I was seven years old, I did not know the names of the kids who lived across the street.

In public, my father and mother spoke a hesitant, accented, not al- 2 ways grammatical English. And they would have to strain—their bodies tense—to catch the sense of what was rapidly said by *los gringos*. At home they spoke Spanish. The language of their Mexican past sounded in counterpoint to the English of public society. The words would come quickly, with ease. Conveyed through those sounds was the pleasing, soothing, consoling reminder of being at home.

During those years when I was first conscious of hearing, my mother 3 and father addressed me only in Spanish; in Spanish I learned to reply. By contrast, English (*inglés*), rarely heard in the house, was the language I came to associate with *gringos*. I learned my first words of English overhearing my parents speak to strangers. At five years of age, I knew just enough English for my mother to trust me on errands to stores one block away. No more.

I was a listening child, careful to hear the very different sounds of 4 Spanish and English. Wide-eyed with hearing, I'd listen to sounds more than words. First, there were English (*gringo*) sounds. So many words were still unknown that when the butcher or the lady at the drugstore said something to me, exotic polysyllabic sounds would bloom in the midst of their sentences. Often, the speech of people in public seemed to me very loud, booming with confidence. The man behind the counter would literally ask, 'What can I do for you?' But by being so firm and so clear, the sound of his voice said that he was a *gringo*; he belonged in public society.

I would also hear then the high nasal notes of middle-class American 5 speech. The air stirred with sound. Sometimes, even now, when I have been traveling abroad for several weeks, I will hear what I heard as a boy. In hotel lobbies or airports, in Turkey or Brazil, some Americans will pass, and suddenly I will hear it again—the high sound of American voices. For a few seconds I will hear it with pleasure, for it is now the sound of my society—a reminder of home. But inevitably—already on the flight headed for home—the sound fades with repetition. I will be unable to hear it anymore.

When I was a boy, things were different. The accent of *los gringos* was 6 never pleasing nor was it hard to hear. Crowds at Safeway or at bus stops would be noisy with sound. And I would be forced to edge away from the chirping chatter above me.

I was unable to hear my own sounds, but I knew very well that I spoke 7 English poorly. My words could not stretch far enough to form complete thoughts. And the words I did speak I didn't know well enough to make into distinct sounds. (Listeners would usually lower their heads, better to hear what I was trying to say.) But it was one thing for *me* to speak English with difficulty. It was more troubling for me to hear my parents speak in public: their high-whining vowels and guttural consonants; their sentences that got stuck with "eh" and "ah" sounds; the confused syntax; the hesitant rhythm of sounds so different from the way *gringos* spoke. I'd notice, moreover, that my parents' voices were softer than those of *gringos* we'd meet.

But then there was Spanish. *Español*: my family's language. *Español*: 8 the language that seemed to me a private language. I'd hear strangers on the radio and in the Mexican Catholic church across town speaking in Spanish, but I couldn't really believe that Spanish was a public language, like English. Spanish speakers, rather, seemed related to me, for I sensed that we shared—through our language—the experience of feeling apart from *los gringos*. It was thus a ghetto Spanish that I heard and I spoke. Like those whose lives are bound by a barrio, I was reminded by Spanish of my separateness from *los otros, los gringos* in power. But more intensely than for most barrio children—because I did not live in a barrio—Spanish seemed to me the language of home. (Most days it was only at home that I'd hear it.) It became the language of joyful return.

A family member would say something to me and I would feel myself 9 specially recognized. My parents would say something to me and I would feel embraced by the sounds of their words. Those sounds said: *I am speaking with ease in Spanish. I am addressing you in words I never use with* los gringos. *I recognize you as someone special, close, like no one outside. You belong with us. In the family.*

Questions About the Reading

1. How did the writer's parents sound to him when they spoke in Spanish? How did that differ from how they sounded in English?
2. How would the writer's experience have been different if he had grown up in a barrio?
3. How have Richard Rodriguez's feelings changed about the English language?

Questions About the Writer's Strategies

1. Is the writer's **mode of development** comparison, contrast, or both? Support your answer.
2. In your own words state the **thesis** of this essay.
3. What **examples** does the writer use to clarify his thesis?
4. Is the writer being judgmental about the sound of Spanish or English? What does he **imply** about being bilingual, no matter what the languages?

Writing Assignments

1. Write an essay that contrasts the comfort you feel with your native language with how you feel about a language you have studied or overheard.
2. Compare and contrast a conversation with someone in your family about cooking a meal to a conversation on the same subject with a clerk in a grocery store.
3. In an essay, compare and contrast how you speak to infants and very young children with how you speak to friends at a party. Use examples to express the differences in language, tone, and sound.

Through the One-Way Mirror

Margaret Atwood

Margaret Atwood is a novelist who lives in Toronto. She has strong opinions about the unequal relationship between Canada and the United States, and in this essay she expresses them with wit and contempt. Although she pokes fun at her own country, the bulk of her criticism is leveled at the United States.

Words to Know

bunion-toed   having a large painful bump on the big toe
construe   interpret
decipherable   understandable
Mr. Magoo   a cartoon character—a funny little, extremely near-sighted man
myopia   nearsightedness
protoplasmic   having the formless, goopy quality of the stuff of which living cells are made

Getting Started

What do you think causes the similarities and differences between neighboring towns, states, or countries?

The noses of a great many Canadians resemble Porky Pig's. This comes 1 from spending so much time pressing them against the longest undefended one-way mirror in the world. The Canadians looking through this mirror behave the way people on the hidden side of such mirrors usually do: they observe, analyze, ponder, snoop and wonder what all the activity on the other side means in decipherable human terms.

The Americans, bless their innocent little hearts, are rarely aware that 2 they are even being watched, much less by the Canadians. They just go on doing body language, playing in the sandbox of the world, bashing one another on the head and planning how to blow things up, same as always. If they think about Canada at all, it's only when things get a bit snowy or the water goes off or the Canadians start fussing over some piddly detail, such as fish. Then they regard them as unpatriotic; for

Americans don't really see Canadians as foreigners, not like the Mexicans, unless they do something weird like speak French or beat the New York Yankees at baseball. Really, think the Americans, the Canadians are just like us, or would be if they could.

Or we could switch metaphors and call the border the longest unde- 3 fended backyard fence in the world. The Canadians are the folks in the neat little bungalow, with the tidy little garden and the duck pond. The Americans are the other folks, the ones in the sprawly mansion with the bad-taste statues on the lawn. There's a perpetual party, or something, going on there—loud music, raucous laughter, smoke billowing from the barbecue. Beer bottles and Coke cans land among the peonies. The Canadians have their own beer bottles and barbecue smoke, but they tend to overlook it. Your own mess is always more forgivable than the mess someone else makes on your patio.

The Canadians can't exactly call the police—they suspect that the 4 Americans are the police—and part of their distress, which seems permanent, comes from their uncertainty as to whether or not they've been invited. Sometimes they do drop by next door, and find it exciting but scary. Sometimes the Americans drop by their house and find it clean. This worries the Canadians. They worry a lot. Maybe those Americans will want to buy up their duck pond, with all the money they seem to have, and turn it into a cesspool or a water-skiing emporium.

It also worries them that the Americans don't seem to know who the 5 Canadians are, or even where, exactly, they are. Sometimes the Americans call Canada their backyard, sometimes their front yard, both of which imply ownership. Sometimes they say they are the Mounties and the Canadians are Rose Marie. (All these things have, in fact, been said by American politicians.) Then they accuse the Canadians of being paranoid and having an identity crisis. Heck, there is no call for the Canadians to fret about their identity, because everyone knows they're Americans, really. If the Canadians disagree with that, they're told not to be so insecure.

One of the problems is that Canadians and Americans are educated 6 backward from one another. The Canadians—except for the Quebecois, one keeps saying—are taught about the rest of the world first and Canada second. The Americans are taught about the United States first, and maybe later about other places, if they're of strategic importance. The Vietnam War draft dodgers got more culture shock in Canada than they did in Sweden. It's not the clothing that is different, it's those mental noises.

Of course, none of this holds true when you get close enough, where 7 concepts like "Americans" and "Canadians" dissolve and people are just people, or anyway some of them are, the ones you happen to approve of. I, for instance, have never met any Americans I didn't like, but I only get to meet the nice ones. That's what the businessmen think too, though they have other individuals in mind. But big-scale national mythologies have a way of showing up in things like foreign policy, and at events like international writers' congresses, where the Canadians often find they have more to talk about with the Australians, the West Indians, the New Zealanders and even the once-loathed snooty Brits, now declining into humanity with the dissolution of empire, than they do with the impenetrable and mysterious Yanks.

But only sometimes. Because surely the Canadians understand the 8 Yanks. Shoot, don't they see Yank movies, read Yank mags, bobble round to Yank music and watch Yank telly, as well as their own, when there is any?

Sometimes the Canadians think it's their job to interpret the Yanks 9 to the rest of the world; explain them, sort of. This is an illusion: they don't understand the Yanks as much as they think they do, and it isn't their job.

But, as we say up here among God's frozen people, when Washington 10 catches a cold, Ottawa sneezes. Some Canadians even refer to their capital city as Washington North and wonder why we're paying those guys in Ottawa when a telephone order service would be cheaper. Canadians make jokes about the relationship with Washington which the Americans, in their thin-skinned, bunion-toed way, construe as anti-American (they tend to see any nonworshipful comment coming from that gray, protoplasmic fuzz outside their borders as anti-American). They are no more anti-American than the jokes Canadians make about the weather: it's there, it's big, it's hard to influence, and it affects your life.

Of course, in any conflict with the Dreaded Menace, whatever it might 11 be, the Canadians would line up with the Yanks, probably, if they thought it was a real menace, or if the Yanks twisted their arms or other bodily parts enough or threatened a "scorched-earth policy" (another real quote). Note the qualifiers. The Canadian idea of a menace is not the same as the U.S. one. Canada, for instance, never broke off diplomatic relations with Cuba, and it was quick to recognize China. Contemplating the U.S.-Soviet growling match, Canadians are apt to recall a line from Blake: "They became what they beheld." Certainly both superpowers suffer from the imperial diseases once so noteworthy among the Romans, the British and the French: arrogance and myopia. But the bodily-parts threat is real enough, and accounts for the observable wimpiness and flunkiness of some Ottawa politicians. Nobody, except at welcoming-committee time, pretends this is an equal relationship.

Americans don't have Porky Pig noses. Instead they have Mr. Magoo 12
eyes, with which they see the rest of the world. That would not be a problem if the United States were not so powerful. But it is, so it is.

Questions About the Reading

1. Why do Canadians "suspect that the Americans are the police" (paragraph 4)?
2. In paragraph 8, what comment is the writer making about Canadian
   culture?
3. In paragraph 10, what is meant by the expression, "When Washington
   catches a cold, Ottawa sneezes"?
4. What is the "Dreaded Menace" (paragraph 11)?
5. In the writer's view, what is the American attitude toward Canada?
   Briefly state her opinion in your own words.

Questions About the Writer's Strategies

1. What is the earlier **metaphor** (the one from which she is switching)
   that the writer refers to in paragraph 3?
2. Which paragraphs make up the **introduction** in this essay? Which
   ones form the **body**? And which ones are the **conclusion**?
3. What is the main contrast between Canadians and Americans? Try to
   isolate and put in your own words the writer's main point.
4. Do you think the writer's presentation is fair to the United States?
   Does it include as much information as it should about the issues the
   writer raises?

Writing Assignments

1. Think of two cities or two states. Write an essay describing how they
   are *alike*. Use the point-by-point method to organize your comparison.
   (If you have ever been to a foreign country, you might prefer to describe points of similarity between that country and the United States.)
2. Write a comparison-and-contrast essay on two kinds of food, such as
   Chinese food and Italian food, food of the southern and northeastern
   United States, Mexican food and Greek food, or food from some other
   pair of cooking traditions. Try to write a mixed comparison and contrast, identifying similarities as well as differences.

Women and Men

Scott Russell Sanders

Scott Russell Sanders grew up among poor farmers, laborers, and factory workers. The men in this world faced endless toil. But Sanders was also exposed as a boy to soldiers on military bases, and he came to view soldiering as the only available alternative to a life of toil—the warrior, faced not with toil, but with waiting, killing, and death. As he explains in this essay, when Sanders reached college and learned that men were viewed as oppressors by the women there, it was not easy for him to relate that idea to his experience of what manhood meant.

Word to Know

fretted   worried

Getting Started

Are the same opportunities for work and pleasure equally available to men and women?

I was slow to understand the deep grievances of women. This was be- 1 cause, as a boy, I had envied them. Before college, the only people I had ever known who were interested in art or music or literature, the only ones who read books, the only ones who ever seemed to enjoy a sense of ease and grace were the mothers and daughters. Like the menfolk, they fretted about money, they scrimped and made-do. But, when the pay stopped coming in, they were not the ones who had failed. Nor did they have to go to war, and that seemed to me a blessed fact. By comparison with the narrow, ironclad days of fathers, there was an expansiveness, I thought, in the days of mothers. They went to see neighbors, to shop in town, to run errands at school, at the library, at church. No doubt, had I looked harder at their lives, I would have envied them less. It was not my fate to become a woman, so it was easier for me to see the graces. Few of them held jobs outside the home, and those who did filled thankless roles as clerks and waitresses. I didn't see, then, what a prison a house could be, since houses seemed to me brighter, handsomer places than any factory. I did not realize—because such things were never spoken of— how often women suffered from men's bullying. I did learn about the wretchedness of abandoned wives, single mothers, widows; but I also learned about the wretchedness of lone men. Even then I could see how exhausting it was for a mother to cater all day to the needs of young children. But if I had been asked, as a boy, to choose between tending a baby and tending a machine, I think I would have chosen the baby. (Having now tended both, I know I would choose the baby.)

So I was baffled when the women at college accused me and my sex of 2 having cornered the world's pleasures. I think something like my bafflement has been felt by other boys (and by girls as well) who grew up in dirt-poor farm country, in mining country, in black ghettos, in Hispanic barrios, in the shadows of factories, in Third World nations—any place where the fate of men is as grim and bleak as the fate of women. Toilers and warriors. I realize now how ancient these identities are, how deep the tug they exert on men, the undertow of a thousand generations. The miseries I saw, as a boy, in the lives of nearly all men I continue to see in the lives of many—the body-breaking toil, the tedium, the call to be tough, the humiliating powerlessness, the battle for a living and for territory.

When the women I met at college thought about the joys and privileges 3 of men, they did not carry in their minds the sort of men I had known in my childhood. They thought of their fathers, who were bankers, physicians, architects, stockbrokers, the big wheels of the big cities. These fathers rode the train to work or drove cars that cost more than any of my childhood houses. They were attended from morning to night by female helpers, wives and nurses and secretaries. They were never laid off, never short of cash at month's end, never lined up for welfare. These fathers made decisions that mattered. They ran the world.

The daughters of such men wanted to share in this power, this glory. 4 So did I. They yearned for a say over their future, for jobs worthy of their abilities, for the right to live at peace, unmolested, whole. Yes, I thought, yes yes. The difference between me and these daughters was that they saw me, because of my sex, as destined from birth to become like their fathers, and therefore as an enemy to their desires. But I knew better. I wasn't an enemy, in fact or in feeling. I was an ally. If I had known, then, how to tell them so, would they have believed me? Would they now?

Questions About the Reading

1. Why did the writer envy women when he was a boy?
2. Explain the "bafflement" the writer feels and believes others feel (paragraph 2).

3. In addition to women and men, what other groups is the writer comparing and contrasting here? What overlaps are there among the different groups?
4. Which of the groups that he describes does the writer identify with most closely? Cite statements from the essay to support your answer.
5. Because he received a scholarship, Sanders was able to go to a university attended by students from wealthy families. What was his attitude toward these students? Why do you think he chose an elite university over a less prestigious one?

Questions About the Writer's Strategies

1. Identify the **introduction, body,** and **conclusion** in this essay.
2. What is the **main idea** of the essay? Is there a **thesis statement**? If so, where is it? If not, state the main idea in your own words.
3. Is this essay written **objectively** or **subjectively**? Identify objective or subjective elements, or both, in the writer's presentation.
4. Is the writer being judgmental? What does he **imply** about the groups he compares and contrasts?

Writing Assignments

1. Compare or contrast two or more social groups at your school—for instance, jocks, nerds, fraternity or sorority types, business majors, art majors, party-goers, or social activists.
2. Look again at the examples essay "My Mother Never Worked" on page 140. Contrast Sanders's view of the women of his childhood with the view presented by Smith-Yackel. In doing so, feel free to offer opinions about each writer's attitude toward women.

Pediatricians

Denise Washington (student)

Most people would agree that being a good doctor demands more than a medical school degree. Before the writer of the following essay became a parent, she might not have been able to describe her ideal doctor. Four years of parenting, however, have made Denise Washington an expert on the subject of pediatricians.

Words to Know

compulsive   caused by obsession or irresistible impulse
unwarranted   unfounded, groundless

Getting Started

What do you think are the most important qualities of a good doctor?

I am a compulsive worrying mother. I am always rushing one of the 1 children to the emergency room or a doctor's office at any sign of abnormality. Consequently, during my four years as a parent, I have come into contact with many pediatricians. Although I can understand what goes through doctors' minds when they encounter an anxious, raving mother, their feelings should have nothing to do with the kind of attention they give to the mother and her children.

For example, my former pediatrician, Dr. Kyle, did not listen to my 2 concerns as a parent. We usually visited Dr. Kyle's office in the afternoon. Perhaps she was sleepy from lunch or had other things on her mind, but she always seemed distracted. The last time she saw the children, she left the examining room four times. Each time she returned, I had to repeat what we had already discussed.

Although I had thought a woman doctor would be especially under- 3 standing of and sympathetic to a mother's concerns, Dr. Kyle was not. Because my younger daughter had respiratory failure at birth, I worry about her development. Instead of reassuring me that my concerns were unwarranted, Dr. Kyle flatly dismissed them as having no merit.

Finally, it seemed to me that Dr. Kyle was less concerned about my 4 children's health than what kind of insurance I carried. The amount of money a doctor is to be paid for attending to my children should not influence her attention to my parental concerns about their health.

Fortunately, I have found a pediatrician who listens to my thoughts 5 and concerns. No matter what is going on outside of the examining room during our visits, Dr. Johnson is courteous enough to ignore the distractions and finish examining my children before leaving the room.

He is also very understanding about my parental concerns. For 6 example, my oldest daughter had trouble learning to walk. Dr. Johnson called in three other doctors to check her leg development, and he also asked me if I wanted to schedule X-rays of her legs if I was not satisfied with the specialists' opinion. Instead of my concern being dismissed as unwarranted, Dr. Johnson's findings reassured me that she would be all right.

Unlike Dr. Kyle, Dr. Johnson does not seem concerned about the kind 7 of insurance I carry. No matter what kind of insurance I have, he always gives me and my children his full attention and is concerned about my concerns for their health and development.

Not all pediatricians are alike. Their treatment of mothers and young 8 children differs as much as their personalities. But every pediatrician should be like Dr. Johnson. The health and development of their young patients may depend on how well they listen to the worried, anxious, and sometimes raving mother.

Questions About the Reading

1. Why is the writer always rushing one of her children to see a doctor?
2. What was Washington's complaint about Dr. Kyle?
3. Why do you think the writer believed that a woman doctor would be the most sympathetic to her needs?
4. According to the writer, what was Dr. Kyle's primary concern?
5. What did Washington like about Dr. Johnson?

Questions About the Writer's Strategies

1. What is the writer contrasting? What method does she use to organize the items she is contrasting?
2. What is the **thesis** of this essay? Is it directly stated? If so, where is it located? If not, state the thesis in your own words.
3. Apart from comparison and contrast, what other **mode of development** does the writer use to develop her essay?

Writing Assignments

1. What is your definition of a good doctor? How is a good doctor different from a bad doctor? Compare and contrast the two. If you wish, you may use **examples,** either made up or from your own experience, to help build your essay.
2. Do you think adequate health care is available to every citizen in this country? How might our health-care system be improved? Write an essay in which you compare and contrast the present state of health care in this country with its future possibilities.

7

Process

IF YOU WANT to learn to make coffee in your new percolator, you will probably follow the directions provided by the manufacturer that explain the whole process. A **process** is a method of doing a task or a job, usually in orderly steps, to achieve a desired result. For example, directions and recipes are both detailed explanations of processes. So are all articles and essays that tell how to prepare for a job interview, how to assemble a stereo system, how to dress for success, or how to operate a microcomputer. So, too, are essays that describe how someone else used a process to accomplish something or complete a task.

In an essay explaining how to carry out a process, the writer tries to give clear and accurate guidance or directions, making the steps as simple as possible for the reader to follow. To do this, the writer must decide exactly what the reader already knows and what he or she needs to be told. The burden is on the writer to provide complete information to enable the reader to perform the task. If the writer forgets to mention how long the cookies should bake, the cook may be left with burned chocolate chip cookies and disappointed friends.

The written explanation of such a process must be organized with particular care. Each step or part of the directions should be discussed in the same order as it occurs in the process. The following sample paragraph is a recipe for shrimp—one you might want to try. Notice that the writer begins with the purchase of the shrimp and then proceeds, step by step, through preparing, cooking, and serving the shrimp.

Topic sentence ☐ When fresh shrimp can be had, have it. What size? Medium
for reasons of economy and common sense. Huge shrimps

Step 1: choose size	are magnificently expensive while small ones come in such numbers per pound that shelling them becomes slave labor.
Step 2: choose quantity	Buy two pounds of fresh shrimp and shell them. First, with
Step 3: shell shrimp	a thumbnail pinch the tail shell hard crosswise (so the tail segments will come out intact), then handle the headless ani- mals like so many pea pods; split them lengthwise, save the contents, and throw the husks away. Sauté the shrimp with
Step 4: cooking directions	three crushed garlic cloves in two-thirds of a stick of butter. When the shrimp turn pink, add a 12-ounce can of Italian to- matoes (which taste better than the fresh supermarket kind), two bay leaves, a teaspoon of dried oregano, a half-cup of dry white wine, and the juice of a lemon. Simmer for ten minutes, sprinkle with chopped parsley and serve with rice.

Philip Kopper,
"Delicacies de la Mer"

Because this paragraph is telling the reader what to do, it is written in the second **person** (*you*), present tense (*come, buy, save, throw*, and so forth), but the word *you* is unstated, which makes the paragraph seem to address the reader even more directly. This **tone** is commonly used in process writing that instructs the reader.

Not all process essays are such clear-cut models of process writing as the previous paragraph. In some cases, a paragraph or essay describing a process may serve a purpose similar to that of a **narrative** or a **description**. That is, whereas strictly process writing is primarily intended to *instruct*, process writing can also be adapted to situations in which the writer mainly wants to *inform* or *describe*. In such cases, a process is often combined with narration and description, as in the following example. Notice that in describing the process—the way the woman packs her suitcases and leaves the house—the writer describes her character. You also know, by the contrast between her habits and those of her husband, that her basic character differs sharply from his. By detailing the process of packing and combining it with other narrative details, the writer tells you indirectly what has previously happened in the woman's life.

Introduction— narrative	He slammed the door angrily behind him, and she heard the squeal of the tires as he raced off in the car. For a moment, she felt her usual fear. She knew he shouldn't drive after he'd been drinking heavily.	1
Step 1: preparation	But then she turned, went to the linen closet, and took out a clean towel. She spread the towel out on her neatly made bed.	2
Step 2: finding suitcases	Next, she got her overnight bag and a larger suitcase from the closet and put them carefully on the towel on her bed.	3
Step 3: packing suitcases	Methodically, she took neatly folded underwear, stockings, and nightgowns from her drawers and packed them in neat rows in the two bags. One set in the overnight bag, and five	

in the larger suitcase. She laid aside a nightgown with a matching robe to pack last.

Next, she lifted dresses and suits, carefully hung on the hangers and buttoned up so they wouldn't wrinkle, from her closet and folded them into the larger suitcase. Two extra blouses and a dress went into the overnight bag. She'd wear the suit she had on.   4

She brought plastic bags from the kitchen and put her shoes into them. One pair went into the overnight bag; two pairs, one for the dresses and one for the suits, went into the larger bag. Then she put her bedroom slippers and the night-gown with the matching robe on top of the other clothes in the overnight bag. She would take only the overnight bag into her parents' house, at least at first. No need for them to know right away that this time was for more than one night. They'd always said that she wasn't going to change him and that the marriage wouldn't last.   5

Step 4: final check and look around

She sighed again, closed the suitcases, carried them out to her car, and then went back into the house for one last look around. Almost ready, she took her coat from the hall closet, folded it carefully over her arm, and took a last look at his shoes and socks left beside his chair and the newspaper flung across the couch where it would leave newsprint on the up-holstery. She left the shoes and socks but couldn't resist fold-ing the newspaper and putting it on a table. Finally, she went out, closed the door silently behind her, got into her car, and drove quietly and slowly away.   6

As you started reading this essay, you probably realized right away that it would be more narrative and descriptive than instructive of a process. Two signals that alerted you are that the writing is in the **third person** (*she*) and in the past tense (*took, packed, lifted, laid,* and so on). Think, for a minute, about how you would go about writing a clear in-structive process description in that person and tense. Experienced writ-ers may use varying **points of view** in process writing, but for clear point-by-point instructions, **second person** (*you*), present tense (*take, pour, measure*), and a straightforward tone are the most common.

Although a process approach can sometimes be useful in writing nar-ratives and descriptions that deal with significant activities or accom-plishments, you will usually use process in writing assignments that in-volve giving directions, describing how a mechanical gadget works, or reporting science experiments. In these situations you may combine process with other modes like **definition** (Chapter 9), **examples** (Chapter 4), and **cause and effect** (Chapter 8). Always remember that three factors are essential to an effective process essay. First, be sure that the steps or procedures are carefully organized, step by step—usually in the same or-der as they should be carried out—so that the reader can understand and follow your explanation. Second, be sure that you include any information that the reader needs about any special materials or preliminary steps. And, third, include *all* the specific steps in the process.

Insert Flap "A" and Throw Away

S. J. Perelman

Have you ever tried to assemble something you bought, only to find out that the instructions provided seemed to match neither the product nor the process required to put it together? In this paragraph, S. J. Perelman describes the process that can result from bad process writing.

Words to Know

capricious   unstable and unpredictable
convulsively   in a fit, thrashing around
dolorous   miserable, pained
procurable   available for purchase
purgatory   temporary suffering

Getting Started

When do you use step-by-step instructions to explain specific tasks?

One stifling summer afternoon last August, in the attic of a tiny stone house in Pennsylvania, I made a most interesting discovery: the shortest, cheapest method of inducing a nervous breakdown ever perfected. In this technique (eventually adopted by the psychology department of Duke University, which will adopt anything), the subject is placed in a sharply sloping attic heated to 340° F. and given a mothproof closet known as the Jiffy-Cloz to assemble. The Jiffy-Cloz, procurable at any department store or neighborhood insane asylum, consists of half a dozen gigantic sheets of red cardboard, two plywood doors, a clothes rack, and a packet of staples. With these is included a set of instructions mimeographed in pale-violet ink, fruity with phrases like "Pass Section F through Slot AA, taking care not to fold tabs behind washers (see Fig. 9)." The cardboard is so processed that as a subject struggles convulsively to force the staple through, it suddenly buckles, plunging the staple deep into his thumb. He thereupon springs up with a dolorous cry and smites his knob (Section K) on the rafters (RR). As a final demonic touch, the Jiffy-Cloz people cunningly omit four of the staples necessary to finish the job, so that after indescribable purgatory, the best the subject can possibly achieve is a sleazy, capricious structure which would reduce any self-respecting moth to helpless laughter. The cumulative frustration, the tropical heat, and the soft, ghostly chuckling of the moths are calculated to unseat the strongest mentality.

Questions About the Reading

1. What is the person in the paragraph trying to do? Why?
2. What do you think laughing moths sound like? Why does the writer refer to moths in particular?
3. Is the writer ultimately successful in accomplishing his task?

Questions About the Writer's Strategies

1. Identify some points of **irony** in this paragraph.
2. What does "smites his knob" mean? Why does the writer use this language?
3. What is the controlling **metaphor** in this paragraph? That is, the writer is describing the situation as if it were something it is not. What is the substitute situation he is using? (Hint: An important clue is the word *subject*.)

Writing Assignments

1. Write a paragraph of advice to the writer of this paragraph. Using a process format, explain how to successfully follow step-by-step instructions without becoming impatient or frustrated. Try to illustrate the process by pointing out some things the writer did wrong.
2. In a process paragraph, explain how to wash a casserole dish left on the counter overnight, clean up a Coke or Pepsi spilled on the floor, freshen up a pair of smelly sneakers, clean a greasy engine, or perform some other unattractive task.

Rescuing Oily Birds

Rachael Bishop

Oil spills have become a common ecological disaster. We have all seen the horrifying pictures of wildlife, especially waterfowl, covered in black oil. Although many of these animals die, some survive thanks to the hard work of wildlife professionals and volunteers who work around the clock to clean and feed them. In 1988, after a 231,000-gallon oil spill in Washington State, Rachael Bishop was one of those who took part in the complicated process that eventually saved nearly three thousand seabirds.

Words to Know

esophagus   a tube for passage of food from the throat to the stomach

slurry   a thin mixture of a liquid

syringe   a medical instrument used to inject fluids

Getting Started

What would you be willing to do to help save some element of the environment?

The birds were tube-fed at least three times a day, twice with a slurry made from trout chow (a cereal product used as feed in hatcheries), vegetable oil, supplements, and electrolyte solution, and once or twice with the electrolyte solution alone. Tube-feeding ensured that each bird got adequate nutrition immediately. Volunteers worked in pairs. Wearing two rubber gloves on each hand, for protection from nips and bites, one person caught and held the bird around its wings and upper body. The second person filled a syringe with the meal, pried open the bird's beak, and carefully inserted a foot-long tube (about an eighth of an inch in diameter) into the bird's throat, pushing gently until the tube reached the stomach opening. The volunteer pressed the syringe, sending a bit less than two ounces of food into the bird's stomach, kinked the tube at the top, and gently withdrew it. Only specially trained people were allowed to do the feeding. One needed to be very careful to send the tube down the bird's esophagus and not down its windpipe, since a mistake would flood the bird's lungs and kill it. One needed to be patient and mindful; the birds had already gone through considerable trauma, and handling distressed and flustered them. Volunteers also offered smelt by hand to the birds, and the healthier ones usually took it.

Questions About the Reading

1. What ingredients did the birds need three times a day?
2. Why were tubes used to feed the birds?
3. Why did the people doing the feeding need to be specially trained?
4. Why was it so important to be patient with the birds?

Questions About the Writer's Strategies

1. Is the writer's **purpose** to **inform, describe,** or **instruct?** Explain your answer.
2. What kind of **order** does the writer use to organize her information?
3. Why is this labeled a process essay? List the steps in the process.

Writing Assignments

1. In a process paragraph, explain how to care for a young child or an elderly person who is sick in bed.
2. Write an informative process essay that describes how to feed a pet you have owned. Describe each step as if you were explaining it to someone who had never fed an animal before.
3. What have you done to improve the environment? Write a process essay describing what steps you could take to do something positive for your immediate environment.

The Right Way to Eat an Ice-Cream Cone

L. Rust Hills

Rust Hills was fiction editor of Esquire *and* The Saturday Evening Post, *and is now a freelance writer. In this paragraph, taken from his book* How to Do Things Right, *he explains his technique, which was perfected through years of taking his children to ice-cream cone stands. Having given us the preliminary pitfalls—melted ice cream on car upholstery, choosing a flavor, holding more than one cone at once—he delivers the ultimate instructions on eating the cone.*

Words to Know

forgoing   deciding against
jostling   bumping together
molecules   very small particles
stance   a way of standing

Getting Started

How can use of detail make even a simple activity sound complex?

Grasp the cone with the right hand firmly but gently between thumb and at least one but not more than three fingers, two-thirds of the way up the cone. Then dart swiftly away to an open area, away from the jostling crowd at the stand. Now take up the classic ice-cream-cone-eating stance: feet from one to two feet apart, body bent forward from the waist at a twenty-five-degree angle, right elbow well up, right forearm horizontal, at a level with your collarbone and about twelve inches from it. But don't start eating yet! Check first to see what emergency repairs may be necessary. Sometimes a sugar cone will be so crushed or broken or cracked that all one can do is gulp at the thing like a savage, getting what he can of it and letting the rest drop to the ground, and then evacuating the area of catastrophe as quickly as possible. Checking the cone for possible trouble can be done in a second or two, if one knows where to look and does it systematically. A trouble spot some people overlook is the bottom tip of the cone. This may have been broken off. Or the flap of the cone material at the bottom, usually wrapped over itself in that funny spiral construction, may be folded in a way that is imperfect and leaves an opening. No need to say that through this opening—in a matter of perhaps thirty or, at most, ninety seconds—will begin to pour hundreds of thousands of sticky molecules of melted ice cream. You know in this case that you must instantly get the paper napkin in your left hand under and around the bottom of the cone to stem the forthcoming flow, or else be doomed to eat the cone far too rapidly. It is a grim moment. No one wants to eat a cone under that kind of pressure, but neither does anyone want to end up with the bottom of the cone stuck to a messy napkin. There's one other alternative—one that takes both skill and courage: Forgoing any cradling action, grasp the cone more firmly between thumb and forefinger and extend the other fingers so that they are out of the way of the dripping from the bottom, then increase the waist-bend angle from twenty-five to thirty-five degrees, and then eat the cone, *allowing* it to drip out of the bottom onto the ground in front of you! Experienced and thoughtful cone-eaters enjoy facing up to this kind of sudden challenge.

Questions About the Reading

1. How many ways are there to eat an ice-cream cone?
2. With all the problems with ice-cream cones, does the writer like to eat them?
3. Why is it necessary to be so careful and systematic when eating an ice-cream cone?

Questions About the Writer's Strategies

1. Which words or phrases in this paragraph have a "scientific" precision that makes this process clear to the reader?
2. Why does the writer take such a serious **tone** in writing the paragraph? Isn't eating an ice-cream cone supposed to be fun? What will happen to someone who eats an ice-cream cone incorrectly?
3. This writer describes a number of problems associated with ice-cream cones. Which words or phrases does he use to help the reader know when he is about to identify those problems?
4. Which words or phrases does the writer use to make eating an ice-cream cone seem more important than it really is?

Writing Assignments

1. Imagine that you are sitting down to a heaping plate of spaghetti and meatballs while wearing a brand-new white suit or dress. In a process paragraph, describe how you would eat the meal.
2. Choose some simple, everyday activity such as making a bed or brushing your teeth and write a paragraph describing the process. Use a serious, authoritative tone.

The Cook

Barbara Lewis (student)

*Barbara Lewis takes us through the process of preparing dinner at a busy
restaurant. She juggles meat, potatoes, and a seemingly endless stream of
sauces and other delectables in a two-hour race with the dinner bell. And
she does all this after a day of classes at Cuyahoga Community College in
Cleveland, Ohio.*

Words to Know

au jus   natural unthickened juices or gravy
escargots   snails
requisition   a formal written order
sauté   to fry food quickly in a little fat
scampi   shrimp

Getting Started

When have you felt that you were the busiest, most pressured person in the world?

Preparing food for the sauté line at the restaurant where I work is a hectic two-hour job. I come to work at 3:00 P.M. knowing that everything must be done by 5:00 P.M. The first thing I do is to check the requisition for the day and order my food. Then I have to clean and season five or six prime rib roasts and place them in the slow-cooking oven. After this, I clean and season five trays of white potatoes for baking and put them in the fast oven. Now I have two things cooking, prime ribs and potatoes, at different times and temperatures, and they both have to be watched very closely. In the meantime, I must put three trays of bacon in the oven. The bacon needs very close watching, too, because it burns very easily. Now I have prime ribs, potatoes, and bacon all cooking at the same time—and all needing constant watching. Next, I make popovers, which are unseasoned rolls. These also go into an oven for baking. Now I have prime ribs, baking potatoes, bacon, and popovers cooking at the same time and all of them needing to be closely watched. With my work area set up, I must make clarified butter and garlic butter. The clarified butter is for cooking liver, veal, and fish. The garlic butter is for stuffing escargots. I have to make ground meat stuffing also. Half of the ground meat will be mixed with wild rice and will be used to stuff breast of chicken. The other half of the ground meat mixture will be used to stuff mushrooms. I have to prepare veal, cut and season scampi, and clean and sauté mushrooms and onions. In the meantime, I check the prime ribs and potatoes, take the bacon and the popovers out of the oven, and put the veal and chicken into the oven. Now I make au jus, which is served over the prime ribs, make the soup for the day, and cook the vegetables and rice. Then I heat the bordelaise sauce, make the special for the day, and last of all, cook food for the employees. This and sometimes more has to be done by five o'clock. Is it any wonder that I say preparing food for the sauté line at the restaurant where I work is a very hectic two-hour job!

Questions About the Reading

1. Run through the cook's list again. About how many people do you think she is preparing food for?
2. Classify the food the cook is responsible for.
3. Do you think the cook likes her job? Explain your answer.

Questions About the Writer's Strategies

1. Where is the **topic sentence** of the paragraph? Does the writer restate the topic sentence anywhere in the paragraph? If so, where? Does the sentence then serve a second purpose? What is that purpose?
2. Do you think *hectic* is an effective word for describing this job?
3. The cook states at the beginning that she has two things to watch carefully. The list of things she watches continues to grow during the paragraph. Identify the sentences where she re-emphasizes this point. Does this help support her statement that the job is hectic?
4. What **order** does the writer use to organize her information in the paragraph?

Writing Assignments

1. We all have moments when we feel under pressure. Write a process paragraph illustrating one of your busy days.
2. Imagine that the restaurant has decided to hire a helper for the cook and that you are to be that helper. Write a process paragraph explaining the steps you would take to assist the cook and how you would blend your activities with hers.

How to Write a Personal Letter

Garrison Keillor

Writing personal letters is an activity that many people believe they do not have the time to undertake. However, as Garrison Keillor explains in this essay, letter writing is a step-by-step process that leads to a unique kind of two-way communication.

Words to Know

anonymity   namelessness, obscurity
declarative   serving to state, announce, or say
obligatory   required, necessary

Getting Started

When was the last time you wrote a letter to a friend?

We shy persons need to write a letter now and then, or else we'll dry   1
up and blow away. It's true. And I speak as one who loves to reach for the
phone and talk. The telephone is to shyness what Hawaii is to February,
it's a way out of the woods. *And yet*: a letter is better.

Such a sweet gift—a piece of handmade writing, in an envelope that is   2
not a bill, sitting in our friend's path when she trudges home from a long
day spent among wahoos and savages, a day our words will help repair.
They don't need to be immortal, just sincere. She can read them twice and
again tomorrow: *You're someone I care about, Corinne, and think of often, and
every time I do, you make me smile.*

We need to write, otherwise nobody will know who we are. They will   3
have only a vague impression of us as A Nice Person, because, frankly,
we don't shine at conversation, we lack the confidence to thrust our faces
forward and say, "Hi, I'm Heather Hooten, let me tell you about my
week." Mostly we say "Uh-huh" and "Oh really." People smile and look
over our shoulder, looking for someone else to talk to.

So a shy person sits down and writes a letter. To be known by another   4
person—to meet and talk freely on the page—to be close despite distance. To escape from anonymity and be our own sweet selves and express the music of our souls.

We want our dear Aunt Eleanor to know that we have fallen in love, 5
that we quit our job, that we're moving to New York, and we want to say
a few things that might not get said in casual conversation: *Thank you for
what you've meant to me. I am very happy right now.*

The first step in writing letters is to get over the guilt of *not* writing. 6
You don't "owe" anybody a letter. Letters are a gift. The burning shame
you feel when you see unanswered mail makes it harder to pick up a pen
and makes for a cheerless letter when you finally do. *I feel bad about not
writing, but I've been so busy*, etc. Skip this. Few letters are obligatory, and
they are *Thanks for the wonderful gift* and *I am terribly sorry to hear about
George's death.* Write these promptly if you want to keep your friends.
Don't worry about the others, except love letters, of course. When your
true love writes *Dear Light of My Life, Joy of My Heart*, some response is
called for.

Some of the best letters are tossed off in a burst of inspiration, so keep 7
your writing stuff in one place where you can sit down for a few minutes
and—*Dear Roy, I am in the middle of an essay but thought I'd drop you a line.
Hi to your sweetie too*—dash off a note to a pal. Envelopes, stamps, address
book, everything in a drawer so you can write fast when the pen is hot.

A blank white 8″ x 11″ sheet can look as big as Montana if the pen's not 8
so hot—try a smaller page and write boldly. Get a pen that makes a sen-
suous line, get a comfortable typewriter, a friendly word processor—
whichever feels easy to the hand.

Sit for a few minutes with the blank sheet of paper in front of you, and 9
let your friend come to mind. Remember the last time you saw each other
and how your friend looked and what you said and what perhaps was
unsaid between you; when your friend becomes real to you, start to
write.

Write the salutation—*Dear You*—and take a deep breath and plunge in. 10
A simple declarative sentence will do, followed by another and another.
As if you were talking to us. Don't think about grammar, don't think
about style, just give us your news. Where did you go, who did you see,
what did they say, what do you think?

If you don't know where to begin, start with the present: *I'm sitting at* 11
*the kitchen table on a rainy Saturday morning. Everyone is gone and the house
is quiet.* Let the letter drift along. The toughest letter to crank out is one
that is meant to impress, as we all know from writing job applications; if
it's hard work to slip off a letter to a friend, maybe you're trying too hard
to be terrific. A letter is only a report to someone who already likes you
for reasons other than your brilliance. Take it easy.

Don't worry about form. It's not a term paper. When you come to the 12
end of one episode, just start a new paragraph. You can go from a few
lines about the sad state of rock 'n' roll to the fight with your mother to

your fond memories of Mexico to the kitchen sink and what's in it. The more you write, the easier it gets, and when you have a True True Friend to write to, a soul sibling, then it's like driving a car; you just press on the gas.

Don't tear up the page and start over when you write a bad line—try to write your way out of it. Make mistakes and plunge on. Let the letter cook along and let yourself be bold. Outrage, confusion, love—whatever is in your mind, let if find a way to the page. Writing is a means of discovery, always, and when you come to the end and write *Yours ever* or *Hugs and Kisses*, you'll know something you didn't when you wrote *Dear Pal*. 13

Probably your friend will put your letter away, and it'll be read again a few years from now—and it will improve with age. 14

And forty years from now, your friend's grandkids will dig it out of the attic and read it, a sweet and precious relic of the ancient Eighties that gives them a sudden clear glimpse of the world we old-timers knew. You will have then created an object of art. Your simple lines about where you went, who you saw, what they said, will speak to those children and they will feel in their hearts the humanity of our times. 15

You can't pick up a phone and call the future and tell them about our times. You have to pick up a piece of paper. 16

Questions About the Reading

1. Why does Keillor believe a letter is better than a phone call?
2. Why is it especially important for shy people to write letters?
3. Why does the writer believe that style and grammar aren't important in a personal letter?
4. What is the first step to letter writing that Keillor suggests most people never get past?

Questions About the Writer's Strategies

1. Is the author's **purpose** to **inform, describe,** or **instruct?** What is it about the **point of view** of this essay that makes it more than a set of instructions?
2. What kind of **order** does the writer use in listing his points?
3. Why is this labeled a process essay? List the steps suggested in the process of writing a letter.
4. The writer uses the mode of **comparison and contrast** in the beginning and conclusion of the essay. To what does he compare writing letters?

Writing Assignments

1. In a process paragraph, explain how to plan a party, go on a first date, or invite someone new to dinner. Try to use a casual, friendly tone.
2. Write a process essay that describes how to respond to a very friendly letter from someone you wish hadn't written to you.
3. Rewrite "How to Write a Personal Letter" in a purely instructional manner with numbered steps. Use the **second person** point of view.

Eating Alone in Restaurants

Bruce Jay Friedman

The human mind is inventive and analytical. If you looked hard enough, you could probably find careful, precise instructions for doing just about anything. Bruce Jay Friedman's writing here is tongue-in-cheek. That should be evident from the title of the book this essay appeared in: The Lonely Guy's Book of Life. *But he's also telling us something useful: with the right attitude, you can pull off anything. In a sense, this piece is telling us how to have that attitude.*

Words to Know

audacious   daring
conviviality   the quality of being warm and festive
disdain   to despise, look down upon
Feydeau   a French writer of bedroom comedies and farces
foreboding   a feeling that something bad will happen
gaucho   a South American cowboy
hors d'oeuvre   an appetizer
imperiously   arrogantly, domineeringly
inconspicuous   not noticeable
Pilgrim stocks   wooden frames for punishment
ploys   tricks
scenario   a sequence of events
suffice   be sufficient

Getting Started

How do you deal with those situations in your life that make you extremely anxious?

Hunched over, trying to be as inconspicuous as possible, a solitary 1 diner slips into a midtown Manhattan steakhouse. No sooner does he check his coat than the voice of the headwaiter comes booming across the restaurant.

"Alone again, eh?" 2

As all eyes are raised, the bartender, with enormous good cheer, 3 chimes in: "That's because they all left him high and dry."

And then, just in case there is a customer in the restaurant who isn't 4
yet aware of the situation, a waiter shouts out from the buffet table:
"Well, we'll take care of him anyway, won't we fellas!"

Haw, haw, haw, and a lot of sly winks and pokes in the ribs. 5

Eating alone in a restaurant is one of the most terrifying experiences in 6
America.

Sniffed at by headwaiters, an object of scorn and amusement to 7
couples, the solitary diner is the unwanted and unloved child of Restaurant Row. No sooner does he make his appearance than he is whisked out
of sight and seated at a thin sliver of a table with barely enough room on
it for an hors d'oeuvre. Wedged between busboy stations, a hair's
breadth from the men's room, there he sits, feet lodged in a railing as if he
were in Pilgrim stocks, wondering where he went wrong in life.

Rather than face this grim scenario, most Lonely Guys would prefer to 8
nibble away at a tuna fish sandwich in the relative safety of their
high-rise apartments.

What can be done to ease the pain of this not only starving but silent 9
minority—to make dining alone in restaurants a rewarding experience?
Absolutely nothing. But some small strategies *do* exist for making the experience bearable.

Before You Get There

Once the Lonely Guy has decided to dine alone at a restaurant, a sense of 10
terror and foreboding will begin to build throughout the day. All the
more reason for him to get there as quickly as possible so that the experience can soon be forgotten and he can resume his normal life. Clothing
should be light and loose-fitting, especially around the neck—on the off
chance of a fainting attack during the appetizer. It is best to dress modestly, avoiding both the funeral-director-style suit as well as the bold, eye-
arresting costume of the gaucho. A single cocktail should suffice; little
sympathy will be given to the Lonely Guy who tumbles in, stewed to the
gills. (The fellow who stoops to putting morphine in his toes for courage
does not belong in this discussion.) En route to the restaurant, it is best to
play down dramatics, such as swinging the arms pluckily and humming
the theme from *The Bridge on the River Kwai.*

Once You Arrive

The way your entrance comes off is of critical importance. Do not skulk 11
in, slipping along the walls as if you are carrying some dirty little secret.
There is no need, on the other hand, to fling your coat arrogantly at the
hatcheck girl, slap the headwaiter across the cheeks with your gloves and

demand to be seated immediately. Simply walk in with a brisk rubbing of the hands and approach the headwaiter. When asked how many are in your party, avoid cute responses such as "Jes lil ol' me." Tell him you are a party of one; the Lonely Guy who does not trust his voice can simply lift a finger. Do not launch into a story about how tired you are of taking out fashion models, night after night, and what a pleasure it is going to be to dine alone.

It is best to arrive with no reservation. Asked to set aside a table for 12 one, the restaurant owner will suspect either a prank on the part of an ex-waiter, or a terrorist plot, in which case windows will be boarded up and the kitchen bombswept. An advantage of the "no reservation" approach is that you will appear to have just stepped off the plane from Des Moines, your first night in years away from Marge and the kids.

All eyes will be upon you when you make the promenade to your 13 table. Stay as close as possible to the headwaiter, trying to match him step for step. This will reduce your visibility and fool some diners into thinking you are a member of the staff. If you hear a generalized snickering throughout the restaurant, do not assume automatically that you are being laughed at. The other diners may all have just recalled an amusing moment in a Feydeau farce.

If your table is unsatisfactory, do not demand imperiously that one for 14 eight people be cleared immediately so that you can dine in solitary grandeur. Glance around discreetly and see if there are other possibilities. The ideal table will allow you to keep your back to the wall so that you can see if anyone is laughing at you. Try to get one close to another couple so that if you lean over at a 45-degree angle it will appear that you are a swinging member of their group. Sitting opposite a mirror can be useful; after a drink or two, you will begin to feel that there are a few of you.

Once you have been seated, and it becomes clear to the staff that you 15 are alone, there will follow The Single Most Heartbreaking Moment in Dining Out Alone—when the second setting is whisked away and yours is spread out a bit to make the table look busier. This will be done with great ceremony by the waiter—angered in advance at being tipped for only one dinner. At this point, you may be tempted to smack your forehead against the table and curse the fates that brought you to this desolate position in life. A wiser course is to grit your teeth, order a drink and use this opportunity to make contact with other Lonely Guys sprinkled around the room. A menu or a leafy stalk of celery can be used as a shield for peering out at them. Do not expect a hearty greeting or a cry of "huzzah" from these frightened and browbeaten people. Too much excitement may cause them to slump over, curtains. Smile gently and be content if you receive a pale wave of the hand in return. It is unfair to imply that you have come to help them throw off their chains.

When the headwaiter arrives to take your order, do not be bullied into 16 ordering the last of the gazelle haunches unless you really want them. Thrilled to be offered anything at all, many Lonely Guys will say "Get them right out here" and wolf them down. Restaurants take unfair advantage of Lonely Guys, using them to get rid of anything from withered liver to old heels of roast beef. Order anything you like, although it is good to keep to the light and simple in case of a sudden attack of violent stomach cramps.

Some Proven Strategies

Once the meal is under way, a certain pressure will begin to build as 17 couples snuggle together, the women clucking sympathetically in your direction. Warmth and conviviality will pervade the room, none of it encompassing you. At this point, many Lonely Guys will keep their eyes riveted to the restaurant paintings of early Milan or bury themselves in a paperback anthology they have no wish to read.

Here are some ploys designed to confuse other diners and make them 18 feel less sorry for you.

- After each bite of food, lift your head, smack your lips thought- 19 fully, swallow and make a notation in a pad. Diners will assume you are a restaurant critic.
- Between courses, pull out a walkie-talkie and whisper a message 20 into it. This will lead everyone to believe you are part of a police stake-out team, about to bust the salad man as an international dope dealer.
- Pretend you are a foreigner. This is done by pointing to items on 21 the menu with an alert smile and saying to the headwaiter: "Is good, no?"
- When the main course arrives, brush the restaurant silverware off 22 the table and pull some of your own out of a breastpocket. People will think you are a wealthy eccentric.
- Keep glancing at the door, and make occasional trips to look out at 23 the street, as if you are waiting for a beautiful woman. Half-way through the meal, shrug in a world-weary manner and begin to eat with gusto. The world is full of women! Why tolerate bad manners! Life is too short.

The Right Way

One other course is open to the Lonely Guy, an audacious one, full of per- 24 ils, but all the more satisfying if you can bring it off. That is to take off your dark glasses, sit erectly, smile broadly at anyone who looks in your direction, wave off inferior wines, and begin to eat with heartiness and enormous confidence. As outrageous as the thought may be—enjoy your own company. Suddenly, titters and sly winks will tail off, the headwaiter's disdain will fade, and friction will build among couples who will turn out to be not as tightly cemented as they appear. The heads of other Lonely Guys will lift with hope as you become the attractive center of the room.

If that doesn't work, you still have your fainting option.   25

Questions About the Reading

1. What steps should a person eating alone take to be less uncomfortable?
2. In your own words, describe *why* single diners receive the treatment the writer describes.
3. What is the "Single Most Heartbreaking Moment" of dining out alone? What makes it so?
4. What is the writer suggesting in paragraph 24? Why might this option be the best one the Lonely Guy could pursue?

Questions About the Writer's Strategies

1. Identify the **thesis statement** of this essay.
2. What is the writer's **tone**?
3. Identify five places where the writer uses exaggeration or overstatement. What is the effect?
4. What makes this a process essay? Briefly list the steps in the process.
5. In what **order** does the writer present the process?

Writing Assignments

1. Think of a situation that causes you fear or serious embarrassment, such as being called on in class when you haven't read your assignment, going to the dentist to have a cavity filled, asking for an extension on a paper's due date, or being confronted by a snarling dog. Write an essay in which you explain the steps for dealing with the situation. Feel free to use exaggeration to describe the causes of your discomfort.

2. Write a process essay that describes giving a speech in public and the steps you recommend to overcome any possible stage fright. Use a serious, authoritative tone.
3. Write an essay in which you explain the process of introducing yourself to a total stranger and beginning a conversation—at a party, for instance, or on a train.

The Wine Experience

Leo Buscaglia

In contemporary life we are often too far removed from the actual process of growing and making things. We buy all our food and clothes in stores without any knowledge of their original sources. This essay describes the joyful step-by-step procedure of wine making in a traditional Italian-American home.

Words to Know

connoisseur   someone with shrewd, clever discrimination concerning matters of taste
cylindrical   circular
dissertation   a speech, lecture
oenophile   someone who loves the study of wine
precariously   lacking stability, balance
prelude   an introduction

Getting Started

Why is it so satisfying to make something from scratch?

Like all good Italians, Papa loved his wine, although I never knew him 1 to drink to excess. A glass or two of wine to accompany his dinner was his limit. He never touched hard liquor.

Papa's love of wine went far beyond the simple enjoyment of drinking 2 it. He was truly an oenophile, a connoisseur. He always made his own wine, from ripened grapes to dated label. His cool, dark cellar was full of dusty bottles and cylindrical, wooden barrels of varying sizes, all carefully marked to indicate the type of grape and the year of the harvest.

When I was growing up, we had many festivities in our home. None, 3 except Christmas and Easter, topped the one night each year that we made the new wine. The anticipation and preparation began in July and August, long before the eventful September evening when the truckload of grapes was delivered. By then Papa had made several visits to his friends—grape growers in Cucamonga, about forty miles from our home—to observe the progress of his grapes. He had spent hours scouring the barrels in which the wine would be made and stored, and applying antirust varnish on every visible metal part of the wine-making equipment. The fermenting vat had been filled with water to swell the wood.

On the appointed evening, the truck would arrive after nightfall, brimming with small, tough-skinned, sweet-smelling Cabernet grapes. The boxes of grapes were hand-carried about two hundred feet to the garage, where a giant empty vat awaited. A hand-powered crusher was positioned precariously on top of the vat, ready to grind noisily into the night, as thousands of grapes were poured into it. It was an all-male operation that included Papa, his relatives, and friends. Dressed in their undershirts, bodies glistening with perspiration, they took turns cranking the crusher handle. My job was to stack the empty crates neatly out of the way as a prelude to what for me was the most exciting part of the evening. 4

After all the grapes had been mashed and the empty boxes stacked, it was time for us to remove our shoes, socks, and pants and slip into the cool, dark moisture for the traditional grape stomping. This was done, of course, to break up the skins, but I couldn't have cared less why it was necessary. For me it was a sensual experience unlike any other, feeling the grape residue gushing between my toes and watching as the new wine turned my legs the rich, deep color of Cabernet Sauvignon. 5

While this "man's work" was being accomplished, the "woman's work" was progressing in the kitchen. The heady fragrance of the crushed grapes, mingled with the savory aromas of dinner wafting from the house, caused our feet to move in step with our growing appetites. The traditional main course for our wine-making dinner was gnocchi, a small, dumplinglike pasta that would be cooked to perfection and topped with a wonderful sauce that had been simmering for hours. 6

Like Christmas Eve, this particular night was unique in many ways. Throughout the rest of the year, we routinely sat down to dinner by 5:30 each evening. But for this occasion dinner was never served until the wine making was finished, sometimes as late as 10 P.M. By then, we were all purple from grape juice, exhausted, and famished. 7

No matter how tired and hungry we were, however, Papa always prefaced the dinner with a dissertation on "the wine experience." This ceremony called for his finest wines, which had been aging in his modest but efficient wine cellar. Drinking wine, he would remind us, was a highly respected activity, not to be taken lightly. The nectar of the grape had brought joy to human beings long before recorded history. 8

"Wine is a delight and a challenge and is never meant to be drunk quickly. It's to be savored and sipped slowly," he'd tell us. "All the senses are awakened when you drink wine. You drink with your eyes, your 9 tongue, your throat, your nose. Notice the colors the wine makes in the glass—all the way from dark purple, like a bishop's robe, to the golden amber of an aspen leaf."

He would hold up the glass to the light as if we were about to share a 10 sacrament, then swirl the wine around in his glass, guiding us through the whole ritual, from the first sip to the final, all-important swallow.

"*Alla salute!*" 11

Questions About the Reading

1. How do you think the writer feels about his father? What leads you to this conclusion?
2. How often did the Buscaglia family make wine?
3. What happened to the grapes after they were crushed?
4. What did wine making and Christmas have in common to the writer as a child?

Questions About the Writer's Strategies

1. What is the writer's **thesis**? Can you identify the thesis statement, or is the thesis **implied**?
2. What is the **point of view** in the essay? Could another point of view be used?
3. In what ways is this paragraph **subjective**? In what ways is it **objective**?
4. Is the writer's purpose to instruct a beginner in how to make wine? If so, what are the main steps? If not, what else would you need to know?

Writing Assignments

1. Write a first-person essay about a family tradition in your home that involves a holiday or a special event. Write it as a process so that your readers could try to duplicate the celebration at home.
2. Choose a skill you have learned from one of your parents and write a **second person** process essay describing how to perform that skill.
3. Think of something you have eaten, worn, or used today and explain the steps that were taken to produce it.

How to Put Off
Doing a Job

Andy Rooney

In this essay, Andy Rooney turns the process approach around, using it to show some steps you can follow to avoid *accomplishing something.*

Word to Know

philosophize   to speculate or think about

Getting Started

When it's time to get down to work, why do we suddenly find other things to do?

February is one of the most difficult times of the year to put off doing 1
some of the things you've been meaning to do. There's no vacation coming up, there are no long weekends scheduled in the immediate future; it's just this long, grim February. Don't tell me it's a short month. February is the longest by a week.

Because I have so many jobs that I don't like to do, I've been reviewing 2
the notebook I keep with notes in it for how to put off doing a job. Let's see now, what could I use today?

—Go to the store to get something. This is one of my most dependable 3
putter-offers. If I start a job and find I need some simple tool or a piece of hardware, I stop right there. I put on some better clothes, get in the car and drive to the store. If that store doesn't have what I'm looking for, I go to another. Often I'm attracted to some item that has nothing whatsoever to do with the job I was about to start and I buy that instead. For instance, if I go to the hardware store to buy a new snow shovel so I can clean out the driveway, but then I see a can of adhesive spray that will keep rugs in place on the floor, I'm apt to buy the adhesive spray. That ends the idea I had to shovel out the driveway.

—Tidy up the work area before starting a job. This has been useful to 4
me over the years as a way of not getting started. Things are such a mess in my workshop, on my desk, in the kitchen and in the trunk of the car

that I decide I've got to go through some of the junk before starting to work.

—Make those phone calls. There's no sense trying to do a job if you ⁵ have other things on your mind, so get them out of the way first. This is a very effective way of not getting down to work. Call friends you've been meaning to call, or the distant relative you've been out of touch with. Even if someone is in California, Texas or Chicago and you're in Florida, call. Paying for a long-distance call is still easier and less unpleasant than actually getting down to work.

—Study the problem. It's foolish to jump right into a job before you've ⁶ thought it through. You might be doing the wrong thing. There might be an easier way to accomplish what you want to do, so think it over carefully from every angle. Perhaps someone has written a how-to book about the job you have in front of you. Buy the book and then sit down and read it. Ask friends who have had the same job for advice about the best way to do it.

Once you've studied the problem from every angle, don't make a ⁷ quick decision. Sleep on it.

—Take a coffee break. Although the term "coffee break" assumes that ⁸ you are drinking coffee in an interim period between stretches of solid work, this is not necessarily so. Don't be bound by old ideas about when it's proper to take a coffee break. If taking it before you get started is going to help keep you from doing the work, by all means take your coffee break first.

—As a last resort before going to work, think this thing over. Is this ⁹ really what you want to do with your life? Philosophize. Nothing is better for putting off doing something than philosophizing. Are you a machine, trapped in the same dull, day-after-day routine that everyone else is in? Or are you a person who makes up his or her own mind about things? Are you going to do these jobs because that's what's expected of you, or are you going to break the mold and live the way you feel like living?

Try these as ways for not getting down to work. ¹⁰

———————

Questions About the Reading

1. In paragraph 1, what does the second sentence mean? How do vacations and long weekends make it easier to put off doing things?
2. Why does the writer say that February is the longest month?
3. Which of the writer's methods for putting off a task can someone use when all the others have been tried?

Chapter 7 / Process

Questions About the Writer's Strategies

1. What is the writer's **thesis**? Can you identify a thesis statement, or is the thesis **implied**?
2. In what way is the thesis **ironic**?
3. What makes this a process essay? Does it describe more than one process?
4. In what humorous way does the writer let us know that he is something of an authority on his subject?

Writing Assignments

1. Write a process essay describing how you *do* get down to work—school work, an odd job, or perhaps an athletic activity or practicing a musical instrument. How do you discipline yourself to begin, and what steps do you take to get started?
2. Rewrite the essay you wrote for assignment 1, using the second person singular. That is, write a process essay instructing someone else how to get started on a task.
3. Write a process essay describing the steps you would follow if you wanted to teach someone to read.

Date Decorating:
Preparing Your Home
for His Arrival

Linda Sunshine

We live in an era when self-help books and articles are written about every conceivable subject. Linda Sunshine's book Women Who Date Too Much—and Those Who Should Be So Lucky *is a parody of all the books that profess to advise women on their relationships with men. This essay describes all the steps a woman should take to impress a man with her household possessions.*

Words to Know

demure   coy, flirtatious
frivolous   silly, giddy, not worthy of attention
Hummels   small German figurines
misconception   a misunderstanding
strategically   planned effectively
superficial   lacking intellectual depth, shallow

Getting Started

What does your living space say about you?

For your first date with that special man, it is important to create the right impression. In other words, you want to present an image that will impress him, whether or not that image actually projects the real you. This may be a difficult concept for some women, especially those of us who came of age in the late 1960s, early 1970s.

During that time we were under the misconception that we should "let it all hang out." We told ourselves looks didn't count, we were all beautiful human beings, what was on the inside was much more important than what was on the outside. In hindsight, it's easy to recognize our mistake: We failed to take into account these principles only applied if you were under twenty-three and stoned eighteen hours a day.

Now that we know better, we need to update our standards to be more in keeping with modern times. This is why you must forget all that Be-Yourself, Take-Me-As-I-Am psychobabble from your long-gone past. You are living in the material world. In the eighties, you are what you mortgage. 3

During these competitive times, it is perfectly permissible to use any deceit necessary to snag yourself a good date. 4

Your living space says a lot about who you are and how you see yourself. Consequently, it is vital that your home project an image he will admire. This is no time to split hairs, if he thinks you're rich, he may find you even more attractive. 5

Projecting a rich and successful image may take a lot of effort and time, depending on your bank account and on how much of a slob you really are. (This is something only you can honestly judge.) In all probability, however, you will have to spend at least as much time getting your apartment together as you would yourself. 6

You want to really make this guy envious of your space, so here are a few of the steps you will need to take. 7

First, hide all evidence that you are frivolous, superficial, or just plain stupid. Remove from view: *TV Guide*, all your confession/decorating magazines, astrology books, and/or comic books. 8

Store all stuffed animals in the laundry hamper. (If this is too painful, send your furry friends on an overnight sleepover with an understanding neighbor. While you're at it, deposit cat(s) and all their toys with the same neighbor. Remove all traces of kitty litter from sight and scent.) 9

Get rid of anything wicker, straw, or gingham. Hummels have to go. Knickknacks are definitely not eighties. 10

Hide all record albums or tapes by John Denver, the Boston Pops, or whales. 11

Stock your refrigerator with cold cuts (late night snack), lots of liquids, and breakfast (just in case). 12

Get out candles (but none that are carved into cute little animals or mushrooms). Stemmed candles that fit into candle holders only! 13

Buy yourself fresh flowers. If he asks who sent the flowers, be demure and smile. Then lie through your teeth. Say: "Just an old friend." Sigh deeply. 14

Hide Tampax and all other yucky personal hygiene items. You want him to think that, inside and out, you are put together as cleanly as a Barbie doll. 15

Try to be neat. Pick up all your dirty laundry and hide it under your bed. Stack dirty dishes in the oven or under the sink. For the sake of the female population (and his mother), you always want to maintain the illusion single women are not as messy as single men. 16

Overall, your apartment should be clean but not sterile. Unlike your 17 mother, your date will not look under your couch for dustbunnies. (If he does, he should be dating your mother, not you.)

Strategically placed bits of clutter—an opened letter here, an assort- 18 ment of Playbills there—tells him you are orderly but not fanatic and, more important, that your life is interesting.

If you are doing well financially, don't keep it to yourself. Display your 19 latest tax return on the coffee table.

A computer report that you lifted from the office tells him you're in- 20 volved with your job. (If he asks about the printout, reply that you don't feel like "talking shop" tonight.)

Remember that first impressions are important. To insure that he'll 21 like you, don't be yourself. Be Susan Anton.

Questions About the Reading

1. According to the writer, how has the world changed since the 1970s?
2. What is the most important image to project to your date?
3. Why do you think stuffed and real animals need to be removed?
4. Why is it important to find a balance between cleanliness and clutter?

Questions About the Writer's Strategies

1. What is the writer's **thesis**? List three places where the thesis is stated or restated.
2. What is the **point of view** in the essay? Could another point of view be used?
3. Identify four places where the writer has used **irony** to amuse the reader.
4. Although this selection is ridiculing a how-to essay, it still describes a process. Briefly list the steps in the process.

Writing Assignments

1. Rewrite this essay in the first person. Try to retain the ironic, humorous tone.
2. Choose your own living space or the home of one of your friends and write a process essay describing how to improve the space so that it would impress a first-time visitor.
3. Write a process essay that **instructs** your readers on how to prepare a romantic meal for an important date.

Pithing a Frog

Irene Szurley (student)

Irene Szurley is offering us more than instructions here. Her running commentary on the process she is describing leaves us asking more questions than just "Are we doing it right?" She wants us to wonder, "Are we right to do this?" Be careful. After she gets through with you, you may never want to go to biology class again.

Words to Know

annihilation   death
cephalic   of the head
cranial   pertaining to the brain
dubiously   questionably
flaccid   soft, limp
grotesque   distorted
intricate   complex
middorsal   mid-back
occipital   the back part of the head
posteriorly   along the back part of the body
procure   to obtain
vertebrae   the bones of the spinal column

Getting Started

How does humor or sarcasm help you endure unpleasant tasks?

During the course of biological events, it often becomes necessary 1
to kill in order to learn about life. Biologists have devised many intricate procedures to accomplish this annihilation, and pithing is one of
these.

This procedure is used as a means of destroying the central nervous 2
system in order to eliminate sensation and response in the frog, so that it
can be properly dissected. Anaesthesis cannot possibly be used as an alternative method, because it wears off, and that could prove disastrously
disadvantageous.

To begin this dubiously humane procedure, you, the aspiring mutila- 3
tionist, must hold the cool, dry frog in your left fist, positioning your fingers and thumbs in the grotesque attitude of a vise-like grip. The index
finger must press down on top of the poor, defenseless frog's head, exert-
ing pressure so that the spinal cord will be bent at the neck.

Next, take your right index finger and use your nail—the longer, the 4
better tactile response—to find the junction of the frog's vertebral column with its occipital bone. If a nail doesn't work, bring the point of a
dull dissecting needle—we don't want any more pain than is absolutely
necessary—posteriorly along the animal's middorsal line until the first
bulge of a vertebra can be felt twinging through the skin.

Now cast aside your dull needles. You are ready to begin the actual 5
rupturing—the mutilation. Procure a sharp needle and puncture the skin
at the junction you have just located. Neatness is important, so remember
to make only a *hole* in the skin; no lengthy gashes, please.

Retrieve your dull needle and insert it through this gaping hole, plung- 6
ing it into the spinal cord as far as it will go. Don't be timid now. At this
point, the frog will become totally limp and flaccid, as he is in a state of
spinal shock. You will no longer have to worry about his squirming and
wiggling efforts to free himself, all in vain. Tsk.

As soon as the probe is in the cord up to the hilt, turn it and direct 7
it forward into the cranial cavity. Move it parallel to the external surface, which by this time is awash with cephalic blood, but don't let
this minor problem deter you. If the needle is positioned correctly in
the cranial cavity, it will be possible to feel bone on all sides of the
needle.

Begin, slowly at first, then progressively more rapidly, to twist the 8
needle; thrash it right and left. Complete destruction of the brain is inevitable, even if you are clumsy.

After this step, the frog is single-pithed. Since our knowledge must 9
know no bounds, we must invariably explore further. Place the needle at
right angles to the body surface, turn its handle towards the vacant head,
parallel to the external surface. *Gently*, since we must maintain the essence of humanity at all times, push the needle into the spinal cord. A
quick way to test your aim, and to amuse your friends, is to see if the
frog's legs have spastically jerked out straight. If so, then you may proceed to slowly rotate your implement of destruction until all the nerves
are disconnected and frayed. The frog is now double-pithed and unable
to offer any resistance to your further exploratory efforts in the name of
science.

Questions About the Reading

1. What does the writer mean by the phrase "kill in order to learn about life"?
2. What is *pithing*? First describe it as you understand it from the essay and then check a dictionary.
3. What is the purpose of destroying the frog's brain?
4. What further steps are necessary to *double-pith*?

Questions About the Writer's Strategies

1. What **tone** is established in this essay? What words or phrases establish the tone? What is the effect of this tone on the reader?
2. Is the technical terminology clearly defined for the nonscientist? What additional terms would you like to see defined by the writer?
3. Where does the writer define *pithing*? Is the definition necessary? Is that the most effective placement for it?
4. In what **order** does the writer organize her material?

Writing Assignments

1. **Describe** any other common procedure, using descriptive words to convey your personal feeling about the procedures. For example, tell how to iron a shirt, wash the car, clean the bathtub, or take out the garbage. Tell your feelings and reactions after each step.
2. Rewrite the paragraph eliminating the emotionally charged or sarcastic words, and compare the effectiveness of the two paragraphs.
3. Give a new owner an explanation of how to housebreak a dog or how to care for a bird or cat. Describe some of the less pleasant sides of these tasks.

8

Cause and Effect

IN YOUR LOCAL newspaper you notice a story about a car accident that took place late on a Saturday night. The driver missed a curve, slammed into a tree, and was badly injured. Police investigators reported that the young victim had been drinking heavily with friends and lost control of the car on the way home. This news article is a relatively clear example of a **cause**, heavy consumption of alcohol, and an **effect**, a serious accident.

Sometimes you can recognize immediately that cause and effect is part of a writer's **mode of development** because the writer uses words that signal a cause-and-effect relationship—words like *because, therefore, as a result*, and *consequently*. However, writers will not necessarily indicate cause and effect so directly. Sometimes a cause-and-effect relationship will be clear only from the arrangement of ideas or the narrative sequence of events. Usually, though, the **topic sentence** or **thesis statement** will indicate that the writer is describing a cause-and-effect situation.

A cause-and-effect explanation tells *why* something turns out the way it does. In some cases, a single cause may contribute to one or more effects. In the following paragraph, the writer says that a single cause—the early release of prisoners—led to an increase in crimes.

Cause

> To save money in the early 1980s, Illinois released 21,000 prisoners an average of three months early. James Austin of

Effects

> the National Council on Crime and Delinquency calculates that the early releases produced 23 homicides, 32 rapes, 262 arsons, 681 robberies, 2,472 burglaries, 2,571 assaults and more than 8,000 other crimes. According to Harvard re-

Effect searchers David P. Cavanaugh and Mark A. R. Kleiman, the $60 million the state saved cost Illinois crime victims $304 million, directly or indirectly.

Eugene H. Methvin,
"Pay Now—Or Pay Later"

At other times, the writer explains that several causes contributed to or resulted in a particular effect.

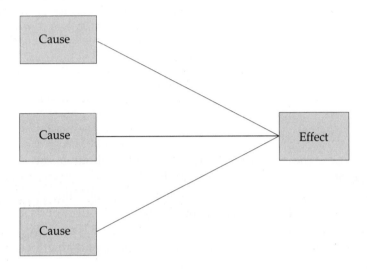

For example, in the following essay, the writer suggests three causes for the disappearance of moonshining—the undercover manufacturing of whiskey—as a fine art.

The manufacture of illicit whiskey in the mountains is not dead. Far from it. As long as the operation of a still remains so financially rewarding, it will never die. There will always be men ready to take their chances against the law for such an attractive profit, and willing to take their punishment when they are caught.   1

Effect

Cause 1: decline in use of home remedies containing corn whiskey
Cause 2: young people finding easier ways to make money

Moonshining as a fine art, however, effectively disappeared some time ago. There were several reasons. One was the age of aspirin and modern medicine. As home doctoring lost its stature, the demand for pure corn whiskey as an essential ingredient of many home remedies vanished along with those remedies. Increasing affluence was another reason. Young people, rather than follow in their parents' footsteps, decided that there were easier ways to make money, and they were right.   2

Third, and perhaps most influential of all, was the arrival,   3
even in moonshining, of that peculiarly human disease
known to most of us as greed. One fateful night, some force
whispered in an unsuspecting moonshiner's ear, "Look.
Add this gadget to your still and you'll double your production. Double your production, and you can double your
profits."

Soon the small operators were being forced out of busi-   4
ness, and moonshining, like most other manufacturing en-
terprises, was quickly taken over by a breed of men bent on
making money—and lots of it. Loss of pride in the product,
and loss of time taken with the product increased in direct
proportion to the desire for production; and thus moonshining as a fine art was buried in a quiet little ceremony attended only by those mourners who had once been the
proud artists, known far and wide across the hills for the ex-
cellence of their product. Too old to continue making it themselves, and with no one following behind them, they were reduced to reminiscing about "the good old days when the
whiskey that was made was *really* whiskey, and no questions
asked."

Suddenly moonshining fell into the same category as   5
faith healing, planting by the signs, and all the other vanishing customs that were a part of a rugged, self-sufficient culture that is now disappearing.

Eliot Wigginton,
"Moonshining as a Fine Art"

In still other cases, one cause may have several effects.

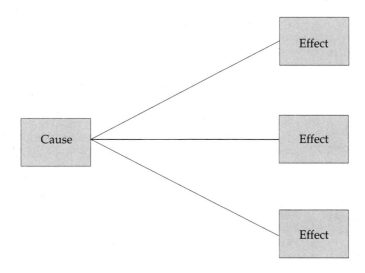

In the following paragraph, the writer explains that the explosion of a nuclear bomb (the cause) has five primary effects. Notice, too, as you read, that the writer combines process with the cause-and-effect explanation.

Topic

Cause

Effect 1: initial
nuclear radiation

Effect 2:
electromagnetic
pulse

Effect 3: thermal
pulse

Effect 4: blast
wave

Effect 5: radioactive
fallout

Whereas most conventional bombs produce only one destructive effect—the shock wave—nuclear weapons produce many destructive effects. At the moment of the explosion, when the temperature of the weapon material, instantly gasified, is at the superstellar level, the pressure is millions of times the normal atmospheric pressure. Immediately, radiation, consisting mainly of gamma rays, which are a very high-energy form of electromagnetic radiation, begins to stream outward into the environment. This is called the "initial nuclear radiation," and is the first of the destructive effects of a nuclear explosion. In an air burst of a one-megaton bomb—a bomb with the explosive yield of a million tons of TNT, which is a medium-sized weapon in present-day nuclear arsenals—the initial nuclear radiation can kill unprotected human beings in an area of some six square miles. Virtually simultaneously with the initial nuclear radiation, in a second destructive effect of the explosion, an electromagnetic pulse is generated by the intense gamma radiation acting on the air. In a high-altitude detonation, the pulse can knock out electrical equipment over a wide area by inducing a powerful surge of voltage through various conductors, such as antennas, overhead power lines, pipes, and railroad tracks. . . . When the fusion and fission reactions have blown themselves out, a fireball takes shape. As it expands, energy is absorbed in the form of X rays by the surrounding air, and then the air re-radiates a portion of that energy into the environment in the form of the thermal pulse—a wave of blinding light and intense heat—which is the third of the destructive effects of a nuclear explosion. . . . The thermal pulse of a one-megaton bomb lasts for about ten seconds and can cause second-degree burns in exposed human beings at a distance of nine and a half miles, or in an area of more than two hundred and eighty square miles. . . . As the fireball expands, it also sends out a blast wave in all directions, and this is the fourth destructive effect of the explosion. The blast wave of an air-burst one-megaton bomb can flatten or severely damage all but the strongest buildings within a radius of four and a half miles. . . . As the fireball burns, it rises, condensing water from the surrounding atmosphere to form the characteristic mushroom cloud. If the bomb has been set off on the ground or close enough to it so that the fireball touches the surface, a so-called ground burst, a crater will be formed, and tons of dust and debris will be fused with the intensely radioactive fission products and sucked up into the mushroom cloud. This mixture will return to earth as radioactive fallout, most of it in the form of fine ash, in the fifth

Chapter 8 / Cause and Effect

destructive effect of the explosion. Depending upon the composition of the surface, from 40 to 70 percent of this fallout—often called the "early" or "local" fallout—descends to earth within about a day of the explosion, in the vicinity of the blast and downwind from it, exposing human beings to radiation disease, an illness that is fatal when exposure is intense.

Jonathan Schell,
The Fate of the Earth

You should notice still another characteristic in this sample paragraph: the writer describes both main causes and subordinate causes, main effects and subordinate effects. One main cause, the explosion of the bomb, causes a series of five initial (main) effects. However, these effects become the causes for still other effects. The initial nuclear radiation (a main effect), for example, is also a cause that results in the death of unprotected human beings in a six-square-mile area (a subordinate effect). The electromagnetic pulse that is generated by the explosion is the cause, in turn, of the knocking out of electrical equipment (an effect). The thermal pulse (effect 3) causes second-degree burns in exposed humans in a 280-square-mile area. The blast wave (effect 4) causes the destruction of buildings, and the radioactive fallout (effect 5) exposes humans to radiation disease (an effect). So you can see that the cause-and-effect relationships can be complicated and require careful analysis by the writer.

You should keep two factors in mind when you are writing and **revising** a cause-and-effect essay. First, be sure that you have actually thought through the causes and effects very carefully. You should not be satisfied with considering only the most obvious or simple causes. For example, we tend to oversimplify and cite one cause as the reason for most wars—the attack on Pearl Harbor for the United States entering World War II, the firing on Fort Sumter for the start of the Civil War, and so on. For the most part, these tend to be the last of many contributing causes that have led to the war. A thoughtful discussion of such a topic in your writing would include an explanation of some of the contributing, less obvious but perhaps more important causes.

Second, you should be careful that you do not mistake some event as a cause simply because it preceded a particular effect. For instance, if a child swallows a coin and then comes down with measles, it would be inaccurate and faulty reasoning to assume that swallowing the coin was a cause of the measles.

Even though you need to guard against faulty assumptions, you should also be aware that writers do not always state a cause-and-effect relationship directly. Sometimes they leave it to the reader to **infer** such a relationship. That is, the writer does not state the relationship, but gives certain information arranged in such a way that the reader will be able to conclude that the relationship exists, as in the following sentences.

> On the ground next to the parked Jeep, the compass glinted in the moonlight. Deep in the woods, shielded from the moon, the hungry teenager circled in the dark with little idea where he had been or how to get where he wanted to go.

Although the writer does not directly state what happened, it is not hard to infer that the teenager dropped his compass without realizing it, with the effect that he is now lost.

You will need to make inferences when you read cause-and-effect writing as well as other modes of development. When you make an inference, be sure that you can pinpoint the information and trace the logic on which your inference is based. When you are writing cause and effect, be sure to give enough information, directly or indirectly stated, so that your reader can determine the cause-and-effect relationship.

You use cause-and-effect reasoning every day in solving problems and making decisions. Legislators create laws to address or prevent the causes of certain problems. In a similar way, scientists find cures for diseases when they are able to isolate the causes of those diseases. Understanding the relation between causes and effects is extremely important both in day-to-day living and in long-range planning. Communicating your understanding in writing is significant evidence of your ability to reason clearly and accurately.

A Momentous Arrest

Martin Luther King, Jr.

Martin Luther King, Jr., was catapulted into international fame when, working for the Southern Christian Leadership Conference, he organized blacks in Montgomery, Alabama, to boycott that city's segregated buses in 1955 and 1956. King, preaching nonviolent resistance to segregation, became the most important leader in the civil rights movement that changed American life so radically over the next decade. Here, in a simple, matter-of-fact tone, King tells of the incident that sparked the Montgomery bus boycott.

Words to Know

accommodate   to make space for, oblige
complied   carried out willingly

Getting Started

Can you imagine having the courage of Mrs. Rosa Parks as she rode into history on a December evening in 1955?

On December 1, 1955, an attractive Negro seamstress, Mrs. Rosa Parks, boarded the Cleveland Avenue Bus in downtown Montgomery. She was returning home after her regular day's work in the Montgomery Fair—a leading department store. Tired from long hours on her feet, Mrs. Parks sat down in the first seat behind the section reserved for whites. Not long after she took her seat, the bus operator ordered her, along with three other Negro passengers, to move back in order to accommodate boarding white passengers. By this time every seat in the bus was taken. This meant that if Mrs. Parks followed the driver's command she would have to stand while a white male passenger, who had just boarded the bus, would sit. The other three Negro passengers immediately complied with the driver's request. But Mrs. Parks quietly refused. The result was her arrest.

Questions About the Reading

1. Was Mrs. Parks breaking any law or custom in sitting where she did?
2. Why didn't Mrs. Parks move when the bus driver asked her to? Do you think she would have moved if the white passenger had been a woman instead of a man?
3. Was Mrs. Parks thinking about the civil rights movement when she refused to move? Explain your answer.

Questions About the Writer's Strategies

1. Which sentence states the cause in this paragraph? Which one states the effect?
2. Do you think the writer presents the incident **objectively** or **subjectively**? Use words and phrases from the paragraph to support your answer.
3. Other than cause and effect, what **mode of development** dominates in this paragraph?
4. What is the **order** in which the incidents in the paragraph are arranged?
5. Do you sympathize with Mrs. Parks? Explain your answer, citing **examples** from the essay that influence your feelings.

Writing Assignments

1. Think of a situation that has made you angry enough to defy authority and risk discipline or even arrest. Perhaps you have protested an unfair grade, a school rule, an unjust traffic ticket, or something of more consequence, like contamination of your city's water supply. Using cause and effect as your mode of development, describe in a paragraph what happened. Try to write objectively.
2. The civil rights movement of the 1950s and 1960s brought about many positive changes in our country's attitude toward minorities. There are, however, still steps that can be taken. In a paragraph, suggest one possible change the country can make, and speculate on the effects it could have on the lives of minority citizens.

The Golden Years

Frances Fitzgerald

*As they get older, most people dream about their ideal version of retire-
ment. But the reality of retirement is often very different from our daydreams. Frances Fitzgerald's paragraph, from her book* Cities on a Hill,
*offers some fascinating data on the contemporary generation of retired
Americans.*

Words to Know

avant-garde   a group who invents and applies new ideas
correlate   to connect, relate
demographics   human population data
migration   moving from one area to another

Getting Started

What will your life be like in your golden years?

$\mathbf{A}$mericans now in their sixties and seventies are surely the first generation of healthy, economically independent retired people in history—
and, in the absence of significant economic growth, they may well be the
last one. But, whatever the economic arrangements of the future, this
generation remains the cultural avant-garde for the increasingly large
generations of the elderly which are to follow them. Already, its members
have broken with many of the traditions of the past, shattering the con-
ventions of what older people should look like and do. And in the process they have changed the shape of American society. The census statis-
tics describe a part of this transformation. They tell us, for one thing, that
this generation has used its economic independence to get out of the
house—or to get its children out. In 1900, some 60 percent of all Americans sixty-five and over lived with an adult child. Today, only about 17
percent live with one. The figures do not tell us who initiated the move,
but they correlate very well with the increasing wealth of the elderly.
Today, a majority of Americans over sixty-five live in the same community as at least one of their children, and live in the place in which they

spent most of their lives. However, a significant minority of them have altered the traditional pattern by moving away from their families and out of their hometowns to make new lives for themselves elsewhere. Retired people—so the census shows—have contributed greatly to the general American migration to the Sun Belt; indeed, they have gone in such numbers as to make a distinct impression on the demographics of certain states. New Mexico, Arizona, and Southern California now have large populations of retirees, but it is Florida that has the highest proportion of them. People over sixty-five constitute 17.3 percent of the population of Florida—as opposed to the national average of 11.3 percent. These elderly migrants have not distributed themselves evenly around the state but have concentrated themselves on the coasts and in the area of Orlando. As a result, there are three counties on the west coast where the median age is between fifty and sixty, and eleven counties around the state where it is between forty and fifty.

Questions About the Reading

1. Why does the writer call the present generation of retired Americans "the cultural avant-garde" for the elderly who will follow them?
2. According to the writer, how have today's retirees changed the shape of American society?
3. How have some retired people altered the traditional pattern of aging?
4. What percentage of the population of Florida is over sixty-five?
5. Why is the median age between fifty and sixty for citizens in three counties on the west coast of Florida?

Questions About the Writer's Strategies

1. Is the **main idea** of this paragraph implied or stated directly? If it is stated directly, where is it located? If it is implied, state the main idea in your own words.
2. Identify the cause-and-effect elements in this paragraph.
3. Besides cause and effect, what other **mode of development** does the author use in this paragraph? List the details that support your answer.
4. Is this paragraph written **subjectively** or **objectively**? Explain your answer.

Writing Assignments

1. Can you imagine yourself as a retired person? Using cause and effect as a mode of development, write a paragraph describing your ideal future as a retiree and how you can go about planning for it now.
2. Do you think the United States will be in reasonable shape by the time you retire? Using cause-and-effect elements, write a paragraph discussing how current problems such as pollution will affect our lives in the future.

Why Eat Junk Food?

Judith Wurtman

Each day, Americans eat 50 million pounds of sugar, 3 million gallons of ice cream, and 5.8 million pounds of chocolate candy. Yet junk foods, as they are commonly known, contain few if any of the nutrients needed to maintain good health. Why, then, do people eat so much junk food? In the following paragraph, taken from Eating Your Way Through Life, *Judith Wurtman suggests two reasons.*

Words to Know

confectionaries   sweets, candies
depicted   shown, represented
euphoria   a feeling of well-being

Getting Started

How often do you think seriously about the food you consume?

We crunch and chew our way through vast quantities of snacks and confectionaries and relieve our thirst with multicolored, flavored soft drinks, with and without calories, for two basic reasons. The first is simple: the food tastes good, and we enjoy the sensation of eating it. Second, we associate these foods, often without being aware of it, with the highly pleasurable experiences depicted in the advertisements used to promote their sale. Current television advertisements demonstrate this point: people turn from grumpiness to euphoria after crunching a corn chip. Others water ski into the sunset with their loved ones while drinking a popular soft drink. People entertain on the patio with friends, cook over campfires without mosquitoes, or go to carnivals with granddad munching away at the latest candy or snack food. The people portrayed in these scenarios are all healthy, vigorous, and good looking; one wonders how popular the food they convince us to eat would be if they would crunch or drink away while complaining about low back pain or clogged sinuses.

Questions About the Reading

1. Why do people consume snacks and soft drinks?
2. How do television advertisements portray people eating snack foods?
3. What do you think would happen if television advertisements showed people complaining about poor health while eating snack foods?

Questions About the Writer's Strategies

1. Is the **topic** of this paragraph stated directly or **implied?** If it is stated directly, where is it located? If it is implied, state it in your own words.
2. Identify the cause-and-effect elements of this paragraph.
3. Explain the ways in which commercials use cause and effect to create false or misleading impressions.

Writing Assignments

1. Write a paragraph or an essay in which you describe the long-term ill effects of a poor diet—one that includes too much junk food or, in a quite different case, one that leads to undernourishment owing to hunger. You may want to research this topic in the library.
2. Think of a time when you consumed way too much of something—caffeine, cake or ice cream, spicy chili, or pizza or spaghetti. In a paragraph, describe the effects of your overindulgence.
3. Write a paragraph in which you identify some of the effects on your body of some activity in which you participate—for instance, jogging, tennis, yoga, or dance.

Bonding at Birth

Douglas A. Bernstein, Edward J. Roy, Thomas K. Srull, and Christopher Wickens

Cause-and-effect development offers a useful format for objective, informative writing. In this paragraph from a psychology textbook, notice how the writers use cause and effect to summarize, clearly and concisely, the point to be learned.

Word to Know

pediatricians   doctors who specialize in the care of children

Getting Started

In what ways does maternal-infant bonding play an important role in our psychological well-being?

In 1976 a book called *Maternal-Infant Bonding* was published. It changed the way that newborn infants are treated from the moment of birth. The authors, pediatricians Marshall Klaus and John Kennell, had observed mothers and their newborns and found that, during the first hour or so after birth, babies are usually awake and will gaze at the mother's face while the mother gazes at and touches the infant. The importance of this early contact was demonstrated by Klaus and Kennell's experiments on the effect of leaving mothers and newborns together for the hour after birth or giving them extra opportunities to be together during their hospital stay. They found that women who were given early and extended contact with their babies were later more emotionally attached to them than mothers given only the routine contact allowed by usual hospital procedures. Further, mothers given early and extended contact with their infants felt more competent and were more reluctant to leave their infants with another person. They stayed closer to their infants, often gazing into their eyes, touching and soothing them, and fondling and kissing them. This difference occurred in the hospital and lasted for a year or more (Hales et al., 1977; Kennell et al., 1974).

Questions About the Reading

1. How are newborn infants now treated? How do you think they were treated formerly?
2. How did Klaus and Kennell arrive at their findings? Make up a more detailed description of how you think the actual activities in their experiment went.
3. Procedures surrounding what fathers do during delivery have also changed in recent years. Judging from this paragraph, what do you think fathers should be doing while the baby is being born and just afterward?

Questions About the Writers' Strategies

1. What is the cause in this paragraph? Is there more than one cause?
2. What is the effect? Is there more than one?
3. Is there a **topic sentence** in this paragraph? If so, where is it? If not, state the **main idea** in your own words.
4. The paragraph describes observed behavior but not underlying internal causes of that behavior. Why?

Writing Assignments

1. Look at the bonding effect from a different angle. Write a paragraph in which you speculate about the psychological causes of the effect. That is, discuss possible reasons *why* early contact strengthens bonding.
2. Have you ever seen the reactions of an older brother or sister to the arrival of a new baby? Or can you remember how you reacted to this situation? Using the birth of a new baby as the cause, write a paragraph describing its effects on the older sibling(s). Illustrate with **examples,** if you can.

On Being Unemployed

Nelliejean Smith (student)

In the paragraph that follows, we learn of the many effects that unemployment can have on a person's life. The writer makes us see—and feel with her—that unemployment is a traumatic experience. Nelliejean Smith has proven, however, that she can cope, for she wrote this paragraph as a student at Cuyahoga Community College.

Words to Know

bureaucracy   government marked by spread of authority among numerous offices, inflexible rules of operation, and unwieldy administration

evoke   to summon or call forth, elicit

Getting Started

In what ways do the effects of unemployment reach deeper than an empty bank account?

Being unemployed creates many problems for my family and me. First of all, there are financial problems. We have cut back on the quality of groceries we purchase. We now buy two pounds of hamburger in place of two pounds of sirloin. This hamburger is also divided into quantities sufficient for three meals: one may be creole beef, one chili, and the other spaghetti. There is also less money for clothing. Dresses must be altered and made into blouses; pants make nice skirts after some alteration. I have two more very sticky problems. I've fallen behind in the rental payments for our apartment, and now I am experiencing difficulties trying to pay the back rent. The other sticky problem is my son's tuition payments. There does not seem to be any way that I can send a complete payment to his college. These are not the only problems I face. I also have psychological problems as a result of unemployment. Often I wonder why this has happened to me. Then depression and confusion take over, and I feel drained of all my abilities. The one question that fills my mind most often is the following: Why can't I get employment? This question evokes in me a lack of self-confidence and self-worth. I am haunted by an overall feeling of uselessness. My other problems center on trying to cope with the bureaucracy of the Employment Bureau. Once I get to the Employment Bureau, I stand in line to sign up. I then wait in another line to which I must report. Once I go through all of this, I am sent out for job interviews, only to find that the employer wants someone with more experience. To top everything off, I had to wait almost six months to receive my first unemployment check. As you can see, there is often a frustratingly long delay in receiving benefits. My family and I have suffered through many problems because of my unemployment.

Questions About the Reading

1. What do you think makes the inability to pay rent and her son's tuition particularly "sticky" problems for the writer?
2. What makes the writer feel "drained" of her abilities?
3. What psychological effects do you think the writer's unsuccessful job interviews have on her?

Questions About the Writer's Strategies

1. What is the **main idea** of this paragraph? Where is this idea first introduced? Where is it repeated?
2. **Transitional** words and expressions provide a bridge between points in this paragraph. Identify the writer's transitions.
3. The writer uses many examples to illustrate the effects of unemployment she names. Identify any two effects that are mentioned. Then identify two examples for each of these effects.
4. What **order** does the writer use in discussing the problems?

Writing Assignments

1. Is the employment bureau the writer describes doing a good job? In a paragraph, describe the effects of the bureau's procedures.
2. What are the effects unemployment has had on the American people as a whole? Do you think it has changed our image of ourselves as a nation? Write a cause-and-effect paragraph or essay in which you indicate some of the social effects of unemployment. You may want to read some articles on this topic in the library before you write.
3. Although being employed has more positive than negative effects, work does have effects that may not always be pleasant. Write a paragraph on how a particular job or certain types of jobs can have negative effects.

It Took This Night to Make Us Know

Bob Greene

Eleven Israeli athletes were murdered by Palestinian terrorists at the 1972 summer Olympics in Munich, West Germany. The news shocked and horrified the world. It also made at least one man—Chicago newspaper columnist Bob Greene—look deep inside himself and think, for perhaps the first time, about where he came from, who he was, and what it means to be born Jewish in today's world.

Words to Know

abstraction   a general idea representing a physical concept
patronized   treated in an offensive, condescending manner

Getting Started

In what ways can racial prejudice and violence be seen as integral parts of the human experience?

WASHINGTON:—It is not supposed to be very strong in us, for we cannot remember. We are the young Jews, born after Hitler, and we have never considered the fact that we are Jewish to be a large part of our identity. A lot of us have not been near a temple in ten years, and we laugh along with the Jewish jokes to show that we are very cool about the whole thing. We are Americans, we have told ourselves, we do not go around calling ourselves Jews: that is for the elderly men with the tortured faces, the old Jews we feel a little embarrassed to be around. Let them recall the centuries of hurt, we think; it is over now, so let them recall those years while we live our good todays.

It is not supposed to be very strong in us, and yet I am sitting at a typewriter in a hotel room hundreds of miles from home trying to write a story about a presidential campaign, and I cannot do it. For the television has just got done telling the story, the story of how once again people who hate the Jews have knocked on a door in the middle of the night and done their killing, and I can think of nothing else. Now the lesson is being taught all over again; it is not up to us to decide how to treat our Jewishness. That was decided for us centuries ago.

It is not supposed to be very strong in us, because all the barriers are 3 down now, and a hotel will not turn us away or a restaurant will not deny us a table if our name does not sound right. And yet when the killings began, they thought to get a young man named Mark Spitz out of Germany, because he may be the best swimmer in the world, but first of all he is a Jew, and no one wanted to think what might happen to him. Many of the people who thrilled as he won his gold medals were very surprised to find out now that Spitz is a Jew. Later they will say that of course it doesn't matter what his religion is. But Spitz knew that it mattered; we all knew that it mattered, and that it would be smarter for him to go.

It is not supposed to be very strong in us, and we have heard the term 4 "six million Jews are dead" so often that it is just an abstraction to us. And yet if the Dachau concentration camp, just a few miles from the Olympic site, was not enough to remind us, the killers in the Munich darkness made sure that we remembered. There is a hate for us that goes back centuries, and every time it seems to have weakened with the years there is another band of men ready to show us that the hate is still strong enough to make them kill in the night.

When the news was certain, when there was no question but that the 5 young Jewish men were dead, I called some friends and we talked about it. They were thinking the same way I was. For all these years we have acted bored with the Jewish traditions, smirked at the ancient, detailed ceremonies, patronized the old ones who insisted on showing their link with the past.

And for us, it took this one night to make us know that maybe it will 6 never go away. We are all Jews who were born into a world where money and education and parents who speak with no accent were part of the package, and that can fool you. But this is the oldest hate the world has ever seen, and 25 years of Jewish prosperity in the United States is hardly enough to erase it from the earth.

It is nothing that we young ones have ever talked much about, and 7 there are not many words to tell it now. Words cannot tell it as well as the look we have seen for years in the faces of the oldest Jews, the look of deepest sorrow that has been there for as many centuries as the hate.

This time the look is there because of a group of Arab terrorists. But it 8 goes so far beyond Middle Eastern politics; the look was there in this same Germany 30 years ago, it was there in Egypt centuries ago, it has been there in every place there have ever been Jews who were not wanted because they were Jews. And because there have been so many of these places, the look has been reborn and reborn and reborn.

There are young men who are dead this week who should be alive, and 9
it would be a horrible thing no matter who they were. But of course they
were Jews; the reason that they are dead is because they were Jews, and
that is why on this night there are so many of us starting to realize for the
first time what that means.

It is not supposed to be very strong in us, for we cannot remember. We 10
grew up laughing at the solemn old Jewish phrases that sounded so
mournful and outmoded and out of date in the second half of the twen-
tieth century. Ancient, outmoded phrases from the temples, phrases like
"Let my people go." Phrases that we chose to let mean nothing, because
it is not supposed to be very strong in us.

Questions About the Reading

1. Why, according to the writer, are young Jews embarrassed to be
   around old Jews with "tortured faces"?
2. Why is the writer having difficulty writing a story about a presidential
   campaign?
3. What effect does the killing of several Jewish men at the Olympics
   have on the young Jewish people living in the United States?
4. What "is not supposed to be very strong" in young American Jews?
5. Consider the title of the essay. What is it that the writer and his con-
   temporaries now know?

Questions About the Writer's Strategies

1. In your own words, express the **main idea** or **thesis** of the essay. Does
   the writer ever state this idea explicitly in a single sentence, or must
   the reader **infer** it?
2. What is the writer's **tone** in the essay? What attitude does he have toward the event described—and toward himself and his friends as a result of the event?
3. Identify the cause-and-effect elements in the essay.
4. How does the writer use repetition in the essay? What is its effect?

Writing Assignments

1. Write an essay in which you discuss what you perceive to be the
   causes of racial violence and their effects on society.

2. Do the Olympic Games decrease tensions among people of different nations, cultures, and races? Write a cause-and-effect essay on this topic.
3. Recall an incident in which you were ridiculed, harassed, or mistreated for no apparent reason other than groundless hostility. If you have never experienced anything like this, maybe someone among your friends could describe such an incident for you. Using the incident as your cause, write an essay about how it affected you or your friend.

Ozone

Ruth Caplan

The Earth is too precious a commodity for us to squander without thought for the future. This passage from Our Earth, Ourselves *focuses on one element of human pollution and its deadly implications for future generations and the world's ecosystem.*

Words to Know

burgeoning   increasing, rising

CFCs   chlorofluorocarbons, chemicals used as propellants and refrigerants that also cause the breakdown of ozone

depletion   exhaustion, gradually using up

ecosystem   relationship between organisms and environment viewed as a unit

epidemics   outbreaks of contagious diseases

inoculation   the process of communicating the virus of a disease in order to immunize

microorganisms   animals or plants that can be seen only with the aid of a microscope

ozone   a form of oxygen gas that makes up the protective layer shielding the Earth from the sun's ultraviolet radiation

photosynthesis   a process by which light is converted to chemical energy

polar vortex   the flow involving rotation about the polar axis

stratospheric   pertaining to a part of the atmosphere

ultraviolet radiation   radiation wavelengths beyond the visible spectrum

Getting Started

How important is ozone to the well-being of our planet and its inhabitants?

———————

Just as scientists have measured ozone loss over Antarctica, they have   1
recorded higher levels of ultraviolet radiation reaching that continent and beyond. The extremely high readings in Antarctica have deadly implications for its ecosystem. Laboratory experiments show that reproduc-

tion of algae, the base of the food chain, can be disrupted when exposed to sunlight unfiltered by ozone. Algae in Antarctic waters are necessary for the development of krill, the tiny surface-dwelling creature that is the main diet of a number of species, including many types of whales.

Recent studies have confirmed that the ozone hole is becoming larger 2 each year, spreading outward to the inhabited land masses surrounding Antarctica. In addition, in December 1987, three out of five Australian ozone-monitoring stations reported a sharp drop in stratospheric ozone levels shortly after the polar vortex broke up. In 1989, researchers reported elevated ultraviolet readings in portions of Australia.

However, danger signs exist closer to our own homes. Lower ozone 3 readings have been found above Bismarck, North Dakota; Caribou, Maine; Canada, Switzerland, and West Germany. During a recent 3½-month trek through Siberia, members of a Canadian-Soviet expedition received unusually severe sunburns. The suspected cause was higher levels of ultraviolet radiation reaching the trekers as a result of ozone depletion.

Not only does ultraviolet radiation cause sunburn, it also can promote 4 skin cancer. There has been a steady rise in this disease in the United States for the past 10 years, especially among Caucasians. Incidences of squamous and basal cell carcinoma, the two most common—but rarely fatal—forms of skin cancer are increasing in the United States at the rate of 600,000 new cases each year. The most deadly form of skin cancer, melanoma, attacks more than 25,000 Americans annually and accounts for about 8,000 deaths. If we continue to destroy the ozone layer, the numbers could become far more staggering.

The Environmental Protection Agency [EPA] recently warned that un- 5 less action is taken to halt ozone depletion, "the United States can expect 40 million additional skin cancer cases and 800,000 deaths of people alive today and those born during the next 88 years." The EPA's warning was based on the assumption that worldwide production of CFCs would grow at 2.5 percent a year. Some estimates show they're already growing faster than that.

Ultraviolet radiation is also a major cause of cataracts, a clouding of 6 the lens of the eye that causes blurred vision and eventual blindness. The EPA estimates that unchecked ozone depletion would bring this affliction to anywhere from 555,000 to 2.8 million Americans born before 2075. Like mild forms of skin cancer, cataracts can be treated with relatively simple surgery. Needed medical services would be available to residents of the developed world, albeit with the increasing cost to national resources. But a lack of medical treatment in less-developed countries would leave an escalating percentage of the world's burgeoning population at far greater risk of going blind or dying from skin cancer. The bulk of this neglected population would be the poor who live closer to the Equator and who now contribute least to ozone destruction.

There is yet another danger to humans from increased exposure to ul- 7 traviolet radiation. Too strong a dose can lower the body's ability to resist such attacking organisms as infectious diseases and tumors. Some medical experts worry that excess exposure will undermine the inoculation programs that have controlled diseases that once caused epidemics. Instead of protecting people from a disease, an inoculation could inflict the disease on those whose immune system has been damaged by excessive exposure to ultraviolet radiation.

Other species will share the sad results of ozone depletion. For the 8 many plants that are sensitive to ultraviolet radiation, continued exposure at higher-than-normal levels can impede photosynthesis, resulting in lower crop yields. A study by the University of Maryland found that soybean yields can drop up to 25 percent when these vital food crops are subjected to a 25 percent ozone loss. As with global warming, there is a danger that ozone loss may be occurring too rapidly for some plant species to adapt. The faster the depletion, the less chance there is for a particular species' survival.

At the foundation of the aquatic ecosystem are small organisms 9 known as phytoplankton. They live on the surface of water and depend on sunlight for survival, making them extremely vulnerable to changes in levels of ultraviolet radiation. Too much exposure to ultraviolet rays can kill phytoplankton, setting off a destructive, possibly deadly, reaction in the marine food chain—first affecting larger microorganisms, then fish larvae that feed on them, then small fish, then larger fish and marine mammals, and even aquatic birds that depend on water creatures for their food. There is no real timetable for this environmental destruction. But marine biologists warn that in recent years there have been reduced populations of krill.

Questions About the Reading

1. Why are algae important to the food chain?
2. According to the author, why are people in less-developed countries at greater risk from the depletion of the ozone layer?
3. What effect does ultraviolet radiation have on plant life?
4. What are the effects of the ozone loss for our planet's ecosystem? What are the effects for human beings?

Questions About the Writer's Strategies

1. Does this essay have a stated or implied **thesis statement**? If it is stated, what is it and where is it located? If it is implied, write it in your own words.
2. Identify the cause-and-effect elements in the essay.
3. Besides cause and effect, what other **mode of development** does the writer use? Support your answer with **details** from the text.

Writing Assignments

1. Write an essay discussing some of the causes and effects of human pollution. Choose one topic such as the forests or the oceans, or write more broadly about the general issue of pollution.
2. Imagine you are a historian writing in the year 2500. Write an essay discussing the historical causes and effects of pollution. Be as positive or as negative as you wish in imagining what the world will be like in five hundred years.

My First Lesson in How to Live as a Negro

Richard Wright

Richard Wright was an important black American writer. Born in Mississippi in 1908, Wright left school after the ninth grade and moved to Chicago, where he worked as a postal clerk. In 1946, he moved to Paris, where he lived until his death in 1960. In the essay, taken from Wright's Uncle Tom's Children, *he describes his first lesson in what it meant to be a young black in the United States in the early part of this century.*

Words to Know

appalling frightful
barrage a vigorous projection of many things at one time
embankments mounds of earth used for support or protection
fortifications things that strengthen or defend
Jim Crow systematic discrimination against blacks
overreaching reaching beyond
profusely in great quantities
stave a narrow strip of wood that forms the sides of a barrel

Getting Started

Can you describe a childhood incident in which you learned a very painful lesson?

My first lesson in how to live as a Negro came when I was quite small.   1
We were living in Arkansas. Our house stood behind the railroad tracks. Its skimpy yard was paved with black cinders. Nothing green ever grew in that yard. The only touch of green we could see was far away, beyond the tracks, over where the white folks lived. But cinders were good enough for me and I never missed the green growing things. And anyhow cinders were fine weapons. You could always have a nice hot war with huge black cinders. All you had to do was crouch behind the brick pillars of a house with your hands full of gritty ammunition. And the first woolly black head you saw pop out from behind another row of pillars was your target. You tried your very best to knock it off. It was great fun.

I never fully realized the appalling disadvantages of a cinder environ- 2
ment till one day the gang to which I belonged found itself engaged in a
war with the white boys who lived beyond the tracks. As usual we laid
down our cinder barrage, thinking that this would wipe the white boys
out. But they replied with a steady bombardment of broken bottles. We
doubled our cinder barrage, but they hid behind trees, hedges, and the
sloping embankments of their lawns. Having no such fortifications, we
retreated to the brick pillars of our homes. During the retreat a broken
milk bottle caught me behind the ear, opening a deep gash which bled
profusely. The sight of blood pouring over my face completely demoral-
ized our ranks. My fellow-combatants left me standing paralyzed in the
center of the yard, and scurried for their homes. A kind neighbor saw me
and rushed me to a doctor, who took three stitches in my neck.

I sat brooding on my front steps, nursing my wound and waiting for 3
my mother to come from work. I felt that a grave injustice had been done
me. It was all right to throw cinders. The greatest harm a cinder could do
was leave a bruise. But broken bottles were dangerous; they left you cut,
bleeding, and helpless.

When night fell, my mother came from the white folks' kitchen. I raced 4
down the street to meet her. I could just feel in my bones that she would
understand. I knew she would tell me exactly what to do next time. I
grabbed her hand and babbled out the whole story. She examined my
wound, then slapped me.

"How come yuh didn't hide?" she asked me. "How come yuh aw- 5
ways fightin'?"

I was outraged, and bawled. Between sobs I told her that I didn't have 6
any trees or hedges to hide behind. There wasn't a thing I could have
used as a trench. And you couldn't throw very far when you were hiding
behind the brick pillars of a house. She grabbed a barrel stave, dragged
me home, stripped me naked, and beat me till I had a fever of one
hundred and two. She would smack my rump with the stave, and, while
the skin was still smarting, impart to me gems of Jim Crow wisdom. I was
never to throw cinders any more. I was never to fight any more wars. I
was never, never, under any conditions, to fight *white* folks again. And
they were absolutely right in clouting me with the broken milk bottle.
Didn't I know she was working hard every day in the hot kitchens of the
white folks to make money to take care of me? When was I ever going to
learn to be a good boy? She couldn't be bothered with my fights. She finished by telling me that I ought to be thankful to God as long as I lived
that they didn't kill me.

All that night I was delirious and could not sleep. Each time I closed 7
my eyes I saw monstrous white faces suspended from the ceiling, leering
at me.

From that time on, the charm of my cinder yard was gone. The green 8
trees, the trimmed hedges, the cropped lawns grew very meaningful, became a symbol. Even today when I think of white folks, the hard, sharp
outlines of white houses surrounded by trees, lawns, and hedges are
present somewhere in the background of my mind. Through the years
they grew into an overreaching symbol of fear.

Questions About the Reading

1. What was the difference between fighting with cinders and fighting
   with broken bottles?
2. Why do you think Wright expected his mother to understand what
   had happened? Why do you think she beat him instead?
3. Why did the green trees, trimmed hedges, and cropped lawns become
   "meaningful" and "an overreaching symbol of fear" for Wright?

Questions About the Writer's Strategies

1. Does this essay have a direct **thesis statement**? If so, what is it and
   where is it located? If not, state it in your own words.
2. What two **modes of development** are used to develop the thesis?
3. Identify the cause-and-effect elements of the essay.
4. Compare the first and last paragraphs of the essay, and explain the
   purpose of each.

Writing Assignments

1. Recall an incident from your childhood that has had a long-lasting effect on you. Write an essay that describes that incident and its effects.
2. Have you ever been involved in a fight or an argument that you knew
   you couldn't win? Describe the incident and discuss its effects on you.
3. Try to recall an incident that brought home to you the painful meaning
   of discrimination or prejudice. Write an essay describing the incident
   and its effects on you.

The Bounty of the Sea

Jacques Cousteau

Jacques Cousteau, the famous French oceanographer, has brought the world of the oceans to us through his books and television documentaries. His love for the oceans has extended to a lifelong concern for protecting and conserving the marine environment. In the following essay, written in the mid-1960s, he vividly describes the sickening of the ocean and the effects that the death of the oceans would have on humankind.

Words to Know

buffer   something that protects
cheek by jowl   very close together
effluents   sewage
insupportable   unbearable
plankton algae   microscopic plant life that floats in water
remorseless   without regret or pity
stench   stink, bad smell
teemed   swarmed
trawlers   fishing boats that drag large nets along the bottom of the ocean

Getting Started

How can the world community understand—and undo—the effects of pollution before it's too late?

———————————————

During the past thirty years, I have observed and studied the oceans 1 closely, and with my own two eyes I have seen them sicken. Certain reefs that teemed with fish only ten years ago are now almost lifeless. The ocean bottom has been raped by trawlers. Priceless wetlands have been destroyed by landfill. And everywhere are sticky globs of oil, plastic refuse, and unseen clouds of poisonous effluents. Often, when I describe the symptoms of the oceans' sickness, I hear remarks like "they're only fish" or "they're only whales" or "they're only birds." But I assure you that our destinies are linked with theirs in the most profound and fundamental manner. For if the oceans should die—by which I mean that all life in the sea would finally cease—this would signal the end not only for marine life but for all other animals and plants of this earth, including man.

With life departed, the ocean would become, in effect, one enormous 2 cesspool. Billions of decaying bodies, large and small, would create such an insupportable stench that man would be forced to leave all the coastal regions. But far worse would follow.

The ocean acts as the earth's buffer. It maintains a fine balance between 3 the many salts and gases which make life possible. But dead seas would have no buffering effect. The carbon dioxide content of the atmosphere would start on a steady and remorseless climb, and when it reached a certain level a "greenhouse effect" would be created. The heat that normally radiates outward from the earth to space would be blocked by the CO_2, and sea level temperatures would dramatically increase.

One catastrophic effect of this heat would be melting of the icecaps at 4 both the North and South Poles. As a result, the ocean would rise by 100 feet or more, enough to flood almost all the world's major cities. These rising waters would drive one-third of the earth's billions inland, creating famine, fighting, chaos, and disease on a scale almost impossible to imagine.

Meanwhile, the surface of the ocean would have scummed over with 5 a thick film of decayed matter, and would no longer be able to give water freely to the skies through evaporation. Rain would become a rarity, creating global drought and even more famine.

But the final act is yet to come. The wretched remnant of the human 6 race would now be packed cheek by jowl on the remaining highlands, bewildered, starving, struggling to survive from hour to hour. Then would be visited upon them the final plague, anoxia (lack of oxygen). This would be caused by the extinction of plankton algae and the reduction of land vegetation, the two sources that supply the oxygen you are now breathing.

And so man would finally die, slowly gasping out his life on some bar- 7 ren hill. He would have survived the oceans by perhaps thirty years. And his heirs would be bacteria and a few scavenger insects.

Questions About the Reading

1. How does Cousteau know that the oceans are sick? What evidence does he give?
2. What is the "greenhouse effect"?
3. What is CO_2?

Questions About the Writer's Strategies

1. What is the **thesis** of this essay? Is it directly stated or **implied**? If it is directly stated, where in the essay is it stated?
2. Identify the cause-and-effect elements of this essay.
3. Apart from cause and effect, does the writer use any other **modes of development**?
4. How are you affected by the use of such words as "scummed over," "thick film of decayed matter," and "cesspool" to describe the ocean?

Writing Assignments

1. Write an essay discussing some of the causes and effects of air pollution. You may want to do some reading in the library before you write.
2. What personal steps can you take to stop pollution? Write an essay that describes what you as an individual can do and what effects you think your actions would have.
3. Why do people pollute? Write an essay identifying some of the things that cause people to harm the environment and the types of pollution that result.

The Thirsty Animal

Brian Manning

In this personal essay, Brian Manning recounts how he developed into a problem drinker and describes his ongoing life as an alcoholic who has quit drinking. Straightforwardly, he tells of his bittersweet memories of drinking and of his struggle, successful so far, to keep the thirsty "animal living inside" locked in its cage.

Words to Know

accouterments   the things that go along with something, accompanying effects or activities
Bordeaux   a type of French wine, usually red
lolling   lounging, relaxing

Getting Started

Can you describe, from a firsthand experience, some of the negative effects of alcohol?

I was very young, but I still vividly remember how my father fascinated 1 my brothers and me at the dinner table by running his finger around the rim of his wineglass. He sent a wonderful, crystal tone wafting through the room, and we loved it. When we laughed too raucously, he would stop, swirl the red liquid in his glass and take a sip.

There was a wine cellar in the basement of the house we moved into 2 when I was eleven. My father put a few cases of Bordeaux down there in the dark. We played there with other boys in the neighborhood, hid there, made a secret place. It was musty and cool and private. We wrote things and stuck them in among the bottles and imagined someone way in the future baffled by our messages from the past.

Many years later, the very first time I drank, I had far too much. But I 3 found I was suddenly able to tell a girl at my high school that I was mad about her.

When I drank in college with the men in my class, I was trying to de- 4 fine a self-image I could feel comfortable with. I wanted to be "an Irishman," I decided, a man who could drink a lot of liquor and hold it. My favorite play was Eugene O'Neill's *Long Day's Journey into Night,* my model the drunken Jamie Tyrone.

I got out of college, into the real world, and the drunk on weekends 5 started to slip into the weekdays. Often I didn't know when one drunk ended and another began. The years were measured in hangovers. It took a long time to accept, and then to let the idea sink in, that I was an alcoholic.

It took even longer to do anything about it. I didn't want to believe it, 6 and I didn't want to deny myself the exciting, brotherly feeling I had whenever I went boozing with my friends. For a long time, in my relationships with women, I could only feel comfortable with a woman who drank as much as I did. So I didn't meet many women and spent my time with men in dark barrooms, trying to be like them and hoping I'd be accepted.

It is now two years since I quit drinking, and that, as all alcoholics 7 know who have come to grips with their problem, is not long ago at all. The urge to have "just one" includes a genuine longing for all the accouterments of drink: the popping of a cork, the color of Scotch through a glass, the warmth creeping over my shoulders with the third glass of stout. Those were joys. Ever since I gave them up I remember them as delicious.

I go to parties now and start off fine, but I have difficulty dealing with 8 the changing rhythms as the night wears on. Everyone around me seems to be having a better time the more they drink, and I, not they, become awkward. I feel like a kid with a broken chain when everyone else has bicycled around the corner out of sight. I fight against feeling sorry for myself.

What were the things I was looking for and needed when I drank? 9 I often find that what I am looking for when I want a drink is not really the alcohol, but the memories and laughter that seemed possible only with a glass in my hand. In a restaurant, I see the bottle of vintage port on the shelf, and imagine lolling in my chair, swirling the liquid around in the glass, inhaling those marvelous fumes. I think of my neighbor, Eileen, the funniest woman I ever got smashed with, and I want to get up on a bar stool next to her to hear again the wonderful stories she told. She could drink any man under the table, she claimed, and I wanted to be one of those men who tried. She always won, but it made me feel I belonged when I staggered out of the bar, her delighted laughter following me.

I had found a world to cling to, a way of belonging, and it still attracts 10 me. I pass by the gin mills and pubs now and glance in at the men lined up inside, and I don't see them as suckers or fools. I remember how I felt sitting there after work, or watching a Sunday afternoon ball game, and I long for the smell of the barroom and that ease—toasts and songs, jokes and equality. I have to keep reminding myself of the wasting hangovers, the lost money, the days down the drain.

I imagine my problem as an animal living inside me, demanding a 11 drink before it dies of thirst. That's what it says, but it will never die of thirst. The fact an alcoholic faces is that this animal breathes and waits. It is incapable of death and will spring back to lustful, consuming life with even one drop of sustenance.

When I was eighteen and my drinking began in earnest, I didn't play 12 in the wine cellar at home anymore; I stole there. I sneaked bottles to my room, sat in the window and drank alone while my parents were away. I hated the taste of it, but I kept drinking it, without the kids from the neighborhood, without any thought that I was feeding the animal. And one day, I found one of those old notes we had hidden down there years before. It fell to the ground when I pulled a bottle from its cubbyhole. I read it with bleary eyes, then put the paper back into the rack. "Beware," it said, above a childish skull and crossbones, "all ye who enter here." A child, wiser than I was that day, had written that note.

I did a lot of stupid, disastrous, sometimes mean things in the years 13 that followed, and remembering them is enough to snap me out of the memories and back to the reality that I quit just in time. I've done something I had to do, something difficult and necessary, and that gives me satisfaction and the strength to stay on the wagon. I'm very lucky so far. I don't get mad that I can't drink anymore; I can handle the self-pity that overwhelmed me in my early days of sobriety. From time to time, I daydream about summer afternoons and cold beer. I know such dreams will never go away. The thirsty animal is there, getting a little fainter every day. It will never die. A lot of my life now is all about keeping it in a very lonely cage.

Questions About the Reading

1. What went along with drinking for the writer? Why did he need alcohol to achieve those effects?
2. Why are parties difficult for the writer?
3. Why did the writer stop drinking?
4. When you finished reading the essay, what opinions had you formed of the writer's personality and character? Cite specific examples from the essay to support your opinions.

Questions About the Writer's Strategies

1. What is the **main idea** of this essay? In which sentences is it most clearly suggested?
2. What are the causes in this essay? What are the effects? Do they overlap at all?
3. Other than cause and effect, what **modes of development** does the writer use? Cite some specific paragraphs in which he uses other modes.
4. The "animal" introduced in paragraph 11 is a **metaphor**. What does it stand for? Interpret it in your own words.
5. Identify the **simile** in paragraph 8. Is it effective in helping you understand how the writer feels?

Writing Assignments

1. Describe in an essay the effects that alcohol has on you. If you do not drink, describe the effects that you have seen it have on others.
2. Do you know anyone who abuses alcohol or other drugs? If not, you have surely heard or read in the media or in school awareness programs about the lure of drugs. Based on what you know (and on what you have learned from reading this essay), write an essay describing the causes and effects of drug abuse.

The Spoils of War

Lynne Sharon Schwartz

When Lynne Sharon Schwartz became curious about an arrogant student in her literature class, she assumed that his anger had to do with the general antiestablishment feeling of the Vietnam era. The last thing she expected was that he would have something to teach her.

Words to Know

ascetic   stern, somber, self-disciplined
demeanor   manner, behavior
eloquent   articulate, expressive
formidably   admirably
impassive   unresponsive, indifferent
impromptu   spontaneous
innate   natural, built-in
microcosm   a smaller system representative of the larger system
prehensile   adapted to seize or grasp
rueful   sorrowful, pitiful
scrutinizing   inspecting, examining
Socratic method   a method of teaching whereby the teacher
    guides student learning by asking leading questions
spoils   property seized unlawfully
strident   loud, shrill
volatile   erratic, unpredictable

Getting Started

When a war is over, why doesn't the suffering end?

H e always sat in the back row, as far away as he could get: long skinny   1
body and long face, thin curly hair, dark mustache. Sometimes his bony
shoulders were hunched as he peered down at his notebook lying open
on that bizarre prehensile arm that grows out of college classroom chairs.
Or else he leaned way back, the lopsided chair balanced on two legs and
propped against the rear wall, his chest appearing slightly concave be-

neath his white shirt, and one narrow leg, in jeans, elegantly stretched out to rest on a nearby empty chair.

Casual but tense, rather like a male fashion model. Volatile beneath the 2 calm: someone you would not want to meet on a dark street. His face was severely impassive in a way that suggested arrogance and scorn.

He must have been about twenty-seven years old, an extremely thin 3 young man—ascetic, stripped down to the essentials. His body looked so brittle and so electrically charged that I almost expected crackling noises when he moved, but in fact he slipped in and out silently, in the wink of an eye. His whole lanky, scrutinizing demeanor was intimidating. He would have no patience with anything phony, I imagined; would not suffer fools gladly.

About every fourth or fifth class he was absent, common enough for 4 evening-session students, who had jobs, families, grown-up lives and responsibilities. I was a trifle relieved at his absences—I could relax—yet I missed him, too. His presence made a definite and compelling statement, but in an unintelligible language. I couldn't interpret him as readily as I could the books on the reading list.

I was hired in the spring of 1970. It was wartime. Students were en- 5 raged. When I went for my interview at Hunter College I had to walk past pickets into a building where black flags hung from the windows. I would use the Socratic method, I earnestly told the interviewer, since I believed in the students' innate intelligence. To myself, I vowed I would win their confidence. After all, I was scarcely older than they were and I shared their mood of protest. I would wear jeans to show I was one of them, and even though I had passed thirty and was married and had two children, I would prove that I could be trusted. I was prepared—even eager—for youthful, strident, moral indignation.

Far from strident, he was totally silent, never speaking in class discus- 6 sions, and I was reluctant to call on him. Since he had a Spanish name, I wondered whether he might have trouble with English. Bureaucratic chaos was the order of the day, with the City University enacting in microcosm the confusion in the nation at large; it was not unusual for barely literate or barely English-speaking students to wind up in an Introduction to Literature class. His silence and his blank arrogant look could simply mean bewilderment. I ought to find out, but I waited.

His first paper was a shocker. I was surprised to receive it at all—I had 7 him pegged as the sullen type who would give up at the first difficult assignment, then complain that college was irrelevant. On the contrary, the paper, formidably intelligent, jarred my view of the fitness of things. It didn't seem possible—no, it didn't seem *right*—that a person so sullen and mute should be so eloquent. Someone must have helped him. The truth would come out in impromptu class papers, and then I would confront him. I bided my time.

After the first exam he tossed his blue book onto my desk, not meeting 8 my eyes, and, wary and feline, glided away, withdrawing into his body as if attempting a disappearing act. The topic he had chosen was the meaning of "the horror" in Joseph Conrad's *Heart of Darkness*, the novella we had spent the first few sessions on.

He compared it to Faulkner's *Intruder in the Dust*. He wrote at length 9 about racial hatred and war and their connection in the dark, unspeakable places in the soul from which both spring, without sentimentality but with a sort of matter-of-fact, old knowledge. He knew Faulkner better than I did; I had to go back and skim *Intruder in the Dust* to understand his exam. I do know that I had never before sat transfixed in disbelief over a student paper.

The next day I called him over after class and asked if he was aware 10 that he had an extraordinary mind. He said, yes, he was. Close up, there was nothing arrogant about him. A bit awkward and shy, yet gracious, with something antique and courtly in his manner.

Why did he never speak in class, I asked.   11

He didn't like to speak in front of people. His voice and his eye turned 12 evasive, like an adolescent's, as he told me this. Couldn't, in fact. Couldn't speak.

What do you mean, I said. You're not a kid. You have a lot to say. You 13 write like this and you sit in class like a statue? What's it all about?

He was in the war, he said, and he finally looked at my face and spoke 14 like the adult that he was. He was lost for a long time in the jungles of Vietnam, he explained patiently, as if I might not know what Vietnam was, or what a jungle was, or what it was to be lost. And after that, he said, he couldn't. He just found it hard to be with people. To speak to people.

But you're so smart. You could do so much.   15

I know. He shrugged: a flesh-and-blood version of the rueful, devil- 16 may-care, movie war-hero shrug. Can't be helped.

Anything can be helped, I insisted.   17

No, he insisted back, quietly. Not after that jungle.   18

Hunter had a counseling service, free. Go, I pleaded.   19

He had already gone. They keep asking me questions about my child- 20 hood, he said, my relationship with my parents, my toilet training. He grinned quickly, turning it on and off. But it doesn't help. It's none of that. It's from when I was lost in that jungle.

You must work, I said. Don't you have to talk to people when you 21
work?

No, he was a meter man. 22

A what? 23

He went around checking on cars, to see if they had overstayed their 24
time at the parking meters.

You can't do that forever, I said. With your brains! 25

Well, at least he didn't have to talk to people, he said sweetly. For now. 26
Maybe later on he would get braver.

And what would he do if I called on him in class? If I made him talk? 27

Oh no, don't do that, he said, and flashed the wry grin again. If you did 28
that I'd probably run out of the room.

I never called on him because I didn't want to risk seeing him run out 29
of the room. But at least we stopped being afraid of each other. He gave
up his blank look, and occasionally I would glance at his face, to see if I
was still making sense or drifting off into some seductive, academic
cloud of words.

I thought of him a lot this summer after I saw young men lined up at 30
post offices to register for military service. I thought of him also when I
heard Ronald Reagan and John Anderson, on television, solemnly pledge
themselves to the defense of this country's shores. No candidate has yet
pledged himself to the defense of this country's young men, to "taking
every measure necessary" to "insure" that their genius does not turn
mute and their very lives become the spoils of war.

Questions About the Reading

1. What was the writer's first impression of the young man in her class?
   Why did she think you wouldn't want to meet him on a dark street?
2. Why did the writer believe she had to prove to her students that she
   could be trusted?
3. What was shocking about the student's paper?
4. What made the young man's genius "turn mute"?

Questions About the Writer's Strategies

1. What are the causes and effects in this essay?
2. Is the **thesis** stated in this essay? If so, what is it? If not, state the thesis
   in your own words.
3. Other than cause and effect, which **mode of development** does the
   writer employ?

4. What **simile** is used in the second paragraph? What does it imply about the student's looks?
5. What is the **tone** of this essay? How does the tone change in the last paragraph?

Writing Assignments

1. Write an essay that describes the positive effects military service can have on young people.
2. Write a cause-and-effect essay explaining how the survivors of war can also become some of its victims. Include people from both sides of the conflict in your explanation.
3. Think of a current situation in which the government could intervene to help people. Using cause and effect as your mode of development, describe how you believe the country's leaders should act.

9

Definition

When writers use words that they think may be unfamiliar to their readers, they will usually define the words. A **definition** is an explanation of the meaning of a word or term.

In its shortest form, the definition may be simply a **synonym**—a familiar word or phrase that has the same meaning as the unfamiliar word. For example, in "she shows more *empathy* for, or true understanding of, older people than her sister," the word *understanding* is a synonym for *empathy*. Or the writer may choose to use an **antonym**—a word or phrase that has the opposite meaning of the unfamiliar word—as in "she is a compassionate rather than an *inconsiderate* person." Here the word *inconsiderate* gives the reader the opposite of the meaning of *compassionate*.

The writer may also choose to use the kind of precise definition found in dictionaries, called a *formal definition*. In a formal definition, the writer first uses a form of **classification**, assigning the word to the **class** of items to which it belongs—and then describing the characteristics that distinguish it from other items of that same class. Here is an example of a formal definition.

Word defined:
class

Description of
characteristics

⌐ A tiger, a member of the cat family, is native to Asia, usually
⌐ weighs over 350 pounds, and has tawny and black-striped
∟ fur.

Many complex words and abstract ideas—such as *truth* and *justice*—require longer and more detailed explanations, which are called **extended definitions**. In an extended definition, the writer may use one or more of the methods of development—description, examples, classification, and so forth—that you have learned about in the earlier chapters of this book. For instance, in the sample paragraphs that follow, the writer first defines the word **symbol** by a formal definition and then, in the third sentence, continues to explain by saying what symbols are *not*, using an antonym. In the second paragraph, the writer completes the definition by using several clear-cut **examples** of symbols.

Formal definition
  A symbol is a person, place, or thing that stands for or 1
strongly suggests something in addition to itself, generally an abstract idea more important than itself. Don't let this def-

Antonym
inition intimidate you. Symbols are not fancy literary de-vices that readers have to wrestle with. In fact, the daily, non-literary lives of readers are filled, quite comfortably and naturally, with more symbols than exist in any book ever written.

Example
  A mink coat, for example, is a piece of clothing made from 2
the pelt of an animal in the weasel family, but for many peo-ple it stands for something else: it is a symbol of success or status or good taste. People do not make sacrifices and sounds of ecstasy over the pelt of a weasel, but over a sym-

Example
bol. A beard, to cite another example, is a hairy growth on a man's face, but a person would have to be a recent arrival from another planet not to realize that a beard is often viewed as a symbol of anything from youthful self-assertion to political radicalism. Our lives are pervaded, perhaps

Examples
dominated, by symbols. Think about the different symbolic meanings everyone gives to the following: a Cadillac, a new house, money, rats, a college diploma, a trip to Europe, a cru-cifix, a date with a popular and goodlooking girl, the Ameri-can flag, a blind date, Lawrence Welk, the F.B.I., Niagara Falls, Valley Forge, a fireplace.

David Skwire and Francis Chitwood,
Student's Book of College English, 2d ed.

Connotation, which refers to the feelings or qualities we associate with a word, and **denotation**, the dictionary definition of a word, are im-portant in writing a definition. Think of the word *pig*, for instance. The dictionary may tell you that a pig is simply a domestic animal with hooves, short legs, bristly hair, and a blunt snout; and a farmer may tell you that a pig is rather intelligent and cleaner than other farm animals. However, the negative connotations of this word are so strong that you are likely to have trouble thinking of a pig without thinking of filth, fat, and greed.

In writing definitions, it is particularly important to choose your words in such a way that their connotations, as well as their denotations, will give your readers the correct impression of what you are defining.

As you are writing and revising, remember to search for the single best word for conveying your ideas.

When you search for connotative words and expressions to use in your writing, beware of **clichés**. Clichés are words or phrases—like "rosy red," "silly goose," "bull in a china shop," "weird," or "outrageous" —that have become so overused that they indicate a lack of imagination and thought on the part of the writer who uses them. Symbols, too, can be clichés. If you are defining *courage*, for example, using Rambo as a symbol to enhance your definition is unlikely to impress your readers. Experienced writers may sometimes use clichés to achieve certain effects, such as humor or ridicule. As a student writer, however, you should try to avoid them so that your writing will seem fresh and original. You should also be aware that many clichés take the form of **similes**—"as filthy as a pig"—and try to make sure your similes are always of your own creation, not ones you have heard before.

In addition to examples, several other **modes of development** can be used to write an extended definition. For example, the writer might use **description** or **narration** or both as the main method of development.

Topic sentence: formal definition	A glacier is an accumulation of snow and ice that continually flows from a mountain ice field toward sea level. Glaciers are
	formed when successive snowfalls pile up, creating pressure on the bottom layers. Gradually, the pressure causes the snow on the bottom to undergo a structural change into an extremely dense form of ice called glacier ice, a process that may take several years. Once the ice begins to accumulate, gravity causes the mass to move downhill. Glaciers usually take the path of least resistance, following stream beds or
Extended definition: descriptive narration	other natural channels down the mountainside. As they move, they scrape along the surface of the earth, picking up rocks and other sediment on the way. The ice and the debris carve a deep U-shaped valley as they proceed down the mountain. If they advance far enough, they will eventually reach the sea and become tidewater glaciers that break off, or calve, directly into salt water. Southeast Alaska is one of only three places in the world where tidewater glaciers exist. (They also are found in Scandinavia and Chile.) Other glaciers, called hanging glaciers, spill out of icy basins high up on valley walls and tumble toward the valley floor.

Sarah Eppenbach,
Alaska's Southeast

Or, as in the example that follows, the writer may use a formal definition combined with **classification, examples,** and **comparison** and **contrast.**

Formal definition Classification: area of land, sea, or sky	A map is a <u>conventional picture</u> of an <u>area of land, sea, or sky</u>. Perhaps the maps most widely used are the <u>road maps</u> 1
Example: road maps	given away by the oil companies. They show the cultural features such as states, towns, parks, and roads, especially
Example: simple maps	paved roads. They show also natural features, such as rivers and lakes, and sometimes mountains. As <u>simple maps</u>, most automobile drivers have on various occasions used sketches drawn by service station men, or by friends, to show the best automobile route from one town to another.
Contrast: chart— represents water: map— represents land	The distinction usually made between "maps" and 2 "charts" is that a chart is a representation of an area consisting chiefly of water; a map represents an area that is predominantly land. It is easy to see how this distinction arose
Contrast: chart— for navigation	in the days when there was no navigation over land, but a truer distinction is that charts are specially designed for use in navigation, whether at sea or in the air.
	Maps have been used since the earliest civilizations, and 3 explorers find that they are used in rather simple civiliza-
Example: use of maps	tions at the present time by people who are accustomed to traveling. For example, Arctic explorers have obtained considerable help from maps of the coast lines showing settle-
Example: features of some maps	ments, drawn by Eskimo people. Occasionally maps show not only the roads, but pictures of other features. One of the earliest such maps dates from about 1400 B.C. It shows not only roads, but also lakes with fish, and a canal with croco-
Comparison: features of early maps with modern maps	diles and a bridge over the canal. This is somewhat similar to the modern maps of a state which show for each large town some feature of interest or the chief products of that town.

C. C. Wylie,
Astronomy, Maps, and Weather

As you can see, you may use any method of development that is appropriate when you need to extend a definition of a word or term.

Whether you are writing an extended definition or relying primarily on some other mode of development, always remember to define any words or terms you use that may be unfamiliar to your readers—particularly any words they must know to understand your meaning. You should also define words with any special or technical meaning that you include in your writing.

The Ultimate Kitchen Gadget

Robert Capon

Anyone who likes to cook owns a number of kitchen gadgets. What is your favorite: a garlic press, a food processor, or a blender? In the following selection, Robert Capon, an Episcopal priest and lover of cooking, defines the ultimate kitchen gadget.

Word to Know

trice a very short time

Getting Started

What is your favorite household appliance?

It is the ultimate kitchen gadget. It serves as a juicer for lemons, oranges and grapefruit, and as a combination seed remover and pulp crusher for tomatoes. It functions as a bowl scraper, an egg separator and a remover of unwelcome particles—the stray bit of eggshell, the odd grain of black rice—from mixing bowl or saucepan. It is a thermometer capable of gauging temperatures up to 500 degrees Fahrenheit and, in addition, is a measuring device for dry ingredients in amounts from 1 tablespoon down to 1/8 teaspoon or less, and for whatever liquids may be called for in the cooking of grains and stocks. It can be used as tongs for removing hot cup custards from the oven, as a mixer of water into pastry dough and as a kneader of bread. Best of all, it cleans up in a trice, presents no storage problems, will not chip, rust or tarnish and, if it cannot be said to be unlosable or indestructible, it nevertheless comes with a lifetime guarantee to remain the one household convenience you will have the least desire either to lose or to destroy. It is, of course, the human hand.

Questions About the Reading

1. Temperatures above about 160 degrees will burn a person's hand. How can the hand be used to gauge temperatures up to 500 degrees?
2. What is the lifetime guarantee of the ultimate kitchen gadget?

3. At what point in the paragraph did you guess what the ultimate kitchen gadget is?

Questions About the Writer's Strategies

1. What is the predominant **mode of development** used to define the ultimate kitchen gadget?
2. Why doesn't the writer identify what he is defining until the very last sentence?
3. What is the **tone** of this paragraph?
4. What **connotations** does the word *gadget* have? Would you normally associate these connotations with the human hand?
5. What is the **irony** in this paragraph?

Writing Assignments

1. Write a paragraph in which you define a household appliance (such as a blender, a vacuum cleaner, or a toaster) by giving examples of its uses and the purpose it serves.
2. Write a definition of the human hand from another point of view. Instead of giving examples of what it can do in the kitchen, describe its physical anatomy—what it looks like underneath the skin. You may want to consult a biology or anatomy textbook.
3. Write a definition of the human body by giving examples of some of the things it can do.

"I Love You"

Robert C. Solomon

Some words and ideas are almost impossible to define. In this paragraph, however, Robert Solomon shows that a definition can express a great deal about a phrase that has no conclusive, final meaning.

Words to Know

elusive   hard to grasp
precipitate   cause

Getting Started

Can you define those three small but important words, *I love you?*

"I love you" does not always have the same meaning, and this, too, should tell us something about the elusive nature of love. The first time it is always a surprise, an invasion, an aggressive act, but once said, "I love you" can only be repeated. It is unthinkable that it should not be said again, and again, and again. When one has not said it for a while, this may itself precipitate a crisis. ("Now why haven't you said that in all of these months!") On the other hand, "I love you" can also serve as a threat ("Don't push me on this; you might lose me"), emotional blackmail ("I've said it, now you have to respond in kind"), a warning ("It's only because I love you that I'm willing to put up with this"), an apology ("I could not possibly have meant what I have said to you, *to you* of all people"). It can be an instrument—more effective than the loudest noise—to interrupt a dull or painful conversation. It can be a cry, a plea, a verbal flag ("Pay attention to me!") or it can be an excuse ("It's only because I love you. . ."). It can be a disguise ("I love you," he whispered, looking awkwardly askance at the open door.). It can be an attack ("How can you do this to me?") or even an end ("So that's that. With regrets, good-bye."). If this single phrase has so many meanings, how varied and variable must be the emotion.

Questions About the Reading

1. What does the writer say happens the first time someone hears "I love you"? Why do you think this occurs?
2. Why must "I love you" be repeated once it has been said?
3. In what way can love be an excuse? Make up an ending for the "It's only because I love you . . ." sentence from the reading.

Questions About the Writer's Strategies

1. Do you think the writer is qualified to tell you what "I love you" means? Why or why not?
2. Why does the writer give so many examples of what "I love you" can mean?
3. What **mode of development** is the writer using in the essay from which this paragraph is taken? How do you know?

Writing Assignments

1. Write a paragraph or essay defining marriage—what it is and what it should be. Use specific examples from marriages you know of to illustrate your definition.
2. Write a paragraph defining the word *emotion*. You might try using **cause-and-effect** development for your definition, showing that something must cause certain effects to qualify as an emotion.

Maestria

Mario Suarez

Some words take on different meanings in different cultures. In the following paragraph, Mario Suarez defines maestria *and* maestro *in the context of a Mexican village.*

Words to Know
bolero   Spanish dance and the music for this dance
folly   foolish behavior

Getting Started
What is it in your life that you do best?

Whenever a man is referred to as a *maestro*, it means that he is master of whatever trade, art, or folly he practices. If he is a shoemaker, for example, he can design, cut, and finish any kind of shoe he is asked for. If he is a musician, he knows composition, direction, execution, and thereby plays Viennese waltzes as well as the bolero. If he is a thief, he steals thousands, for he would not damn his soul by taking dimes. That is *maestria*. It is applied with equal honor to a painter, tailor, barber, printer, carpenter, mechanic, bricklayer, window washer, ditchdigger, or bootblack if his ability merits it. Of course, when a man is graying and has no apparent trade or usefulness, out of courtesy people may forget he is a loafer and will call him a *maestro*. Whether he is or not is of no importance. Calling him a *maestro* hurts no one.

Questions About the Readings

1. Why would a maestro thief never steal a dime?
2. Do you think a talented window washer in America would be referred to as a maestro?
3. When is someone referred to as a maestro even if he has accomplished little?
4. How would you define *maestria* in your own words?

Questions About the Writer's Strategies

1. Do you think the writer's use of the word *maestro* is the same as the common American definition?
2. Why does the writer give so many **examples** of what *maestro* means?
3. Is this paragraph **objective** or **subjective**?
4. What is the main **mode of development** used to define *maestria*?

Writing Assignments

1. Rewrite the definition of *maestro* by using examples that are **antonyms** of the word.
2. Write an extended definition of a sports star by using the **comparison** and **contrast** mode of development.
3. Write a **narrative** paragraph defining the word *maestria* by using your own strongest ability as an example.

Grandparents

Nancy Pritts Merrell (student)

In the paragraph that follows, the writer provides us with an extended definition of the word grandparents *by telling us what they do and how we feel about them at different times in our lives and theirs. The writer, a recent college graduate, makes us understand her feelings about grandparents, and because her feelings are so human and typical, she makes us aware of our own attitudes toward and feelings about grandparents.*

Words to Know

accomplishments   achievements
appreciated   valued

Getting Started

Apart from the dictionary definitions, how would you define the difference between a parent and a grandparent?

Of all family members, grandparents are probably the least appreciated. They are just people who are always around. They make a fuss over the children in the family, brag to their friends about the accomplishments of this child or that child, and show countless pictures of new babies. Grandfathers can fix anything, and grandmothers always have homemade cookies around. When you are small, it's fun to stay with your grandparents because they always let you do things you can't do at home, and of course they buy you things. They are always available to babysit because they don't go out much and actually prefer to see their grandchildren. They are usually good for a small loan now and then that doesn't need to be paid back because they turn it into a gift. You respectfully listen to their advice but don't follow it because they are old and don't understand how things are in this day and age. You thank them politely for what they do for you, and then don't call or visit them until you need something else. And of course you never tell them how dear they are to you because they know how you feel about them anyway. Then all of a sudden, they are no longer there to do the things that only grandparents do, and you find yourself wishing that you had told them what they meant to you as people and not just as grandparents.

Questions About the Reading

1. What are some of the **examples** that the writer uses to define grandparents? What are some of the examples she uses to tell how we treat grandparents?
2. Do children understand that grandparents will not always be there? Support your answer with statements from the paragraph.
3. What does the writer mean when she says, "you find yourself wishing that you had told them what they meant to you as people and not just as grandparents"?

Questions About the Writer's Strategies

1. What is the main **mode of development** that the writer uses to define grandparents?
2. Do you think the writer's definition of grandparents is correct? Is part of her definition **implied** rather than directly stated?
3. What is the **point of view** in the paragraph? Does it change? If so, could the writer have maintained the same point of view throughout the paragraph? Explain how it could be done.

Writing Assignments

1. Write a paragraph in which you define a true *friend* by giving examples of the person's behavior.
2. Using descriptive **details**, write a paragraph defining what it means to be happy or sad, angry, tired, or hungry.
3. Write a paragraph in which you define what the word *parent* means to you. Use several modes of development: examples, description, narration—whatever is appropriate. You might want to begin by **brainstorming** to see what **connotations** the word *parent* has for you.

Baseball's Hot Dogs

Jim Kaplan

Baseball, the game of inches, requires precision performance and intense concentration. Do grandstanding and posturing constitute unfair psychological interference? In this definition of hot-dogging, Jim Kaplan presents some expert opinions on the question.

Words to Know

imperturbable   not easily disturbed
repertoire   a collection of dramatic skills

Getting Started

What kind of behaviors announce, "Look at me!"?

Here's Rickey Henderson at the plate. Taking forever to situate him- 1
self in the batter's box, the New York Yankees outfielder crouches low
and extends a shy left foot, like a man inching into a cold swimming pool.
A pitch arrives on the inside corner. Henderson twists away and then
looks shocked when the umpire calls it a strike. Finally, Rickey sees a
pitch he likes and rides it out of the park.

Now the real fun begins. Playing shamelessly to the crowd and cam- 2
era, Henderson chucks his bat high over his head, ambles to first by way
of the Yankee dugout, lowers his head and proceeds around the bases in
an endless, mock-serious trot. The fans love it. The opponents do not.

Henderson is baseball's foremost "hot dog"—and his repertoire is so 3
varied and controversial that his employers have actually put pressure
on him to modify his style. This spring, the Yankees proposed banning
Henderson's famous "snatch," a one-handed catch in which he snaps his
glove down like a teacher scrawling a semicircle on a blackboard and finishes with it pressed to his heart.

"They said, 'Rickey, the only snatch you can make is the last out of the 4
World Series,'" explained Henderson, adding that he thought he could
still get away with it on occasion. "I want to show I can do more than
catch. I want to show I can *catch*. To me, the snatch isn't hot-dogging; it's
style. People say I'm a hot dog. What *is* a hot dog?"

Good question. "A hot dog is someone whose actions put down some- 5
one on another team," says Doug DeCinces, the former major-league
third baseman now playing for Tokyo's Yakult Swallows.

"Hot-dogging is unnecessarily calling attention to yourself," adds Roy 6
Smalley, the well traveled former American League infielder.

But there's another point of view: that hot-dogging is flair and zest, the 7
very ingredients that make baseball so entertaining on the air or in person. Hot dogs contribute to baseball science, strategy and style. Some hot
dogs show off; others motivate themselves; still others intimidate the op-
position; most are entertaining.

Henderson may qualify on every count. "I never try to put anyone 8
down," he says. "I take my time getting into the box because I'm thinking
of the pitches I'm going to get." But he knows only too well the effect his
apparent stalling has. Even as imperturbable a pitching pro as the now-
retired Tom Seaver got so flustered that he had to turn his back on the
mound until Henderson had set himself to hit.

"Rickey has always played with flair," says Milwaukee manager Tom 9
Trebelhorn, who handled Henderson in the minors. "When he played for
me, he drove the other side crazy. Now he drives *me* crazy."

National League managers echo those sentiments about the San 10
Francisco Giants' Jeffrey "Hac-Man" Leonard, who showcased his trademark "flap down" homerun trot (one arm pinned to his side) four times
during the 1987 League Championship Series.

"[One flap down] is entertaining, a guy having fun," the unflappable 11
Leonard has told reporters. "Anything that provides energy gets me up.
Like Muhammad Ali, we'll bring out the best in our opponents, and
that'll make us better."

Oh, there are many kinds of baseball hot dogs—kosher and otherwise. 12
Cleveland's Mel Hall used to round the bases with a batting glove in each
back pocket arranged to flap "bye-bye." He has since contained his act.
But there's no containing Dennis "Oil Can" Boyd, the Boston Red Sox
pitcher who celebrates good fortune by variously high-fiving and low-
fiving teammates, waving to the crowd, doing clenched-fist "out" calls
and Michael Jackson struts, and snapping his fingers as he walks off the
mound.

Oil Can (the nickname is Mississippi slang for beer can) grew up play- 13
ing with older men who had starred in the Negro leagues. "I had a lead-
off hitter who drag-bunted with the bat behind his back," says Boyd.
"My fielders would turn [the double play] by throwing the ball between
their legs. A first baseman named Bud Moore said to throw to him in the
dirt so he could pick it and look good. When I punched [struck] a guy
out, I'd say, 'Get outta here—next guy up.' To hot-dog was the way to
play."

TV may be the biggest boon to hot-dogging since the invention of mus- 14
tard. Midway through the 1982 World Series, St. Louis pitcher Joaquin
Andujar was struck on the leg by a line drive and carried off in apparent
agony. NBC sportscaster Bob Costas raced down to the dugout expecting
to report on a broken leg. The Cardinals made faces and winked at him.
"Television time," they were saying. Sure enough, Andujar returned to
pitch and win the final game.

"These days there are fewer characters but more character-acting," 15
says Costas. "You can almost choreograph your own moment, and the
camera will do the rest."

Hot *dog*!   16

Questions About the Reading

1. What *is* a hot dog? Fashion your own definition, based on the essay
   and your personal opinions.
2. What is the difference between catching and *catching* (paragraph 4)?
   Why does Henderson want to show that he can *catch*?
3. What do you think the writer's opinion of hot-dogging is? Does he offer any conclusions about it?

Questions About the Writer's Strategies

1. What two **similes** does the writer use in his description of Henderson?
2. Identify the **subjective** elements in this essay.
3. What primary **mode of development** does the writer use to develop
   his definition?
4. What is the **tone** of the essay? What type of **audience** do you think the
   essay is aimed at?

Writing Assignments

1. Write an essay in which you define some other behavior in which people use different styles or about which they have various opinions, like
   flirting, arguing, dancing, or even walking. Try to talk with people
   about the behavior and use **dialogue** in your definition, as Kaplan
   does.
2. Write an essay defining the term *essay*. (Put this book aside and don't
   refer to it for help in composing your definition.)

Defining Success

Michael Korda

*Michael Korda has written several books with the intention of helping
people get the most out of their work and their lives. The titles of his books
tell you exactly what he has in mind for you—*Power! *and* Success! *But
before he can tell you (as the subtitle of his first book puts it) "how to get
it, how to use it," he wants to be sure you understand what* it *is. In the
first chapter of* Success! *he presents this controversial definition.*

Words to Know

conglomerate   a business corporation made up of many different companies

degenerate   to decrease in quality or size

grandiose   large, great

relative   determined in relation to something else

superseded   taken over, replaced

unethical   lacking in honesty or principles

Getting Started

What is your personal definition of *success?*

O thers may ask how you define success. This is more difficult. Success   1
is relative; not everybody wants to put together a four-billion-dollar conglomerate, or become President of the United States, or win the Nobel
Peace Prize. It is usually a mistake to begin with such grandiose ambitions, which tend to degenerate into lazy daydreams. The best way to
succeed is to begin with a reasonably realistic goal and attain it, rather
than aiming at something so far beyond your reach that you are bound to
fail. It's also important to make a habit of succeeding, and the easiest way
to start is to succeed at something, however small, every day, gradually
increasing the level of your ambitions and achievements like a runner in
training, who begins with short distances and works up to Olympic
levels.

Try to think of success as a journey, an adventure, not a specific desti-   2
nation. Your goals may change during the course of that journey, and
your original ambitions may be superseded by different, larger ones. Suc-

cess will certainly bring you the material things you want, and a good, healthy appetite for the comforts and luxuries of life is an excellent road to success, but basically you'll know you have reached your goal when you have gone that one step further, in wealth, fame or achievement, than you ever dreamed was possible.

How you become a success is, of course, your business. Morality has 3 very little to do with success. I do not personally think it is necessary to be dishonest, brutal or unethical in order to succeed, but a great many dishonest, brutal or unethical people in fact do succeed. You'd better be prepared for the fact that success is seldom won without some tough in-fighting along the way. A lot depends on your profession, of course. There is a great deal of difference between setting out to become a success in a Mafia family and trying to become vice president of a bank, but the differences simply consist of contrasting social customs and of what is the appropriate way to get ahead in a given profession or business. Whether you're hoping to take over a numbers game or an executive desk, you have to make the right moves for your circumstances. In the former example, you might have to kill someone; in the latter, you might only have to find ways of making your rivals look foolish or inefficient. In either case, you have to accept the rules of the game and play to win, or find some other game. This is a book about success, after all, not morality. The field you go into is your choice, but whatever it is, you're better off at the top of it than at the bottom.

Questions About the Reading

1. What does the writer say is the best way to succeed?
2. What does the writer mean when he says to "think of success as a journey, an adventure, not a specific destination"? Does this sentence in any way contradict what he says is the best way to succeed?
3. What does Korda mean by his statement "Morality has very little to do with success"?
4. What does Korda suggest you do if you have to violate your moral standards to achieve success in your field?

Questions About the Writer's Strategies

1. Does the writer actually define success? If so, identify the sentence(s) in which he does so.
2. What is the **main idea** (thesis) of the essay?
3. What are the **tone** and **point of view** of the essay? Why should we consider the writer an authority on success?

4. Do you believe that how a person becomes a success is that person's business only? Why or why not?

Writing Assignments

1. Korda focuses on success in people's professions, but people can be professional successes and personal failures. Write an essay in which you define success in a person's life.
2. Write an essay in which you define one of the following terms: *competition*, *cooperation*, or *ambition*. Give several examples. Develop a paragraph for each example.
3. Write an essay defining *morality*. Use whatever **modes of development** seem appropriate.

It's Failure, Not Success

Ellen Goodman

Not everyone agrees with Michael Korda's get-what-you-can mentality (see pp. 318–319). Ellen Goodman found herself getting more and more disturbed as she read Korda's words to live by. She was certain there must be more to the truly successful life. So she wrote her own definition of suc-cess and applied another term, failure, *to the self-serving life Korda de-scribed. Do you agree with Korda or with Goodman?*

Words to Know

ambivalence   simultaneously having different feelings or atti-tudes

bigot   an intolerant or prejudiced person

edits   cuts out, does away with

excised   removed

Fanny Farmer   author of a well-known cookbook

finesses   glosses over

intent   determined

judgmental   having an opinion about something, criticizing it

machete-ing   using a machete or heavy knife

Machiavellian   having political principles that are based on craftiness and doing anything necessary to get ahead

napalm   a firm jelly used in flame throwers and incendiary bombs

placebo   a substance given as medication that does not contain actual medication

Getting Started

In what ways could success be accompanied by failure?

———————————

I knew a man who went into therapy about three years ago because, as   1
he put it, he couldn't live with himself any longer. I didn't blame him.
The guy was a bigot, a tyrant and a creep.

In any case, I ran into him again after he'd finished therapy. He was   2
still a bigot, a tyrant and a creep, *but . . .* he had learned to live with himself.

Now, I suppose this was an accomplishment of sorts. I mean, nobody 3
else could live with him. But it seems to me that there are an awful lot of
people running around and writing around these days encouraging us to
feel good about what we should feel terrible about, and to accept in ourselves what we should change.

The only thing they seem to disapprove of is disapproval. The only 4
judgment they make is against being judgmental, and they assure us that
we have nothing to feel guilty about except guilt itself. It seems to me that
they are all intent on proving that I'm OK and You're OK, when in fact,
I may be perfectly dreadful and you may be unforgivably dreary, and it
may be—gasp!—*wrong*.

What brings on my sudden attack of judgmentitis is success, or rather, 5
Success!—the latest in a series of exclamation-point books all concerned
with How to Make It.

In this one, Michael Korda is writing a recipe book for success. Like 6
the other authors, he leapfrogs right over the "Shoulds" and into the
"Hows." He eliminates value judgments and edits out moral questions as
if he were Fanny Farmer and the subject was the making of a blueberry
pie.

It's not that I have any reason to doubt Mr. Korda's advice on the way 7
to achieve success. It may very well be that successful men wear handker-
chiefs stuffed neatly in their breast pockets, and that successful single
women should carry suitcases to the office on Fridays whether or not
they are going away for the weekend.

He may be realistic when he says that "successful people generally 8
have very low expectations of others." And he may be only slightly cynical when he writes: "One of the best ways to ensure success is to develop
expensive tastes or marry someone who has them."

And he may be helpful with his handy hints on how to sit next to 9
someone you are about to overpower.

But he simply finesses the issues of right and wrong—silly words, em- 10
barrassing words that have been excised like warts from the shiny surface of the new how-to books. To Korda, guilt is not a prod, but an enemy
that he slays on page four. Right off the bat, he tells the would-be
successful reader that:

- It's OK to be greedy.
- It's OK to look out for Number One.
- It's OK to be Machiavellian (if you can get away with it).
- It's OK to recognize that honesty is not always the best policy
  (provided you don't go around saying so).
- And it's always OK to be rich.

Well, in fact, it's not OK. It's not OK to be greedy, Machiavellian, dis- 11
honest. It's not always OK to be rich. There is a qualitative difference between succeeding by making napalm or by making penicillin. There is a
difference between climbing the ladder of success, and machete-ing a
path to the top.

Only someone with the moral perspective of a mushroom could assure 12
us that this was all OK. It seems to me that most Americans harbor ambivalence toward success, not for neurotic reasons, but out of a realistic
perception of what it demands.

Success is expensive in terms of time and energy and altered beha- 13
vior—the sort of behavior he describes in the grossest of terms: "If you
can undermine your boss and replace him, fine, do so, but never express
anything but respect and loyalty for him while you're doing it."

This author—whose *Power!* topped the best-seller list last year—is in- 14
tent on helping rid us of that ambivalence which is a signal from our conscience. He is like the other "Win!" "Me First!" writers, who try to make
us comfortable when we should be uncomfortable.

They are all Doctor Feelgoods, offering us placebo prescriptions in- 15
stead of strong medicine. They give us a way to live with ourselves, perhaps, but not a way to live with each other. They teach us a whole lot
more about "Failure!" than about success.

Questions About the Reading

1. What does the writer mean when she says, "he leapfrogs right over the 'Shoulds' and into the 'Hows'"?
2. What is the "qualitative difference between succeeding by making na-palm or by making penicillin"?
3. What is the "moral perspective of a mushroom"? Does Korda have such a perspective, in your opinion?
4. What does success demand that makes Americans ambivalent about it? What is it about Korda's brand of success that should make us un-comfortable?

Questions About the Writer's Strategies

1. What is the writer defining in this essay?
2. Does the essay contain a **thesis statement**? State the thesis in a sen-tence of your own. What is the function of the first four paragraphs of the essay?

3. Does the writer indicate that she is being **subjective**? If so, how?
4. Find a **simile** in paragraph 10. What is its effect?

Writing Assignments

1. Write an essay defining *failure.*
2. Write an essay defining *generosity* or *kindness.*
3. Write an essay in which you define something by saying what it is not. Possible topics might include fishing ("Fishing is not a pastime for the impatient"); voting ("Voting is not a chore, nor is it a spur-of-the-moment act"); writing ("Writing is not as hard as it seems, and it should not be threatening"); winning or losing; or being rich or poor.

What Is Intelligence, Anyway?

Isaac Asimov

Many of us think that intelligence is something one is simply born with, or that it has to do with doing well in school or scoring highly on IQ tests. But did you ever stop to think about what IQ tests really measure? In the essay that follows, Isaac Asimov asks us to rethink our definition of intelligence.

Words to Know

aptitude ability
arbiter someone who has the power to judge
complacent self-satisfied
intricate elaborate
KP kitchen patrol
oracles wise expressions
raucously loudly

Getting Started

Do you think that tests can ever really measure intelligence?

What is intelligence, anyway? When I was in the army I received a 1
kind of aptitude test that all soldiers took and, against a normal of 100,
scored 160. No one at the base had ever seen a figure like that, and for
two hours they made a big fuss over me. (It didn't mean anything. The
next day I was still a buck private with KP as my highest duty.)

All my life I've been registering scores like that, so that I have the com- 2
placent feeling that I'm highly intelligent, and I expect other people to
think so, too. Actually, though, don't such scores simply mean that I am
very good at answering the type of academic questions that are considered worthy of answers by the people who make up the intelligence
tests—people with intellectual bents similar to mine?

For instance, I had an auto-repair man once, who, on these intelligence 3
tests, could not possibly have scored more than 80, by my estimate. I
always took it for granted that I was far more intelligent than he was.
Yet, when anything went wrong with my car I hastened to him with
it, watched him anxiously as he explored its vitals, and listened to his

pronouncements as though they were divine oracles—and he always fixed my car.

Well, then, suppose my auto-repair man devised questions for an in- 4 telligence test. Or suppose a carpenter did, or a farmer, or, indeed, almost anyone but an academician. By every one of those tests, I'd prove myself a moron. And I'd *be* a moron, too. In a world where I could not use my academic training and my verbal talents but had to do something intricate or hard, working with my hands, I would do poorly. My intelligence, then, is not absolute but is a function of the society I live in and of the fact that a small subsection of that society has managed to foist itself on the rest as an arbiter of such matters.

Consider my auto-repair man, again. He had a habit of telling me 5 jokes whenever he saw me. One time he raised his head from under the automobile hood to say: "Doc, a deaf-and-dumb guy went into a hardware store to ask for some nails. He put two fingers together on the counter and made hammering motions with the other hand. The clerk brought him a hammer. He shook his head and pointed to the two fingers he was hammering. The clerk brought him nails. He picked out the sizes he wanted, and left. Well, Doc, the next guy who came in was a blind man. He wanted scissors. How do you suppose he asked for them?"

Indulgently, I lifted my right hand and made scissoring motions with 6 my first two fingers. Whereupon my auto-repair man laughed raucously and said, "Why, you dumb jerk, he used his *voice* and asked for them." Then he said, smugly, "I've been trying that on all my customers today." "Did you catch many?" I asked. "Quite a few," he said, "but I knew for sure I'd catch *you*." "Why is that?" I asked. "Because you're so god-damned educated, Doc, I *knew* you couldn't be very smart."

And I have an uneasy feeling he had something there.   7

Questions About the Reading

1. What does the writer mean when he says, "My intelligence, then, is not absolute but is a function of the society I live in. . . . "?
2. What distinction does the writer make between being educated and being smart?
3. Do you think the repairman is smarter than the writer? Why or why not?

Questions About the Writer's Strategies

1. What **mode of development** does the writer use in paragraphs 5 and 6? What is the purpose of these paragraphs?

2. Does the writer actually define *intelligence*? If so, state his definition in your own words. If not, explain why not.
3. In paragraph 6, the writer says he made the scissoring motion "indulgently." What does this tell you about his attitude toward the joke? Why is his attitude **ironic**?
4. Does the essay contain a **thesis statement**? If so, where is it located? If not, state it in your own words.
5. Is the repairman a **symbol**? If so, what does he represent?

Writing Assignments

1. Imagine a society in which intelligence is measured by how well people can work with their hands and fix machinery. Write a definition of intelligence for that society.
2. Write an essay defining the term *joke*. Use examples to illustrate your definition.
3. Pick one of the following concepts and define it in an essay: *beauty, truth, wisdom,* or *quality.*

Democracy

Amy Tan

Democracy is something Americans believe in, something many say they would fight and die for, and something the government tries to encourage in other parts of the world. Yet, as Amy Tan points out in this essay, we might not define democracy in quite the same way as would those who only dream of it.

Words to Know

bourgeoisie   middle class
entomology   study of insects
inalienable   unchanging, undeniable
prestige   honor, status

Getting Started

How do you imagine your life is different from that of a student living in a country that is not democratic?

How much we Americans take our freedoms for granted. We already 1
have the rights: freedom of expression, contracts and legal departments
to protect them, the right to put differences of opinion to a vote. We put
those rights in writing, carry them in our back pockets all over the world,
pull them out as proof. We may be aliens in another country, but we still
maintain that our rights are inalienable.

I try to imagine what democracy means to people in China who dream 2
of it. I don't think they are envisioning electoral colleges, First Amendment rights or civil lawsuits. I imagine that their dreams of democracy
begin with a feeling in the chest, one that has been restrained for so long
it grows larger and more insistent, until it bursts forth with a shout. Democracy is the right to shout, "Listen to us."

That is what I imagine because I was in China in 1987. I saw glimpses 3
of another way of life, a life that could have been mine. And along with
many wonderful things I experienced in my heart, I also felt something
uncomfortable in my chest.

In Shanghai in 1987, I attended the wedding of my niece. After the cer- 4
emony, she and her husband went home to the three-room apartment

Chapter 9 / Definition

shared with her mother, father and brother. "Now that you're married," I said with good humor, "you can't live at home anymore."

"The waiting list for government-assigned housing is sixteen years," 5 replied my niece's husband. "We will both be forty-eight years old when we are assigned our own place."

My mouth dropped. He shrugged. 6

While on a boat trip down the Huangpu River, I asked a tour 7 guide how she had chosen her career. She told me matter-of-factly that people in China did not choose careers. They had jobs assigned to them.

She saw my surprised expression. "Oh, but I'm lucky. So many people 8 can't get any kind of good job. If your family came from a bad background—the bourgeoisie—then, no college. Maybe only a job sweeping the streets." At a family dinner in Beijing, I learned that my sister's husband could not attend our get-together. He was away at his job, said my sister.

"When will he return?" I asked. My mother explained that his job was 9 in a city thousands of miles away. He had been living apart from my sister for the past ten years. "That's terrible," I said to my sister. "Tell him to ask for a transfer. Tell him you miss him."

"Miss, not miss!" my mother sniffed. "They can't even ask." 10

One of my sisters did ask. Several years ago, she asked for a visa to 11 leave China. Now she lives in Wisconsin. A former nurse, she now works six days a week, managing a take-out Chinese restaurant. Her husband, trained as a surgeon, works in the kitchen. And recently I've met others who also asked, a waiter who was once a doctor in China, a taxi driver who was formerly a professor of entomology, a housekeeper who was an engineer. Why did they ask to leave? I found it hard to understand how people could leave behind family, friends, their motherland and jobs of growing prestige.

My sister in Wisconsin helped me understand. After my novel was 12 published, she wrote me a letter. "I was once like you," she said. "I wanted to write stories as a young girl. But when I was growing up, they told me I could not do so many things. And now my imagination is rusted and no stories can move out of my brain."

My sister and I had the same dream. But my brain did not become 13 rusted. I became a writer. And later, we shared another dream, that China and our family were on the verge of a better, more open life. We did not imagine that the blood that is thicker than water would be running through the streets of Beijing. We did not believe that one Chinese would kill another. We did not foresee that an invisible great wall would rise up, that we would be cut off from our family, that letters would stop, that the silence would become unbearable.

These days I can only imagine what has happened to my family in 14 China. And I think about the word democracy. It rolls so easily off my English-speaking tongue. But in Beijing it is a foreign-sounding word, so many syllables, so many clashing sounds. In China, democracy is still not an easy word to say. Many cannot say it.

Hope then. 15

Questions About the Readings

1. What inspired Amy Tan to write about democracy?
2. What is the writer expressing when she says "I don't think they are envisioning electoral colleges, First Amendment rights, or civil lawsuits"?
3. Why did some of the writer's relatives and acquaintances leave their families, homes, and careers?
4. What does Amy Tan mean when she states that the word *democracy* is so hard for the Chinese to say?

Questions About the Writer's Strategies

1. Does the writer actually define the word *democracy* in a formal way? Why do you think she chose to define it, or not define it?
2. What **examples** does the author use to describe the lack of freedom in China?
3. What parts of the essay are **objective**? What parts of the essay are **subjective**?
4. Is the writer emphasizing the **connotation** or **denotation** of the word *democracy?*

Writing Assignments

1. Can you imagine being a student in another culture? Write an essay that **compares** your everyday life with the life of a student in a country with fewer freedoms.
2. Write an essay in which you define the word *dictatorship.* Use a **mode of development** that allows you to use examples from recent history.
3. Write an essay defining the term *immigrant,* using an extended example of someone in your own family background, someone you have known, or someone in American history.

The Bright Cave
Under the Hat

Lance Morrow

During this time in our culture when homelessness is becoming more and more prevalent, agreeing on the definition of home *has become a very important task. In this essay from* Time *magazine, Lance Morrow explores many of the variations of home that can exist in this complex world.*

Words to Know

apocalypse   a revelation, unveiling
concentric   having a common center, focus
configuration   form
emanation   something that comes from a source
forage   search for
hypothetical   presumed, supposed
infinitely   endlessly, immeasurably
ingenious   inventive, creative
interminable   continual, endless
intonations   tone, accent
metaphysical   supernatural, superhuman
nomads   wanderers
obscure   unclear, remote
primal   original, primary
sanctity   sacredness
sentimentalized   romanticized

Getting Started

When you think of home, what exactly comes to mind?

A man in a park in Phoenix showed me how to make a home out of   1
cardboard boxes. Not a home, exactly, but something like a backyard
playhouse built by an ingenious child. The cardboard boxes interlocked,
and the shelter, secret and cozy, kept out the cold of the Arizona night.
The man, named Ernest, had once been an engineer at the Boeing Co.

Ernest, I came to understand, was a sort of brilliant grown-up orphan: 2
he had an air that was both distinguished and tattered. Something in his
mind had broken years before. He survived on technique. Ernest taught
me how to forage for an all-American diet: wait politely behind a fast-
food place at closing time and accept the unsold hamburgers and fries. A
third problem, keeping clean, was difficult but manageable: a cold-water
spigot in the morning sun.

It is not always the physical part of homelessness that is hard: home 3
and homelessness are also ideas, emotions, metaphysical states. Home is
all the civilization that a child knows. Home is one of nature's primal
forms, and if it does not take shape properly around the child, then his
mind will be at least a little homeless all its life.

A child is a precise metaphysician. He (or she) writes down name, 4
house number, street, town, state, ZIP code, country . . . and then, to be exact, "Planet Earth, the Solar System, the Galaxy, the Universe." Creation
is an onion with many skins, all layering outward from the child's self. If
he gets lost in the galaxy, he can find the way back, can fly through the
concentric circles to his own house—from outermost remoteness to in-
nermost home. Nostalgia means the *nostos algos*, the agony to return
home. What got broken long ago in Ernest was his charts and instruments for the journey.

The ideal of home has been grossly sentimentalized from time to time, 5
of course, just as mothers and small towns have been. Both can be suffocating, like an interminable Sunday in an airless house. Home is a place
to run away from when the time comes.

But people want to run back sometimes as well. Home is both mag- 6
netic poles, the start and the finish. T. S. Eliot wrote, "We shall not cease
from exploration/ And the end of all our exploring/ Will be to arrive
where we started/ And know the place for the first time."

People tend to run back at this time of year. If war and recession come 7
banging on the door, as they are doing now, the spirit feels unquiet, dis-
lodged. The news carries with it threats of eviction and violence. . . .

A Connecticut man has been convicted of murder. The man argues in 8
his defense that the police made an illegal search of his "home"—the
cardboard boxes he used as a chest of drawers as he sheltered beneath a
highway overpass—in order to get their evidence. Does the Fourth
Amendment protect cardboard boxes? What is the legal definition of
home? What confers the sanctity of home? A lease or a deed? Four walls?
How thick or thin? Must home have doors and locks?

The womb is the first home. Thereafter, home is the soil you come from 9
and recognize, what you knew before uprooted: creatures carry an imprint of home, a stamp—the infinitely subtle distinctiveness of tempera-

ture and smell and weather and noises and people, the intonations of the familiar. Each home is an unrepeatable configuration; it has personality, its own emanation, its spirit of place. Nature's refugees, like eels and cranes, are neither neurotic nor political, and so steer by a functional homing instinct. Human beings invented national boundaries and the miseries of exile; they have messier, more tragic forms of navigation that often get them lost. The earth is home, and all its refugees, its homeless, sometimes seem a sort of advance guard of apocalypse. They represent a principle of disintegration—the fate of homelessness generalized to a planetary scale.

In later years a person sometimes visits his childhood home and circles 10 it with a sort of alienated wonder. Someone else's lights are burning inside upon someone else's Christmas tree, and the child that once lived there is now a stranger in the skin of a middle-aged man. It seems a sort of obscure outrage that the windows and doors are not all open at once, telling stories. The home, like the mind, is a time capsule. Where are the stories and jokes of the house? Its old animation has become a ghost and gone into memory. The house is someone else's now.

Love is home. But home may be a horror also, a cage with wild animals 11 in it. Home is aligned on the side of life, and so the perversion of it (by incest, for example; by violence; by betrayal) is a filthy business, and sometimes evil.

The myth of Eden records the first trauma of homelessness. Home, af- 12 ter that expulsion, is what we make, what we build. We build our own home again, endlessly, in memory of Eden, or hope of it. Past or future. The present is never contented, perfection is hypothetical, and home is always incomplete.

The flesh is home: African nomads without houses decorate their faces 13 and bodies instead. The skull is home. We fly in and out of it on mental errands. The highly developed spirit becomes a citizen of its own mobility, for home has been internalized and travels with the homeowner. Home, thus transformed, is freedom. Everywhere you hang your hat is home. Home is the bright cave under the hat.

Questions About the Readings

1. Why do you think the writer was inspired to write this essay?
2. What does the writer mean when he says that lacking a physical home may not be the hardest part of homelessness?
3. Why is the legal definition of *home* so important?
4. What do the world's refugees represent to the writer?

Questions About the Writer's Strategies

1. What **figure of speech** does the writer use in the title of the essay? What idea is he trying to express?
2. How does the writer use **irony** in describing the homeless man's diet?
3. What parts of the essay are **objective?** What parts of the essay are **subjective**?
4. What are the main **modes of development** used to define home?
5. Is Ernest a **symbol**? If so, what does he represent?

Writing Assignments

1. Write an essay defining your own interpretation of what the word *home* means.
2. Write an essay that defines home as "a place to run away from when the time comes." Use **examples** in your definition.
3. Write an essay defining the word *family*. Try to give as diverse a definition as you can. Use **brainstorming** to explore the many **connotations** of *family*.

10

Extra Readings

IN THIS SECTION, you will find some additional reading selections. Although some of the readings have one dominant **mode of development**, most of them illustrate combinations of the different modes.

As you read, keep in mind what we have stressed in the earlier sections. Determine the

- topic of each paragraph
- thesis of each essay
- structure of the reading (introduction, development, conclusion)
- supporting details
- modes of development
- point of view (person, time, tone)
- method of organization (time, space, order of importance)
- transitional words
- effective words and sentences

Then, make use of these same strategies to write paragraphs and essays that are as clear and effective as those you have read.

Ode to My Father

Tess Gallagher

*Tess Gallagher is a poet. She seems to have been aware of this calling from early in her youth. When she tells of her experiences with her father, she comes back several times to her central idea, almost a refrain: this was necessary to become a poet. The modes are **narration** and **cause and effect**. At the end, Gallagher is a grown woman with a life of her own and a new view of the father whose actions shaped her.*

Words to Know

defiance   unwillingness to submit
primal   primary, of first importance
psychic   mental, psychological
stamina . endurance, strength
vulnerability   openness or susceptibility to being hurt

On Saturdays my father would drive my mother and my three broth- 1
ers and me into town to shop and then to wait for him while he drank in what he called "the beer joints." We would sit for hours in the car watching the townspeople pass, commenting on their dress and faces, trying to figure out what they did with the rest of their lives. Although it was just a game we played to pass the time, I think it taught me to see deeply at a very young age. Every hour or so my mother would send me on a round of the taverns to try for a sighting of my father. I would peck on the windows and the barmaid would shake her head "no" or motion down the dim aisle of faces to where my father would be sitting on his stool, forgetting, forgetting us all for a while. Back at the car, my brothers were quarreling, then crying. My mother had gone stiff. These times were the farthest I would ever get from home.

My father's drinking and the quarrels he had with my mother because 2
of it terrorized my childhood. There is no other way to put it. And if terror and fear are necessary to the psychic stamina of a poet, I had them in steady doses—just as inevitably as I had the rain. I learned that the world was not just, that any balance was temporary, that the unreasonableness could descend at any minute, thrashing aside everything and everyone in

its path. Love, through all this, was constant, though it had a hoary head. Its blow, brutal as any evil, was perhaps more so for how it raked the quick of my being. The body remembers too, though not with malice, but as one might gaze uncomprehendingly at photographs of family friends, now deceased—but somehow important.

I remember the day I became aware that other families lived differ- 3 ently. I was showering in the junior high school's gym with my best friend, Molly, when she noticed the welts on my back. I could not see them and so could not share her awe and worry for me. What had happened to me? What had I done? Who had done this?

I was sixteen when I had my last lesson from the belt and my father's 4 arm. I had learned that no words, no pleading would save me. I stood still in the yard, in full view of the neighbors, and took "what was coming to me." I looked steadily ahead, without tears or cries, as a tree must look while the saw bites in, then deepens to the core. I felt my spirit reach its full defiance. I stood somehow in the power of my womanhood that day and knew I had passed beyond humiliation. If a poet must know that physical pain and unreasonable treatment can be turned aside by an ultimate act of the will, I learned this then. I did not feel sorry for myself. I did not stop the loving. It was our hurt not to have another way to settle these things. For we had no language between us in those numb years of my changing, of my large hope toward the world. All through my attempts in the poems, this need has been building, the need to forge a language that would give these dead and living lives a way to speak. There was often the feeling that the language might come too late, might even do damage, might not be equal to the love. All these fears. Finally no choice.

The images of these two primal figures, mother and father, condense 5 now into a view of my father's work-thickened hands and my mother's back, turned in hopeless anger at the stove where she fixed eggs for my father in silence. My father gets up from the table, shows me the open palms of his hands: "Threasie," he says, "get an education. Don't get hands like these."

Years later, after returning from a trip to Ireland, it was the work of 6 these hands that I wanted to celebrate and to acknowledge for my father. He had recently retired from the docks and liked to play cards with the men down at Chinook Tavern. I would drive down and pick him up when the game ended at 2:00 A.M. Sometimes I would go early enough to have a beer with his friends in the back room and to listen to them kid him. "Hey Okie, how'd an ole geezer like you get a good lookin' daughter like that?" My father would laugh and wink, giving his head a quick little dip and rise. He didn't need to say anything. They called him Okie because he'd come from Oklahoma and he liked to be called that.

When he got home, we put the coffee pot on and sat at the kitchen ⁷
table and talked. I don't remember when we began this sort of talking but
I think now it happened because my father had caught sight of his death.
He had suffered a heart attack while I had been in Ireland and this had
given him more to say. When I'd been a child fishing with him in the
salmon derbies he had talked more than he usually did—talked "to make
the fish bite"—for just when you got to the most interesting place in the
story, the fish were sure to bite. And they did. But this night there was
another kind of talking. My father knew I was going the next day to a job
in another part of the country. He might not see me again. He began to
tell me his life. And though he told it all plainly and without pity for himself—only some verbal turning of the palms upward—the rhythms of his
speech, his vulnerability before me had a power and beauty I did not
want to see lost to the world.

The next day I got on a bus and waved good-bye to him and my ⁸
mother. The bus was crammed with people headed for Seattle. They were
talking and adjusting their packages. The woman sitting next to me had
some knitting to work on. I took out my notebook with its pale green-
white pages, frog-belly green they were. I was thinking this is no place to
write this; this is too important a poem to be writing here. I put the book
on my knees and tried to hear my father's voice, to get it to speak
through me. This was the only place, the only time.

3 A.M. Kitchen: My Father Talking

For years it was land working me, oil fields,
cotton fields, then I got some land. I
worked it. Them days you could just about
make a living. I was logging.

Then I sent to Missouri. Momma
come out. We got married.
We got some kids. Five kids.
That kept us going.

We bought some land near the water.
It was cheap then. The water
was right there. You just looked out
the window. It never left the window.

I bought a boat. Fourteen footer.
There was fish out there then.
You remember, we used to catch
six, eight fish, clean them right
out in the yard. I could of fished to China.

I quit the woods. One day just
walked out, took off my corks, said that's
it. I went to the docks.
I was working winch. You had to watch
to see nothing fell out of the sling. If
you killed somebody you'd
never forget it. All
those years I was just working
I was on edge, every day. Just working.

You kids. I could tell you
a lot. But I won't.

It's winter. I play a lot of cards
down at the tavern. Your mother.
I have to think of excuses
to get out of the house. You're
wasting your time, she says. You're wasting
your money.

You don't have no idea, Threasie.
I run out of things
to work for. Hell, why shouldn't I
play cards? Threasie,
some days now I just don't know.

———————————

How It Feels to Be Colored Me

Zora Neale Hurston

Zora Neale Hurston was an important black woman writer in the United States. Although her works of fiction, folklore, and essays were popular during the Harlem renaissance in the 1930s, her writing was out of print and she was penniless at the time of her death. Her work has recently been reissued, and an anthology of her writing, I Love Myself When I Am Laughing, *edited by writer and activist Alice Walker, was published in 1979. The following essay, taken from this anthology, describes how Hurston became aware of the color of her skin and how it shaped her attitude toward life.*

Words to Know

assegai   a light spear used by Southern African tribesmen
circumlocutions   roundabout ways of speaking
ebb   the retreat of the tide
extenuating   making less serious
Hegira   a flight from danger
oleander   a poisonous shrub with sweet-smelling flowers
pigmentation   coloring
proscenium   the area of the theater located between the curtain and the first seats in the audience
raiment   clothing
rambunctious   unruly
Reconstruction   the period after the U.S. Civil War (1865–1877)
rending   tearing apart
specter   a ghost
thorax   the chest
veneer   a thin layer, the surface appearance

I am colored but I offer nothing in the way of extenuating circumstances   1
except the fact that I am the only Negro in the United States whose grandfather on the mother's side was *not* an Indian chief.

I remember the very day that I became colored. Up to my thirteenth   2
year I lived in the little Negro town of Eatonville, Florida. It is exclusively a colored town. The only white people I knew passed through the town

going to or coming from Orlando. The native whites rode dusty horses, the Northern tourists chugged down the sandy village road in automobiles. The town knew the Southerners and never stopped cane chewing when they passed. But the Northerners were something else again. They were peered at cautiously from behind curtains by the timid. The more venturesome would come out on the porch to watch them go past and got just as much pleasure out of the tourists as the tourists got out of the village.

The front porch might seem a daring place for the rest of the town, but 3 it was a gallery seat for me. My favorite place was atop the gate-post. Proscenium box for a born first-nighter. Not only did I enjoy the show, but I didn't mind the actors knowing that I liked it. I usually spoke to them in passing. I'd wave at them and when they returned my salute, I would say something like this: "Howdy-do-well-I-thank-you-where-you-goin'?" Usually automobile or the horse paused at this, and after a queer exchange of compliments, I would probably "go a piece of the way" with them, as we say in farthest Florida. If one of my family happened to come to the front in time to see me, of course negotiations would be rudely broken off. But even so, it is clear that I was the first "welcome-to-our-state" Floridian, and I hope the Miami Chamber of Commerce will please take notice.

During this period, white people differed from colored to me only 4 in that they rode through town and never lived there. They liked to hear me "speak pieces" and sing and wanted to see me dance the parse-me-la, and gave me generously of their small silver for doing these things, which seemed strange to me for I wanted to do them so much that I needed bribing to stop. Only they didn't know it. The colored people gave no dimes. They deplored any joyful tendencies in me, but I was their Zora nevertheless. I belonged to them, to the nearby hotels, to the county—everybody's Zora.

But changes came in the family when I was thirteen, and I was sent to 5 school in Jacksonville. I left Eatonville, the town of the oleanders, as Zora. When I disembarked from the river-boat at Jacksonville, she was no more. It seemed that I had suffered a sea change. I was not Zora of Orange County any more, I was now a little colored girl. I found it out in certain ways. In my heart as well as in the mirror, I became a fast brown—warranted not to rub nor run.

But I am not tragically colored. There is no great sorrow dammed up 6 in my soul, nor lurking behind my eyes. I do not mind at all. I do not belong to the sobbing school of Negrohood who hold that nature somehow has given them a lowdown dirty deal and whose feelings are all hurt about it. Even in the helter-skelter skirmish that is my life, I have seen that the world is to the strong regardless of a little pigmentation more or less. No, I do not weep at the world—I am too busy sharpening my oyster knife.

Someone is always at my elbow reminding me that I am the grand- 7 daughter of slaves. It fails to register depression with me. Slavery is sixty years in the past. The operation was successful and the patient is doing well, thank you. The terrible struggle that made me an American out of a potential slave said "On the line!" The Reconstruction said "Get set!"; and the generation before said "Go!" I am off to a flying start and I must not halt in the stretch to look behind and weep. Slavery is the price I paid for civilization, and the choice was not with me. It is a bully adventure and worth all that I have paid through my ancestors for it. No one on earth ever had a greater chance for glory. The world to be won and nothing to be lost. It is thrilling to think—to know that for any act of mine, I shall get twice as much praise or twice as much blame. It is quite exciting to hold the center of the national stage, with the spectators not knowing whether to laugh or to weep.

The position of my white neighbor is much more difficult. No brown 8 specter pulls up a chair beside me when I sit down to eat. No dark ghost thrusts its leg against mine in bed. The game of keeping what one has is never so exciting as the game of getting.

I do not always feel colored. Even now I often achieve the unconscious 9 Zora of Eatonville before the Hegira. I feel most colored when I am thrown against a sharp white background.

For instance at Barnard. "Beside the waters of the Hudson" I feel my 10 race. Among the thousand white persons, I am a dark rock surged upon, and overswept, but through it all, I remain myself. When covered by the waters, I am; and the ebb but reveals me again.

Sometimes it is the other way around. A white person is set down in our 11 midst, but the contrast is just as sharp for me. For instance, when I sit in the drafty basement that is The New World Cabaret with a white person, my color comes. We enter chatting about any little nothing that we have in common and are seated by the jazz waiters. In the abrupt way that jazz orchestras have, this one plunges into a number. It loses no time in circumlocutions, but gets right down to business. It constricts the thorax and splits the heart with its tempo and narcotic harmonies. This orchestra grows rambunctious, rears on its hind legs and attacks the tonal veil with primitive fury, rending it, clawing it until it breaks through to the jungle beyond. I follow those heathen—follow them exultingly. I dance wildly inside myself; I yell within, I whoop; I shake my assegai above my head, I hurl it true to the mark *yeeeeooww!* I am in the jungle and living in the jungle way. My face is painted red and yellow and my body is painted blue. My pulse is throbbing like a war drum. I want to slaughter something—give pain, give death to what, I do not know. But the piece ends. The men of the orchestra wipe their lips and rest their fingers. I creep back slowly to the veneer we call civilization with the last tone and find the white friend sitting motionless in his seat, smoking calmly.

"Good music they have here," he remarks, drumming the table with 12 his fingertips.

Music. The great blobs of purple and red emotion have not touched 13 him. He has only heard what I felt. He is far away and I see him but dimly across the ocean and the continent that have fallen between us. He is so pale with his whiteness then and I am *so* colored.

At certain times I have no race, I am *me*. When I set my hat at a certain 14 angle and saunter down Seventh Avenue, Harlem City, feeling as snooty as the lions in front of the Forty-Second Street Library, for instance. So far as my feelings are concerned, Peggy Hopkins Joyce on the Boule Mich with her gorgeous raiment, stately carriage, knees knocking together in a most aristocratic manner, has nothing on me. The cosmic Zora emerges. I belong to no race nor time. I am the eternal feminine with its string of beads.

I have no separate feeling about being an American citizen and col- 15 ored. I am merely a fragment of the Great Soul that surges within the boundaries. My country, right or wrong.

Sometimes, I feel discriminated against, but it does not make me 16 angry. It merely astonishes me. How *can* any deny themselves the plea- sure of my company? It's beyond me.

But in the main, I feel like a brown bag of miscellany propped against 17 a wall. Against a wall in company with other bags, white, red and yellow. Pour out the contents, and there is discovered a jumble of small things priceless and worthless. A first-water diamond, an empty spool, bits of broken glass, lengths of string, a key to a door long since crumbled away, a rusty knife-blade, old shoes saved for a road that never was and never will be, a nail bent under the weight of things too heavy for any nail, a dried flower or two still a little fragrant. In your hand is the brown bag. On the ground before you is the jumble it held—so much like the jumble in the bags, could they be emptied, that all might be dumped in a single heap and the bags refilled without altering the content of any greatly. A bit of colored glass more or less would not matter. Perhaps that is how the Great Stuffer of Bags filled them in the first place—who knows?

The Momist Manifesto

Alice Kahn

After interviewing several sets of parents for a local support organization, Kahn recounts some of the challenges every parent faces. We learn that many of the things individuals take for granted are soon challenged when they have children. Life suddenly becomes a constant undertaking to be a "good parent," yet Kahn finds hope in knowing that parents as a group are in the struggle together.

Words to Know

compounded   combined
elusive   difficult to define or describe
frivolous   inappropriately silly
manifesto   a public declaration of principles
milieu   surroundings
poignant   appealing to the emotions; touching
rebuffed   refused bluntly
scurry   to go with light, running steps
sprightly   full of life

Recently I was a minor participant in a unique event. Bananas, a pio- 1
neering parent support organization, and the local First Presbyterian
Church held "Parenting Twenty-five Hours a Day: A Special Event for
Families." It was my job to walk around during the lunch hour interviewing members of *the* oppressed group of the '80s—parents.

The entire conference right down to professional child care was free. It 2
included workshops on child *and* parent development, being a single parent, a new parent, a stepparent; one entitled "Dual (Not Duel) Careers,"
and, my favorite, one on "Setting Limits (Formerly Known as Discipline)." You can't even mention the d-word anymore.

At lunchtime, I walked around with Judy Calder, a registered nurse 3
who works full-time with the Bananas organization. Calder operated the
video equipment while I did the interviews. I think Bananas hoped I
would provide some sprightly entertainment for their video files, a little

gal-in-the-street zaniness with those lovable, laughable parents. Instead, as Calder observed, "the interviews were really poignant."

Why is parenting in the '80s such serious business? Why do we find a role that dates back to Adam and Eve so stressful? There are lots of answers, lots of places to put the blame, but I think the major reason is because parents are trying so hard to do the job well. Everyone I know, including myself, is obsessed with trying to be something called "a good parent." This is a particularly elusive concept since the desired outcome is so unclear. What is the goal? A moral child? A successful child? A happy child? A child who loves you? An independent child? All of the above? 4

My impression of the parents I interviewed was that most of them were already in the top ten percentile of parenting. Almost by definition, anyone who would spend their entire Saturday focusing on how to be a better parent is already half there. Other parents were probably spending their time doing chores, fighting with their kids, escaping from their kids, or, rarely, having fun with their kids. 5

Many of the people at the conference were child-care workers in addition to being parents. They discussed the problem of being listened to by their client kids while being rebuffed by their own kids. Parents of teens talked about the pain of being rejected (except, of course, when needed as a funding agent) by their youngsters, who are choosing the support of their peer group. Some parents talked about the problems of balancing career and family. 6

One woman discussed her decision to leave her job as an executive at AT&T to stay home. "I decided I was paying someone to do my job while I was at my other job," she said. I thought of how hard, as a black woman, the road to her executive position must have been, and what a difficult choice that must have been. Her comment will surely strike at the guilt feelings of other mothers who are afraid to leave their jobs because of uncertainty over whether they could come back, because they can't afford it, or because they simply can't stand to be home with the children full-time. Some fathers may feel this conflict, too, but they have not experienced the rapidly changing expectations that women have. While 46 percent of American women were housewives in 1960, today that number has been cut to 20 percent. All indications are that this percentage will continue to decline. But it doesn't change the fact that these mothers still grew up in a world where women were expected to stay home and raise the children. 7

A stepfather talked to me about the importance of being patient in winning the love of his three-year-old stepchild. He observed that he had no more right to expect the child's love than any stranger on the street. 8

But he said after a year of patient attention, the child (whose natural father was named Carl) came up to him one day and said, "You're my Carl."

Two couples with babies less than a year old talked about how the youngsters had changed their relationships. In both cases, the women stayed at home. One man talked about his difficulty with coming home tired from work and finding the wife at the door passing him the baby and saying the equivalent of " You take the little bugger, I'm getting out." 9

All these problems seemed familiar, some I've experienced, some I've only heard about. What struck me was that regardless of class, style, or any other variable, I can always empathize with that struggle to raise a child well. 10

It is a struggle compounded by the fact that in the modern family, the child has replaced the father as house tyrant. We all scurry around trying to meet that child's needs, trying not to cross him. How many times have you seen a mother (and that mother might have been me) standing in the supermarket presenting a reasonable list of alternatives to an unreasonable screaming little person who stood there shouting, "No, no, no, no"? 11

Discipline is a real thorn in the side of those who spent their formative years rejecting all forms of discipline and control. We fear damaging or repressing our children as we complained our parents did to us. In the context of a "question authority" community, it becomes particularly difficult to set limits for our children. That's why we feel such gratitude for anyone who seems to be on our side, anyone who understands that discipline is not the equivalent of child abuse. 12

Recently a woman asked me, in a somewhat confrontational manner, "What are your politics?" The whole presentation of this question had a '60s milieu about it, and I immediately fell into a '60s response, saying somewhat sheepishly and guiltily, "I used to have politics, but I haven't had time since my kids were born." The assumption here is that politics is something you do for The World rather than for you and yours. Increasingly, however, I realize that parenting *is* my politics. I find my allies are those people who make my life as a parent easier, whether it's an arms control advocate or a good teacher or someone like Bill Cosby, who can produce that rarest of all experiences, real family entertainment. 13

I respect people in public life who take care of their families as well as do their job. In this regard, I thought the much maligned Jackie Kennedy Onassis managed to maintain a strong family life against all odds. By contrast, I've been appalled at how few have observed the hypocrisy of Ronald Reagan advocating "family values" while seeming to be quite distant and unavailable to his own children. If someone spends his life making speeches and going to meetings while his own family is in shambles, I find it hard to take him seriously, like the preacher who can't 14 practice what he preaches. It's clear to me that regardless of whatever happens in my life, I won't enjoy it unless my children are doing well.

At the end of the Bananas conference, many spoke of how comforting 15 it was to spend time with other struggling parents, to understand how common the problems are. One father went up to one of the conference organizers and said, "I want you to know how much we appreciate what you're doing for people like us." Although working parents don't have much time for organizing and meeting, I think we are going to increasingly see the end of the parent as wimp. But first we're going to have to learn to stand up to our kids and set those limits. If they want to question authority, they can wait until they're capable of cleaning their rooms or proving themselves otherwise responsible. Once we earn a little self-respect at home, maybe then we can find a way to make our schools, our communities, and our governments help our lives as parents instead of make them more difficult.

Having a child helps you get your priorities straight. You know that 16 you'll never waste a prayer on anything frivolous again. No more, please-God-let-me-get-the-promotion. Never another please-let-him-call-me. Anybody who's ever sat in a hospital emergency room waiting for the results of tests on their child knows exactly what I'm talking about. Although it's easy to forget, there is nothing more important we have to do than raise these children.

When I first walked around with my baby strapped on my chest in her 17 little frontpack, I noticed a lot of people giving me a big smile. I'm not talking about the baby-worshippers who kitchy-cooed my little doll. I mean the other parents who gave me that knowing welcome-to-the-club look. We *are* in this together. We're making the same statement against the dark, violent world that seems to have forgotten the value of life.

———————————

Thanksgiving

Linda Hogan

As far back as our first ancestors on this continent, the land has nourished life. Poet Linda Hogan, a member of the Chickasaw Nation, writes eloquently about the unique relationship between the land and its grateful people. Her vivid images of Native American ceremonies and history capture this sense of human connectedness to the circle of life.

Words to Know

alchemy   the process of turning lead to gold
diffuse   to spread about or scatter
dormant   asleep or lying as if asleep
metate   a square stone used for grinding corn
reciprocity   a cooperative interchange of favors or privileges
verdant   green with vegetation

In Pueblo country, throughout the yearly growing season, the corn 1
dances take place. The dancing begins at the time of planting and ends
with the time of harvest.

It is a serious dance, a long and hard barefoot dance on burning hot 2
southwestern earth. It is a dance of community, not only between people,
but a larger sense of community that includes earth, the new young
plants, and the fiery sun. It's a dance of human generosity, as the dancers
lend their energy to the kernels sowed in newly turned soil. There is
drumming and singing. There is feasting on loaves of bread baked out-
doors in clay ovens, on watermelons the color of the mountains, on
meats, and varieties of chile sauces. But mostly there is prayer in the
dance, and thankfulness.

A few years ago I was asked, as part of a ceremony, to grind light- 3
giving blue corn with a grinding stone and a metate. I didn't know then
that corn was as dependent on people as people have been, throughout history, on corn. But 90-year-old writer Meridel Le Sueur has written
that ancient women gatherers were free travelers who loved the tiny
grass of early corn, hand-pollinated it, and "created the great cob of

nutrition which cannot free itself from the cob without the hand of human."

During that ceremony, I also drank bitter tea, telling the herb in the cup, *thank you*, telling the sun, *thank you*, and thanking the land. Gratitude and a human connectedness with food is part of many ceremonies of life that are centered on hunting, picking, planting, and healing. 4

In my own tribal history, too, corn has meant life. The people eat cornbread and ear corn, parched corn, cornmeal mush. My grandmother, like many other Chickasaw women, made hominy with lye and ashes in a large black kettle on the wood stove. Still, in a single kernel of that swollen white corn, people swallow the light of sun and the rich mineral earth, eat of the rains in the milky sweetness of yellow corn, eat the rich loamy smell of turned earth, of planter's moons, of seeds planted in the sacred land. 5

The reciprocity among land, food, and people also exists farther north where ricers' boats move among the wild rice plants in the swampy, humid land as the boat is pushed with a pole through lily pads and plants and the distant call of a loon. In the diffuse, soft light of the sun, the people are covered with rice dust and dried pollen and insects. They, too, sing their thankful song to the rice, and the songs, like those of others, come to life within the food. 6

Here a woman works with a digging stick. There a child chases crows away from the crops. Old men break ground and turn the soil. Women plant by the moon. There are the berry-pickers, and the grateful people who bring in the twisting, shining fish from the river. The herb gatherers know to pick plants at certain times of the year and month, and they speak with the plants as they work, thanking them. And there is the native woman I met in Hawaii; it fell to her to be the traditional hunter of wild pigs, to take only what was needed, to feed others, and be thankful. Sometimes in the hurry sickness of our time, we forget to return the gift of what we've taken from the rich land that feeds us. Sometimes we do not remember that millions of years of life have grown from this verdant, muddy, yielding terrain where we live in the land of our ancestors. We forget the long years of hunger, the starving times of history we have survived, and the years of living on lard and flour. We forget the meaning of food, which is both beginning and end of a divine alchemy, an infinite movement of sun into fruit, of windborne seeds falling to earth, seeds being carried in the fur of animals and the stomachs of birds, of rain water, of life rising up again. In our food all things come together in an elemental dance of magic and mystery; brother water, sister light, mother land, and the sacred fire all rise up in stalks and stems, opening a blossom and becoming red fruit of grass eaten by the deer, or the ripening yellow ears of corn planted and harvested by our short-lived hands. 7

Thanksgiving / Linda Hogan

Now it is autumn, and in the cool, plastered corners of houses are the 8
seed pots. The pots are smooth, rounded clay that has been painted with
lines thin as a strand of corn silk and they hold the seeds of pumpkin,
beans, and squash in a loving embrace before they go back to land. Even
last summer's sun is held there, dormant and ready to turn over and
surge to life in incredible germinations of renewal.

Near here grew the green spring pastures with onions growing at the 9
borders. Now, in autumn, they are the golden stubble of harvested hay,
the road is damp and silty with fallen red leaves that are turning back
into soil, waiting for spring's rich rains and sun. On the next hill are the
five wild turkeys I saw last month as they walked through the tall, dry
grasses, and beyond them are the caves of mineral salt that generations of
people have used. This is the vulnerable land shared among us. Not far
from here the ancient plants are listening and moving again toward the
ripening.

———————————

The Dare

Roger Hoffmann

Roger Hoffmann recounts an episode from his adolescence when approval by his peers was more important than personal safety. No matter our age or particular adolescent experience, we are able to relate to the pressure Hoffmann felt as a child. The desire for acceptance by friends and colleagues is something we never outgrow.

Words to Know

ambiguous   having multiple meanings
escalated   increased
guerrilla warfare   warfare carried out by an irregular, independent force
implicit   understood although not directly stated
provoke   to cause anger or resentment
silhouette   an outline of something that appears dark against a light background

---

The secret to diving under a moving freight train and rolling out the 1 other side with all your parts attached lies in picking the right spot between the tracks to hit with your back. Ideally, you want soft dirt or pea gravel, clear of glass shards and railroad spikes that could cause you instinctively, and fatally, to sit up. Today, at thirty-eight, I couldn't be threatened or baited enough to attempt that dive. But as a seventh grader struggling to make the cut in a tough Atlanta grammar school, all it took was a dare.

I coasted through my first years of school as a fussed-over smart kid, 2 the teacher's pet who finished his work first and then strutted around the room tutoring other students. By the seventh grade, I had more A's than friends. Even my old cronies, Dwayne and O.T., made it clear I'd never be one of the guys in junior high if I didn't dirty up my act. They challenged me to break the rules, and I did. The I-dare-you's escalated: shoplifting, sugaring teachers' gas tanks, dropping lighted matches into public mailboxes. Each guerrilla act won me the approval I never got for just being smart.

Walking home by the railroad tracks after school, we started playing 3 chicken with oncoming trains. O.T., who was failing that year, always won. One afternoon he charged a boxcar from the side, stopping just short of throwing himself between the wheels. I was stunned. After the train disappeared, we debated whether someone could dive under a moving car, stay put for a 10-count, then scramble out the other side. I thought it could be done and said so. O.T. immediately stepped in front of me and smiled. Not by me, I added quickly, I certainly didn't mean that I could do it. "A smart guy like you," he said, his smile evaporating, "you could figure it out easy." And then, squeezing each word for effect, "I . . . DARE . . . you." I'd just turned twelve. The monkey clawing my back was Teacher's Pet. And I'd been dared.

As an adult, I've been on both ends of life's implicit business and social 4 I-dare-you's, although adults don't use those words. We provoke with body language, tone of voice, ambiguous phrases. I dare you to: argue with the boss, tell Fred what you think of him, send the wine back. Only rarely are the risks physical. How we respond to dares when we are young may have something to do with which of the truly hazardous male inner dares—attacking mountains, tempting bulls at Pamplona—we embrace or ignore as men.

For two weeks, I scouted trains and tracks. I studied moving boxcars 5 close up, memorizing how they squatted on their axles, never getting used to the squeal or the way the air felt hot from the sides. I created an imaginary, friendly train and ran next to it. I mastered a shallow, head-first dive with a simple half-twist. I'd land on my back, count to ten, imagine wheels and, locking both hands on the rail to my left, heave myself over and out. Even under pure sky, though, I had to fight to keep my eyes open and my shoulders between the rails.

The next Saturday, O.T., Dwayne and three eighth graders met me be- 6 low the hill that backed up to the lumberyard. The track followed a slow bend there and opened to a straight, slightly uphill climb for a solid third of a mile. My run started two hundred yards after the bend. The train would have its tongue hanging out.

The other boys huddled off to one side, a circle on another planet, and 7 watched quietly as I double-knotted my shoelaces. My hands trembled. O.T. broke the circle and came over to me. He kept his hands hidden in the pockets of his jacket. We looked at each other. BB's of sweat appeared beneath his nose. I stuffed my wallet in one of his pockets, rubbing it against his knuckles on the way in, and slid my house key, wired to a red-and-white fishing bobber, into the other. We backed away from each other, and he turned and ran to join the four already climbing up the hill.

I watched them all the way to the top. They clustered together as if I 8 were taking their picture. Their silhouette resembled a round shouldered tombstone. They waved down to me, and I dropped them from my mind and sat down on the rail. Immediately, I jumped back. The steel was vibrating.

The train sounded like a cow going short of breath. I pulled my shirt-tail out and looked down at my spot, then up the incline of track ahead of me. Suddenly the air went hot, and the engine was by me. I hadn't pictured it moving that fast. A man's bare head leaned out and stared at me. I waved to him with my left hand and turned into the train, burying my face into the incredible noise. When I looked up, the head was gone. 9

I started running alongside the boxcars. Quickly, I found their pace, held it, and then eased off, concentrating on each thick wheel that cut past me. I slowed another notch. Over my shoulder, I picked my car as it came off the bend, locking in the image of the white mountain goat painted on its side. I waited, leaning forward like the anchor in a 440-relay, wishing the baton up the track behind me. Then the big goat fired by me, and I was flying and then tucking my shoulder as I dipped under the train. 10

A heavy blanket of red dust settled over me. I felt bolted to the earth. Sheet-metal bellies thundered and shook above my face. Count to ten, a voice said, watch the axles and look to your left for daylight. But I couldn't count, and I couldn't find left if my life depended on it, which it did. The colors overhead went from brown to red to black to red again. Finally, I ripped my hands free, forced them to the rail, and, in one convulsive jerk, threw myself into the blue light. 11

I lay there face down until there was no more noise, and I could feel the sun against the back of my neck. I sat up. The last ribbon of train was slipping away in the distance. Across the tracks, O.T. was leading a cavalry charge down the hill, five very small, galloping boys, their fists whirling above them. I pulled my knees to my chest. My corduroy pants puckered wet across my thighs. I didn't care. 12

The Dare / Roger Hoffmann

The First Appendectomy

William A. Nolen, M.D.

In this inside look at the practice of medicine, William Nolen, surgeon and author, recalls the first operation he ever performed. In his minute-by-minute account, the action at times seems almost comical, but Nolen is not laughing. He reminds us at the end what a large and terrifying responsibility it is for a doctor—even with the best of training—to hold a person's life in his hands.

Words to Know

anesthetist   a doctor who gives anesthesia
anticlimactic   having less importance than preceding events
Benchley, Robert   an American humorist
convalescence   recovery
distended   stretched out
equanimity   calmness
hemostats   clamps to stop bleeding
infinitesimal   tiny, minute
intravenous   through the veins
lesion   an injury
ligature   a joining
paean   a song of praise
sutures   stitches

The patient, or better, victim, of my first major surgical venture was a   1
man I'll call Mr. Polansky. He was fat, he weighed one hundred and
ninety pounds and was five feet eight inches tall. He spoke only broken
English. He had had a sore abdomen with all the classical signs and
symptoms of appendicitis for twenty-four hours before he came to Bellevue.

After two months of my internship, though I had yet to do anything   2
that could be decently called an "operation," I had had what I thought
was a fair amount of operating time. I'd watched the assistant residents
work, I'd tied knots, cut sutures and even, in order to remove a skin lesion, made an occasional incision. Frankly, I didn't think that surgery

was going to be too damn difficult. I figured I was ready, and I was chomping at the bit to go, so when Mr. Polansky arrived I greeted him like a long-lost friend. He was overwhelmed at the interest I showed in his case. He probably couldn't understand why any doctor should be so fascinated by a case of appendicitis: wasn't it a common disease? It was just as well that he didn't realize my interest in him was so personal. He might have been frightened, and with good reason.

At any rate, I set some sort of record in preparing Mr. Polansky for surgery. He had arrived on the ward at four o'clock. By six I had examined him, checked his blood and urine, taken his chest x-ray and had him ready for the operating room.

George Walters, the senior resident on call that night, was to "assist" me during the operation. George was older than the rest of us. I was twenty-five at this time and he was thirty-two. He had taken his surgical training in Europe and was spending one year as a senior resident in an American hospital to establish eligibility for the American College of Surgeons. He had had more experience than the other residents and it took a lot to disturb his equanimity in the operating room. As it turned out, this made him the ideal assistant for me.

It was ten o'clock when we wheeled Mr. Polansky to the operating room. At Bellevue, at night, only two operating rooms were kept open—there were six or more going all day—so we had to wait our turn. In the time I had to myself before the operation I had reread the section on appendectomy in the *Atlas of Operative Technique* in our surgical library, and had spent half an hour tying knots on the bedpost in my room. I was, I felt "ready."

I delivered Mr. Polansky to the operating room and started an intravenous going in his arm. Then I left him to the care of the anesthetist. I had ordered a sedative prior to surgery, so Mr. Polansky was drowsy. The anesthetist, after checking his chart, soon had him sleeping.

Once he was asleep I scrubbed the enormous expanse of Mr. Polansky's abdomen for ten minutes. Then, while George placed the sterile drapes, I scrubbed my own hands for another five, mentally reviewing each step of the operation as I did so. Donning gown and gloves I took my place on the right side of the operating-room table. The nurse handed me the scalpel. I was ready to begin.

Suddenly my entire attitude changed. A split second earlier I had been supremely confident; now, with the knife finally in my hand, I stared down at Mr. Polansky's abdomen and for the life of me could not decide where to make the incision. The "landmarks" had disappeared. There was too much belly.

George waited a few seconds, then looked up at me and said, "Go ahead."

"What?" I asked. 10

"Make the incision," said George. 11

"Where?" I asked. 12

"Where?" 13

"Yes," I answered, "where?" 14

"Why, here, of course," said George and drew an imaginary line on the 15 abdomen with his fingers.

I took the scalpel and followed where he had directed. I barely 16 scratched Mr. Polansky.

"Press a little harder," George directed. I did. The blade went through 17 the skin to a depth of perhaps one sixteenth of an inch.

"Deeper," said George. 18

There are five layers of tissue in the abdominal wall: skin, fat, fascia (a 19 tough membranous tissue), muscle and peritoneum (the smooth, glistening, transparent inner lining of the abdomen). I cut down into the fat. Another sixteenth of an inch.

"Bill," said George, looking up at me, "this patient is big. There's at 20 least three inches of fat to get through before we even reach the fascia. At the rate you're going we won't be into the abdomen for another four hours. For God's sake, will you cut?"

I made up my mind not to be hesitant. I pressed down hard on the 21 knife, and suddenly we were not only through the fat but through the fascia as well.

"Not that hard," George shouted, grabbing my right wrist with his left 22 hand while with his other hand he plunged a gauze pack into the wound to stop the bleeding. "Start clamping," he told me.

The nurse handed us hemostats and we applied them to the numerous 23 vessels I had so hastily opened. "All right," George said, "start tying."

I took the ligature material from the nurse and began to tie off the ves- 24 sels. Or rather, I tried to tie off the vessels, because suddenly my knot-tying proficiency had melted away. The casual dexterity I had displayed on the bedpost a short hour ago was nowhere in evidence. My fingers, greasy with fat, simply would not perform. My ties slipped off the vessels, the sutures snapped in my fingers, at one point I even managed to tie the end of my rubber glove into the wound. It was, to put it bluntly, a performance in fumbling that would have made Robert Benchley blush.

Here I must give my first paean of praise to George. His patience dur- 25 ing the entire performance was nothing short of miraculous. The temptation to pick up the catgut and do the tying himself must have been strong. He could have tied off all the vessels in two minutes. It took me twenty.

Finally we were ready to proceed. "Now," George directed, "split the 26 muscle. But gently, please."

I reverted to my earlier tack. Fiber by fiber I spread the muscle which 27 was the last layer but one that kept us from the inside of the abdomen. Each time I separated the fibers and withdrew my clamp, the fibers rolled together again. After five minutes I was no nearer the appendix than I had been at the start.

George could stand it no longer. But he was apparently afraid to sug- 28 gest I take a more aggressive approach, fearing I would stick the clamp into, or possibly through, the entire abdomen. Instead he suggested that he help me by spreading the muscle in one direction while I spread it in the other. I made my usual infinitesimal attack on the muscle. In one fell swoop George spread the rest.

"Very well done," he complimented me. "Now let's get in." 29

We each took a clamp and picked up the tissue-paper-thin perito- 30 neum. After two or three hesitant attacks with the scalpel I finally opened it. We were in the abdomen.

"Now," said George, "put your fingers in, feel the cecum (the portion 31 of the bowel to which the appendix is attached) and bring it into the wound."

I stuck my right hand into the abdomen. I felt around—but what was 32 I feeling? I had no idea.

It had always looked so simple when the senior resident did it. Open 33 the abdomen, reach inside, pull up the appendix. Nothing to it. But apparently there was.

Everything felt the same to me. The small intestine, the large intestine, 34 the cecum—how did one tell them apart without seeing them? I grabbed something and pulled it into the wound. Small intestine. No good. Put it back. I grabbed again. This time it was the sigmoid colon. Put it back. On my third try I had the small intestine again.

"The appendix must be in an abnormal position," I said to George. "I 35 can't seem to find it."

"Mind if I try?" he asked. 36

"Not at all," I answered. "I wish you would." 37

Two of his fingers disappeared into the wound. Five seconds later they 38 emerged, cecum between them, with the appendix flopping from it.

"Stuck down a little," he said kindly. "That's probably why you didn't 39 feel it. It's a hot one," he added. "Let's get at it."

The nurse handed me the hemostats, and one by one I applied them to 40 the mesentery of the appendix—the veil of tissue in which the blood vessels run. With George holding the veil between his fingers I had no trouble; I took the ligatures and tied the vessels without a single error. My confidence was coming back.

"Now," George directed, "put in your purse string." (The cecum is a 41 portion of the bowel which has the shape of half a hemisphere. The appendix projects from its surface like a finger. In an appendectomy the routine procedure is to tie the appendix at its base and cut it off a little beyond the tie. Then the remaining stump is inverted into the cecum and kept there by tying the purse-string stitch. This was the stitch I was now going to sew.)

It went horribly. The wall of the cecum is not very thick—perhaps one 42 eighth of an inch. The suture must be placed deeply enough in the wall so that it won't cut through when tied, but not so deep as to pass all the way through the wall. My sutures were alternately too superficial or too deep, but eventually I got the job done.

"All right," said George, "let's get the appendix out of here. Tie off the 43 base."

I did. 44

"Now cut off the appendix." 45

At least in this, the definitive act of the operation, I would be decisive. 46 I took the knife and with one quick slash cut through the appendix—too close to the ligature.

"Oh oh, watch it," said George. "That tie is going to slip." 47

It did. The appendiceal stump lay there, open. I felt faint. 48

"Don't panic," said George. "We've still got the purse string. I'll push 49 the stump in—you pull up the stitch and tie. That will take care of it."

I picked up the two ends of the suture and put in the first stitch. 50 George shoved the open stump into the cecum. It disappeared as I snugged my tie. Beautiful.

"Two more knots," said George. "Just to be safe." 51

I tied the first knot and breathed a sigh of relief. The appendiceal 52 stump remained out of sight. On the third knot—for the sake of security—I pulled a little tighter. The stitch broke; the open stump popped up; the cecum disappeared into the abdomen. I broke out in a cold sweat and my knees started to crumble.

Even George momentarily lost his composure. "For Christ's sake, 53 Bill," he said, grasping desperately for the bowel, "what did you have to do that for?" The low point of the operation had been reached.

By the time we had retrieved the cecum, Mr. Polansky's peritoneal 54 cavity had been contaminated. My self-confidence was shattered. And still George let me continue. True, he all but held my hand as we retied and resutured, but the instruments were in my hand.

The closure was anticlimactic. Once I had the peritoneum sutured, 55 things went reasonably smoothly. Two hours after we began, the operation was over. "Nice job," George said, doing his best to sound sincere.

"Thanks," I answered, lamely. 56

The scrub nurse laughed. 57

Mr. Polansky recovered, I am happy to report, though not without a 58
long and complicated convalescence. His bowel refused to function normally for two weeks and he became enormously distended. He was referred to at our nightly conferences as "Dr. Nolen's pregnant man." Each
time the reference was made, it elicited a shudder from me.

During his convalescence I spent every spare moment I could at Mr. 59
Polansky's bedside. My feelings of guilt and responsibility were overwhelming. If he had died I think I would have given up surgery for good.

Glossary

Various terms are used throughout this edition of PATTERNS to explain the basic strategies of writing. These terms are boldfaced in the chapter introductions and end-of-selection questions, and they are boldfaced and defined here in the following pages. Terms in bold type within the definitions are also defined in the glossary.

Alternating Method Also called the point-by-point method, the alternating method is used in **comparison** and **contrast** writing. The method compares and contrasts two subjects item by item. (See also **Block Method**.)

Antonym An antonym is a word that has a meaning *opposite* to the meaning of another word. For example, *pleasure* is an antonym of *pain*. Using an antonym is one method used by writers to define an unfamiliar word.

Audience A reader or readers of a piece of writing. More specifically, an audience is that reader or group of readers toward which a particular piece of writing is aimed. (See also **Purpose** and **Occasion**.)

Block Method The block method is used in comparison and contrast writing. In the block method, the writer explains all the characteristics of the first item together in a block, and then explains all the characteristics of the second item in a corresponding block. (See also **Alternating Method**.)

Body The body is the development of the thesis over a group of related paragraphs in an essay. (See also **Introduction** and **Conclusion**.)

Brainstorming A prewriting technique that many writers use to generate ideas for writing. In brainstorming, a writer jots down as many details and ideas on a subject that come to mind.

Cause A cause is a reason for something that happens or an explanation as to why some effect occurs. Writers explain why an **effect** (or result) comes about by explaining its causes. See Chapter 8, "Cause and Effect," for further discussion.

Chronological Order See **Order**.

Class In **classification** and **division**, a writer can classify or divide items if they are of the same type, that is, if they belong to the same class.

Classification Classification is the process of sorting a group of items into categories on the basis of some characteristic or quality that the items have in common. As a **mode of development**, classification is used by writers to organize and develop information included in a paragraph or essay. Classification is sometimes combined with **division** to develop a topic or thesis. See Chapter 5, "Classification and Division," for further discussion.

Cliché Clichés are words or phrases that have become overused and so have lost their expressive power. Examples of clichés are: "rosy red," "silly goose," "bull in a china shop," and "works like a horse."

Coherence Coherence refers to the logical flow of a piece of writing. Writing is coherent when the **main idea** is clearly stated, and the connections between the supporting **details** and the main idea are obvious. (See also **Unified/Unity**.)

Comparison When making a comparison, the writer discusses the similarities of objects or ideas. Writers sometimes combine comparison with **contrast** in developing their main idea. See Chapter 6, "Comparison and Contrast," for further discussion.

Conclusion In writing, the term *conclusion* is used to refer to the sentences or paragraph that completes the composition. Within the conclusion, the writer may restate the main idea of the composition or sum up the important points made in the composition.

In reading, the term *conclusion* refers to the idea the reader can draw from the information in the reading selection. Drawing a conclusion involves making an **inference**, that is, deriving an idea that is implied by the information stated within a composition.

Connotation Connotation refers to the feelings or qualities a reader associates with a word. In persuasive writing, writers often use the connotations of words to appeal to their readers. (See also **Denotation**.)

Contrast When making a contrast, the writer discusses the differences among objects or ideas. Writers sometimes combine contrast with **comparison** in developing an idea. See Chapter 6, "Comparison and Contrast," for further discussion.

Definition A definition explains the meaning of a word or term. Writers frequently use a variety of methods for defining the words and terms they use. They may use a dictionary definition, a **synonym**, or an **antonym**. They may also use any combination of the **modes of development** explained in this text.

An **extended definition** is one that occurs over the course of several sentences or paragraphs. It is often used to define complex objects or concepts. See Chapter 9, "Definition," for further discussion.

Denotation Denotation refers to the exact or dictionary definition of a word. (See also **Connotation**.)

Description In a description, the writer discusses the appearance of a person, place, or object. In descriptions, writers use words and details that appeal to the senses in order to create the *impression* they want the reader to have about what is described.

Details Details are specific pieces of information—examples, incidents, dates, and so forth—that explain and support the general ideas in a composition. Writers use details to make their general ideas clearer and more understandable to the reader.

Development   Development refers to the detailed explanation of the main—and usually more general—ideas in a composition. The main idea (or topic) of a paragraph is explained through the more specific information in the sentences within the paragraph. The **main idea** or **thesis** of an essay is explained or developed through the paragraphs within the essay.

Dialogue   Dialogue is conversation, usually between two or more persons. It is used by writers to give the exact wording used by people introduced in the composition, and thus is always set off by quotation marks. The writer usually uses a new paragraph to indicate a change of speaker. Dialogue is commonly found in narrative writing.

Division   In division, the writer breaks down or sorts a single object or idea into its components or parts and then gives detailed information about each of the parts. Division is sometimes used in combination with **classification**. For further discussion, see Chapter 5, "Classification and Division."

Effect   An effect is the result of certain events or **causes**. An effect may be the result of one or more causes. Writers often combine cause and effect to explain why something happens. For further discussion, see Chapter 8, "Cause and Effect."

Essay   An essay is a written composition based on an idea, which is called its **thesis.** An essay usually consists of at least three paragraphs. In the paragraphs, writers generally introduce and state the thesis, develop or explain the thesis, and conclude the essay. See Chapter 1, "The Basics of Paragraphs and Essays," for further discussion.

Event   An occurrence or happening that a writer will portray, often as part of a **fictional** or **nonfictional narrative**.

Example   An example is a specific illustration of a more general idea or statement. Writers may use one or more examples and may extend a single example over an entire essay in order to illustrate and support their ideas.

Extended Example   An extended example is one example that occurs over several sentences or paragraphs. It is used as a way of providing additional support for a **topic sentence** or **thesis statement**. See Chapter 4, "Examples," for further discussion.

Fact(s)   Anything or things that are known with certainty. Writers often present facts as a way of stating the **objectivity** of their position on a subject. (See also **Opinion.**)

Fiction (Fictional Narrative)   A paragraph or essay that presents a story or event that did not occur, or which differs significantly from a real or true event is called fiction. (By contrast, see **Nonfiction [Nonfictional Narrative].**)

Figure of Speech   A term or phrase that uses nonliteral meaning to create an image or **impression**. (See also **Metaphor** and **Simile.**)

First Person   (See **Person.**)

Freewriting   Freewriting is a prewriting exercise that involves writing without stopping for a set period of time, often five to ten minutes. Freewriting is an effective way to start writing and to generate ideas.

General Idea/General Statement A general idea or statement is broad and sweeping and therefore must usually be explained through more specific information. The **main idea** of a paragraph or essay is a relatively general idea, involving only the main features of the thought. In a paragraph or an essay, the general ideas and statements must be supported by more specific information.

Implied/Imply To imply is to hint at or indicate indirectly. Writers sometimes only imply their ideas rather than stating them directly. An implied idea requires the reader to draw **conclusions** or make **inferences** in order to determine the idea.

Impression The effect, feeling, or image that an author tries to create through **description**.

Incidents Incidents are the more specific, detailed happenings within a particular event. The narrative about an event will include an account of the specific incidents that occurred as part of the event (see **Narration**).

Inference An inference is a conclusion drawn by the reader based on information known or indicated *indirectly*. Writers sometimes indicate their ideas indirectly by suggesting rather than stating them. Readers must make inferences and use the information that is known or stated to determine the writer's ideas.

Inform Inform means to relate or tell about something. Writers often use **process** as a **mode of development** in which to inform their readers, though any of the modes in this text can be used to inform.

Instruct Instruct means to teach or educate. Writers often use **process** as a **mode of development** in which to instruct their readers.

Introduction The introduction of a paragraph or essay is at its beginning. The introduction of an essay is often the place where the writer places the **thesis statement.** (See also **Body** and **Conclusion.**)

Irony The use in writing of a relationship that is contradictory or unexpected. Writers often use irony to amuse, sadden, instruct, or anger their readers.

Main Idea The main idea of a composition is the general concept or broad opinion on which the composition is based. The main idea of a paragraph is referred to as the **topic**. The main idea of an essay is called the **thesis**.

Metaphor A metaphor is a figure of speech that compares unlike items by attributing the qualities or characteristics of one item to the other. A metaphor compares the items without the use of the words *like* or *as*. (See also **Simile**.)

Mixed Method Writers will often use the mixed method form in **comparison** and **contrast** writing, when neither the **alternating method** nor the **block method** alone is sufficient.

Mode of Development The mode of development refers to the kind of information used to support and explain the **main idea** of a paragraph or essay. Writers commonly use, either singly or in combination, the modes included in this text: **narration, description, examples, classification** and **division, comparison** and **contrast, process, cause** and **effect,** and **definition.**

Narration   Narration is a **mode of development** used by writers to tell a story or give an account of a historical or factual event. See Chapter 2, "Narration," for further discussion.

Nonfiction (Nonfictional Narrative)   A paragraph or essay that presents a story or event that actually happened. (By contrast, see **Fiction [Fictional Narrative]**.)

Objective   A paragraph or essay that presents the facts without including the writer's own feelings about interpretation of those facts is said to be objective. (By contrast, see **Subjective**.)

Occasion   An occasion is a set of circumstances under which a particular piece of writing occurs. The writing assignments in this text are occasions for writing paragraphs and essays.

Opinion   An opinion is a writer's belief or conclusion about something that may or may not be based on fact. Writers often use opinion as a way of presenting a subjective account of an event or object. (By contrast, see **Fact[s]**.)

Order   Order refers to the sequence in which the information in a composition is organized or arranged. Information is commonly organized in chronological order, order of importance, or spatial order. In **chronological order**, the information is sequenced according to time. In **order of importance**, the information may be sequenced from the least to the most important—or from the most to the least important. In **spatial order**, the information is presented from a particular vantage point—the door to a room, front to back, floor to ceiling, and so forth.

Order of Importance   See **Order**.

Paragraph   A paragraph is usually a set of two or more sentences that are related to one another in explaining an idea. The major use of a paragraph is to mark a division of the information within a composition. Another use of the paragraph is to set off **dialogue** within a composition. In this text, a paragraph is considered as a unit. The first word of a paragraph is usually indented a few spaces from the left margin of the writing or the print.

Person   Person is indicated by the personal pronouns used in a composition. Writers use the **first person** (*I, we*) to represent themselves as participants or firsthand observers of their subject. They use the **second person** (*you*) to address the reader directly. They use the **third person** (*he, she, it, one, they*) to provide the reader with a less limited and more objective view of the subject than may be conveyed by using first or second person. (See also **Point of View**.)

Point of View   Point of view refers to the way writers present their ideas. Point of view is determined by the **person, time,** and **tone** used in a composition. Person is indicated by the personal pronouns. Time is determined by the words that indicate whether the information included in the composition takes place in the past, in the present, or in the future. Tone refers to the attitude that writers take toward their subjects. Tone may be serious, humorous, formal, informal, cynical, sarcastic, ironic, sympathetic, and so forth.

Process   Process is a **mode of development** used by writers to explain the method of doing a task, making or preparing something, or achieving a particular result. See Chapter 7, "Process," for further discussion.

Purpose   Purpose refers to a writer's reason for writing. Common purposes for writing include writing to inform and to instruct. (See also **Persuade, Inform** and **Instruct.**)

Revise   To evaluate, rework, and rewrite a draft, keeping **audience, purpose, thesis, development**, and, finally, mechanics in mind.

Second Person   See **Person**.

Sentence   A sentence is a group of words that expresses a unit of thought. A sentence usually contains a word or words that express who is doing an action or is being acted upon (the *subject* of the sentence) and a word or words that express the action that is taking place (the *verb* of the sentence). The first word of a sentence begins with a capital letter. The end of the sentence is marked by a period (.), a question mark (?), or an exclamation point (!).

Simile   A simile is a figure of speech in which unlike items are compared. A simile is usually introduced by *like* or *as*, as in "He worked *like a horse* on the project" or "The chicken was as tasteless *as a piece of cardboard*." (See also **Metaphor**.)

Spatial Order   See **Order**.

Subjective   Subjective writing is that in which the writer's own feelings about the topic are expressed. (By contrast, see **Objective**.)

Support   Support refers to the information—specific details, examples, and so forth—used to develop or explain the general idea in a composition.

Symbol   A symbol is a person, place, or object that represents something other than itself, usually something immaterial or abstract.

Synonym   A synonym is a word or phrase that has the same meaning as another word or phrase. Writers sometimes use a synonym to clarify an unfamiliar word or phrase used in their compositions.

Thesis   The thesis is the main idea of an essay. The thesis may be stated directly (see **Thesis Statement**) or only implied (see **Implied/Imply**).

Thesis Statement   The thesis statement is the sentence or sentences in which the **main idea** of an essay is stated. The thesis statement is generally placed at or near the beginning of an essay.

Third Person   See **Person**.

Time   Time refers to the period (past, present, future) when the action mentioned in the composition took place. Time is indicated by the action words (verbs) and such words as *tomorrow, yesterday, next week*, and so on. (See also **Point of View**.)

Tone   Tone refers to the attitude writers take toward their subjects. The attitude in a particular composition may be formal, informal, serious, humorous, and so forth. (See also **Point of View**.)

Topic   The main idea of a paragraph is called its topic. The topic of a paragraph may be stated directly (see **Topic Sentence**) or only implied (see **Implied/Imply**).

Topic Sentence   The topic sentence is the sentence or sentences in which the **main idea** of a paragraph is stated. The topic sentence is commonly placed at or near the beginning of a paragraph, but it may appear at any point in the paragraph.

Transitions   Transitions are words and expressions such as *for example, on the other hand, first, second,* or *to illustrate* that are used to help the reader identify the relation of ideas in a composition.

Unified/Unity   A paragraph must be unified if it is to be effective, which means it must deal with a single idea, and that each sentence in the paragraph must be related to that idea. (See also **Main Idea** and **Coherence**.)

Acknowledgments

Edward Abbey: From DOWN THE RIVER by Edward Abbey. Copyright © 1982 by Edward Abbey. Used by permission of the publisher, Dutton, an imprint of New American Library, a division of Penguin Books USA Inc.

L. O. Anderson: From *Wood-Frame House Construction* by L. O. Anderson (Dover, 1973). Reprinted by permission.

Isaac Asimov: "The Difference Between a Brain and a Computer," from *Please Explain* by Isaac Asimov. Copyright © 1973 by Isaac Asimov. Reprinted by permission of Houghton Mifflin Company. "What Is Intelligence, Anyway?" Reprinted by permission of the author.

Margaret Atwood: Margaret Atwood, "Canada: Through the One-Way Mirror," *The Nation* magazine/The Nation Co. Inc., © 1986. Reprinted by permission.

Russell Baker: "Back to the Dump," Copyright © 1983 by The New York Times Company. Reprinted by permission. "Learning to Write," Copyright © 1982 by Russell Baker. Published by agreement with Congdon and Weed, Inc. "The Plot Against People," Copyright © 1968 by The New York Times Company. Reprinted by permission.

Rachael Bishop: From "Rescuing Oily Birds." Originally appeared in *The Atlantic*. Reprinted by permission of the author.

Suzanne Britt: From "That Lean and Hungry Look." Reprinted by permission of the author.

Stephanie Brush: "The Big Five Popular Fears of Our Times," from *Life: A Warning* by Stephanie Brush. Copyright © 1987 by Stephanie Brush. Reprinted by permission of Linden Press, a division of Simon & Schuster, Inc.

Leo Buscaglia: "The Wine Experience" from *Papa, My Father* by Leo Buscaglia. Published by Slack, Inc. Copyright © 1989 by Leo Buscaglia. Used by permission.

Ruth Caplan: From OUR EARTH, OURSELVES by Ruth Caplan. Copyright © 1990 by Environmental Action, Inc. Used by permission of Bantam Books, a division of Bantam Doubleday Dell Publishing Group, Inc.

John Ciardi: "Dawn Watch" and "The Pencil Rack," from *Manner of Speaking* by John Ciardi. Copyright 1972 Rutgers University Press. Reprinted by permission of the author.

Jacques Cousteau: Selection from *The Bounty of the Sea*. Reprinted by permission of The Cousteau Society, Inc.

Joan Didion: "Marrying Absurd" from SLOUCHING TOWARDS BETHLE-HEM by Joan Didion. Copyright © 1967, 1968 by Joan Didion. Reprinted by permission of Farrar, Straus and Giroux, Inc.

Frances Fitzgerald: "Golden Years" from *Cities on a Hill* by Frances Fitzgerald. Copyright © 1986 by Frances Fitzgerald. Reprinted by permission of Simon & Schuster, Inc.

Richard Ford: From "Accommodations." First published in *Banana Republic Trips.* Copyright © 1988 by Richard Ford. Reprinted by permission of the author.

Bruce Jay Friedman: "Eating Alone in Restaurants," from *The Lonely Guy* by Bruce Jay Friedman. Copyright © 1979. Reprinted by permission of McGraw-Hill Publishing Company.

Tess Gallagher: Excerpt taken from "My Father's Love Letters" by Tess Gallagher in *American Poetry Review*, May/June 1981. Reprinted by permission.

Ellen Goodman: "It's Failure, Not Success," © 1979, The Boston Globe/Washington Post Writers Group.

James Gorman: "What the Nose Knows." Copyright 1986 by James Gorman. Reprinted by permission of the author.

Bob Greene: "It Took This Night to Make Us Know," from *Johnny Deadline: Reporter* by Bob Greene. Copyright © 1976 Nelson-Hall Inc. Reprinted by permission of the publisher.

Gilbert Highet: Reprinted by permission of Curtis Brown, Ltd. Copyright © 1957 by Gilbert Highet.

L. Rust Hills: "How to Eat an Ice Cream Cone" from *How to Do Things Right: The Revelations of a Fussy Man* (New York: Doubleday, 1972). Reprinted by permission of the author.

Suzanne Hilton: Reprinted by permission of Ray Lincoln Literary Agency, Elkins Park House, 107–B, Elkins Park, Pa. as agent for author.

Roger Hoffman: "The Dare." Copyright © 1986 by the New York Times Company. Reprinted by permission.

Linda Hogan: "Thanksgiving" first appeared in *Elle* Magazine, November 1990. Reprinted by permission of the author.

John Holt: "Three Disciplines for Children," from *Freedom and Beyond* by John Holt, copyright © 1972 pp. 102–104. Reprinted with permission.

Robert Johnson: Copyright © Commonweal Foundation 1989.

Alice Kahn: "The Womanly Art of Beast Feeding" and "The Momist Manifesto," from MY LIFE AS A GAL by Alice Kahn. Copyright © 1987 by Alice Kahn. Used by permission of Dell Books, a division of Bantam Doubleday Dell Publishing Group, Inc.

E. J. Kahn, Jr.: From *The Big Drink: The Story of Coca-Cola* by E. J. Kahn, Jr. Copyright © 1950, 1959, 1960 by E. J. Kahn, Jr. Reprinted by permission of Random House, Inc.

Jim Kaplan: From Jim Kaplan, "Baseball's Hot Dogs—Do They Spice Up the Game—or Leave a Bad Taste in Your Mouth?," *TV Guide,* May 28, 1988, pp. 14–15. Reprinted with permission from TV Guide ® Magazine. Copyright © 1988 by News America Publications Inc., Radnor, Pennsylvania.

Garrison Keillor: "How to Write a Personal Letter," by Garrison Keillor from the November 1987 *Reader's Digest.* Originally appeared in *Omni,* August 1987. Reprinted with permission. Reprinted by permission of International Paper Company and the author. Copyright © 1987 by International Paper Company.

Michael Korda: "Defining Success," reprinted by permission of the author. Copyright © 1977.

Charles Kuralt: "Down With the Forests" from *Dateline America* by Charles Kuralt, copyright 1979 by CBS, Inc., reprinted by permission of Harcourt Brace Jovanovich, Inc.

Mary Paik Lee: "The Quiet Odyssey" and "The Next Generation." From *Quiet Odyssey* by Mary Paik Lee. Copyright © 1990. Reprinted by permission of University of Washington Press.

Barry Holstun Lopez: "The Sperm Whale" are paragraphs excerpted from an essay entitled "A Presentation of Whales" from the collection CROSSING OPEN GROUND by Barry Lopez. Copyright © 1980, 1988 Barry Holstun Lopez. (First appeared in *Harper's* March 1980.) Reprinted with permission of Charles Scribner's Sons, an imprint of Macmillan Publishing Company.

William Lutz: Excerpt from DOUBLESPEAK by William Lutz. Copyright © 1989 by William Lutz. Reprinted by permission of HarperCollins Publishers Inc.

David McCullough: Reprinted with permission from *American Heritage,* Volume 37, number 3. Copyright © 1986 by American Heritage, a Division of Forbes, Inc.

Mary T. Madden: Copyright 1968 American Journal of Nursing Company. Reprinted by permission from *American Journal of Nursing,* April 1968, Vol. 68, pp. 778–779. Used with permission. All rights reserved.

Brian Manning: Copyright © 1985 by the New York Times Company. Reprinted by permission.

David Mazie: Excerpted with permission from "Keep Your Teen-Age Driver Alive" by David Mazie, *Reader's Digest* June 1991. Copyright © 1991 by The Reader's Digest Assn., Inc.

Lance Morrow: "The Bright Cave Under the Hat," copyright 1990 The Time Inc. Magazine Company. Reprinted by permission.

William A. Nolen, M.D.: Reprinted by permission of Blassingame, McCauley and Wood.

Deborah Tannen: "Living with Asymmetry" from *You Just Don't Understand* by Deborah Tannen, Ph.D. Copyright © 1991 by William Morrow and Company. Used by permission of William Morrow and Co., Inc. Publishers, New York.

Deems Taylor: Reprinted by permission of Curtis Brown, Ltd. Copyright © 1937 by Deems Taylor.

Paul Theroux: "Healthy Bodies, Healthy Minds?" from *The Old Patagonian Express* by Paul Theroux. Copyright © 1979 by Cape Cod Scriveners Company. Reprinted by permission of Houghton Mifflin Company. All rights reserved.

John Updike: "The Movie House" from *Five Boyhoods,* edited by Martin Levin. (Doubleday) Copyright © 1962. Renewed 1990 by Martin Levin. Reprinted by permission of Martin Levin.

Judith Viorst: Copyright © 1977 by Judith Viorst. Originally appeared in *Redbook.*

Eliot Wigginton: "Moonshining as a Fine Art" from *The Foxfire Book* by Eliot Wigginton. Copyright © 1968, 1969, 1970, 1971, 1972 by The Foxfire Fund, Inc. Used by permission of Doubleday, a division of Bantam Doubleday Dell Publishing Group, Inc.

Richard Wright: Excerpt from *Uncle Tom's Children* by Richard Wright. Copyright 1936, 1937 and 1938 by Richard Wright. Copyright © renewed 1964 by Ellen Wright. Reprinted by permission of HarperCollins Publishers, Inc.

Judith Wurtman: "Why Eat Junk Food?" from *Eating Your Way Through Life* by Judith Wurtman (New York: Raven Press, 1979). Reprinted by permission of Raven Press, Publishers.

Index

To the Student: Your ratings of the reading selections will help us plan future editions of *Patterns*. Please mail your answers to the English Editor, College Division, Houghton Mifflin Company, 222 Berkeley Street, Boston, MA 02116-3764.

Selections	Inter-esting	Not in-teresting	Too difficult	Read-able	Too easy	Didn't read
NARRATION						
The Movie House	___	___	___	___	___	___
Grandma's Last Day	___	___	___	___	___	___
The Discovery of Coca-Cola	___	___	___	___	___	___
Pearl Harbor Echoes in Seattle	___	___	___	___	___	___
Vital Signs	___	___	___	___	___	___
Freedom	___	___	___	___	___	___
Learning to Write	___	___	___	___	___	___
The Pie	___	___	___	___	___	___
The Jeaning of America—and the World	___	___	___	___	___	___
Healthy Bodies, Healthy Minds?	___	___	___	___	___	___
Just Walk on By: A Black Man Ponders His Power to Alter Public Space	___	___	___	___	___	___
The Deli	___	___	___	___	___	___
DESCRIPTION						
The Way to Rainy Mountain	___	___	___	___	___	___
Judy Schoyer	___	___	___	___	___	___
The Marion	___	___	___	___	___	___
The Subway Station	___	___	___	___	___	___
The Sperm Whale	___	___	___	___	___	___
The Quiet Odyssey	___	___	___	___	___	___
Peace and Quiet	___	___	___	___	___	___
Dawn Watch	___	___	___	___	___	___
I Love Washington	___	___	___	___	___	___
The Monster	___	___	___	___	___	___
Marrying Absurd	___	___	___	___	___	___
This Man Has Expired	___	___	___	___	___	___
Aravaipa Canyon	___	___	___	___	___	___
Limbo	___	___	___	___	___	___
EXAMPLES						
Naming Cows	___	___	___	___	___	___
The Pencil Rack	___	___	___	___	___	___
The Shoe as a Strategic Weapon	___	___	___	___	___	___
The Next Generation	___	___	___	___	___	___
Wrappings	___	___	___	___	___	___
Down with the Forests	___	___	_ _	___	___	___
Of Shopping	___	___	___	___	___	___
What the Nose Knows	___	___	___	___	___	___
Living with Asymmetry	___	___	___	___	___	___
Back to the Dump	___	___	___	___	___	___
My Mother Never Worked	___	___	___	___	___	___
CLASSIFICATION AND DIVISION						
A Matter of Perspective	___	___	___	___	___	___
The Three New Yorks	___	___	___	___	___	___
Where I Come from Is Like This	___	___	___	___	___	___
No More Bad Bugs	___	___	___	___	___	___
The Plot Against People	___	___	___	___	___	___
Friends, Good Friends—and Such Good Friends	___	___	___	___		
Doublespeak	___	___	___	___	___	___
The Womanly Art of Beast Feeding	___	___	___	___	___	___
Three Disciplines for Children	___	___	___	___	___	___
The Big Five Popular Fears of Our Time	___	___	___	___	___	___
COMPARISON AND CONTRAST						
Good Girl, Bad Girl	___	___	___	___	___	___
Two Views of Time	___	___	___	___	___	___
Jungle and Desert	___	___	___	___	___	___
That Lean and Hungry Look	___	___	___	___	___	___
Eating American-style	___	___	___	___	___	___
Nursing Practices—England and America	___	___	___	___	___	___
The Difference Between a Brain and a Computer	___	___	___	___	___	___
Aria	___	___	___	___	___	___

Selections	Interesting	Not interesting	Too difficult	Readable	Too easy	Didn't read
Through the One-Way Mirror	___	___	___	___	___	___
Women and Men	___	___	___	___	___	___
Pediatricians	___	___	___	___	___	___
PROCESS						
Insert Flap "A" and Throw Away	___	___	___	___	___	___
Rescuing Oily Birds	___	___	___	___	___	___
The Right Way to Eat an Ice-Cream Cone	___	___	___	___	___	___
The Cook	___	___	___	___	___	___
How to Write a Personal Letter	___	___	___	___	___	___
Eating Alone in Restaurants	___	___	___	___	___	___
The Wine Experience	___	___	___	___	___	___
How to Put Off Doing a Job	___	___	___	___	___	___
Date Decorating: Preparing Your Home for His Arrival	___	___	___	___	___	___
Pithing a Frog	___	___	___	___	___	___
CAUSE AND EFFECT						
A Momentous Arrest	___	___	___	___	___	___
The Golden Years	___	___	___	___	___	___
Why Eat Junk Food?	___	___	___	___	___	___
Bonding at Birth	___	___	___	___	___	___
On Being Unemployed	___	___	___	___	___	___
It Took This Night to Make Us Know	___	___	___	___	___	___
Ozone	___	___	___	___	___	___
My First Lesson in How to Live as a Negro	___	___	___	___	___	___
The Bounty of the Sea	___	___	___	___	___	___
The Thirsty Animal	___	___	___	___	___	___
The Spoils of War	___	___	___	___	___	___
DEFINITION						
The Ultimate Kitchen Gadget	___	___	___	___	___	___
"I Love You"	___	___	___	___	___	___
Maestria	___	___	___	___	___	___
Grandparents	___	___	___	___	___	___
Baseball's Hot Dogs	___	___	___	___	___	___
Defining Success	___	___	___	___	___	___
It's Failure, Not Success	___	___	___	___	___	___
What Is Intelligence, Anyway?	___	___	___	___	___	___
Democracy	___	___	___	___	___	___
The Bright Cave Under the Hat	___	___	___	___	___	___
EXTRA READINGS						
Ode to My Father	___	___	___	___	___	___
How It Feels to Be Colored Me	___	___	___	___	___	___
The Momist Manifesto	___	___	___	___	___	___
Thanksgiving	___	___	___	___	___	___
The Dare	___	___	___	___	___	___
The First Appendectomy	___	___	___	___	___	___

School _____

Course Title _____